PURE-PRO
PUBLISHING

MY LIFE AND FIGHT
TO CURE THE WORLD'S DEADLIEST KILLER

FATE STACKED THE DECK

Dan Clevenger

FROM VAGABOND... TO VISIONARY

PURE-PRO PUBLISHING
Columbus, Ohio

FATE STACKED THE DECK
Copyright © 2021 by Dan Clevenger

All rights reserved. No part of this book may be reproduced in whole or in part without written permission from the author, except by reviewers who may quote brief excerpts in connection with a review in a newspaper, magazine or electronic publication; nor may any part of this book be reproduced, stored in a retrieval system, or transmitted in any form or by any means electronic, mechanical, photocopying, recording, or other, without written permission from the author.

Published by Pure-Pro Publishing and Dan Clevenger

Jacket by Milan Jovanovic, Chameleon Studios
Format by Diana Vara

ISBN 978-057825671-9 (hardback)
ISBN 978-168564145-0 (paperback)
ISBN 978-168564146-7 (ebook)

This book is dedicated to my son Logan's boys—
my grandsons Pauly and Tommy

Grandsons Pauly & Tommy

FORWARD

I've known Dan as my friend for almost sixty years. I've followed his career as a very successful political lobbyist in Columbus, Ohio and through many of his endeavors to help make this world a better place. What always impressed me about him was his tireless commitment to achieve whatever goal he set out to accomplish. He put his heart and soul into succeeding. However, through the years, he faced many obstacles in attempting to get the projects to completion.

He was blessed with former University of Michigan friends, local Ohio businessmen, and contacts throughout the college and professional sports world, who he involved in various walks. They were a tremendous help to Dan. During those many years, there were successes and failures with the ultimate goals not reached. I know first-hand, because I watched Dan's efforts for a long time and got acquainted with many of his friends and family. Failures were due mostly to various agencies either political or private, some of whom didn't fulfill what was asked of them by Dan. His hopes and dreams were of the magnitude that required working with large organizations who ultimately let him down. There were many times that I told Dan to give up, but that was not his nature. He is a fighter.

I think you will enjoy reading his story.

Tom Van Arsdale
3 Time NBA All-Star
Author of *Journey Man*

MY SEMINAL MOMENT

When I submitted "The First Half" draft of my book to Das (my professional writing advisor) for his appraisal among his myriad criticisms was that I needed a "hook" to get my audience "in to" its content. Something they could relate to since I was no one famous and why should many of them care about what happened to me. They would find out if they stuck with it but that was the key. Why should they?

What I settled on was far from what he expected, a challenge to the reader. What was the seminal moment in their life? What single event shaped their future? I had long suppressed mine for its horror but as I searched my memory it came roaring back to haunt me again—my first exposure to pure evil. With all my heart I hope yours were inspirational because that is what breeds leaders and I will forever wish that for my readers and their families. Far less to overcome. My horror was dormant until I began my recollection, then there it was again and on my 80th birthday I started to cry.

As you will hopefully read shortly, my Mother's family was from Jessup, Pennsylvania just outside Scranton in the foothills of the Moosic Mountains, near the Poconos. She and I would visit every summer for two weeks during which her brothers and sisters would reunite and I would get together with my Jessup buddies for some serious pick-up baseball. The high school was a block away with a huge field/"playground," totally undeveloped, in between.

    Dad had bought me a Rawlings glove and a Louisville Slugger bat for the trip. I believe it was 1950 and I was about to be nine years old. My buddies knew of my coming and I was psyched. I still recall what a beautiful morning it was: so bright and fresh in the mountains, a cool breeze. Life was perfect and only to get better. At 9:00 AM I broke free and headed to the field. There was no one there yet where we usually met up. I noticed that down at the end at the heavily shrubbed area seven or eight bigger kids were in what I thought was a rock throwing contest or something. They were bigger kids. Could my buddies have grown that much in a year?

    I headed toward the group searching for familiar faces but then something caught my attention that was out of place. They were not my buddies. They were older kids and they were throwing rocks at something hanging from a small tree. It was a cat, a small one and it was crying as the rocks hit home. I lost all control, dropped my glove and waded in with my bat, smashing everyone in sight. They all ran for the high school on a hilltop a couple hundred yards away. I was crying uncontrollably as I walked over to the cat, no longer swaying or crying, now dead. Christ, it was a kitten, lost in the field. I took it down and found a safe place and covered it with rocks, my first funeral. I remember kneeling by the rocks until I stopped crying, praying for the kitty.

When I got up, I recovered my bat and glove and down where I had come in, my buddies had started to form. I was in no mood to play as I had looked up at the high school where the cat beaters were standing and looking down at me. No longer in a crying mood, I gave my glove to a buddy and with no explanation began running up the hill with my bat to mop things up. They all ran like the cowards they were. They never again surfaced during my two week stay. I hope to reunite with the kitten in heaven.

So my seminal moment was a moment of horror. At least I knew about me. I am the most emotional person I know but that wasn't going to cut it. I would later realize that they weren't afraid of me. Better yet, I had shamed them. That lasts.

More importantly, what evils lurk within children that begin a beautiful summer day by torturing to death a baby animal? What strengths lay dormant in a child that unthinkingly risks all to make them pay?

PROLOGUE

Those of you that used to know me probably wonder what about me merits an autobiography of my life. I'll tell you in five words—<u>circumstances</u>, that and being free and able to advantage them. I'll toss in another: <u>relationships</u>, those which that freedom allowed me to develop. Then <u>opportunity</u>, of which our country is the land of with all of them offering <u>achievement</u> as a <u>reward</u>. Circumstance, Relationships, Opportunity, Achievement and Reward.

Of course this theorem came to me retrospectively as I was trying to figure out how I got here from there myself, and it all comes down to the people I have encountered along the way. From the reprobates to the supreme rulers and the obstacles and opportunities they presented requiring my involvement. This book recounts how I navigated those waters and came out the other side as a survivor and an achiever, albeit somehow ultimately falling short in my primary objectives, which came later in life when it meant the most, especially to me and to millions of others.

Failure is never easy to accept especially after having done one's best and under circumstances beyond one's control. When winning is stolen from you at a potential cost of billions of dollars and millions of lives, one of them potentially your own, by a man-made pandemic and an associate's betrayal on the ultimate challenge of your life it is a tough choke-down.

Some of the people I feature are and will likely remain foreign to the reader but they all mattered to me and helped shape my life, as did the famous and infamous, given equal billing. They all fit and had value in my life, much of which was spent trying to find its purpose. Eventually my family gave me that purpose and in its fullest bloom it was threatened by a diagnosis of Inherent Neuropathy, a nasty burden, a progressive, debilitating version that I have forced myself to manage with the constant assistance of my wife Becky for close to twenty years. It has not been the life she dreamed of and that is my greatest shame. Maybe one of my readers will be inspired to pick up the cause with a similar strategy after our nation's political crisis runs its course.

Everything I write about played a role in what I became and what transpired. I can't write about some of the most critical elements because of confidentiality requirements of huge public companies involved but everything else happened precisely as presented.

America's national sport, football, is featured throughout, as are some of its greatest players, past and present. Believe me this is not a side of it you will be aware of or find elsewhere. As with our country, its future is tenuous. I had that in control too. Even the NIL Law, allowing college athletes to profit from Name, Image and Likeness was under control.

The Columbus, Ohio bicycling event, Pelotonia, was my inspiration for "The Tour for the Cure" that was to be our weapon to fund cures for Neurological Diseases worldwide. It was to be the biggest fundraising event in history. Until Fate Stacked the Deck.

Dan Clevenger, Chairman
Pure-Pro Products, LLC
Retired

INTRODUCTION

I'm pretty much not a right-off-the-rack guy in my 80th year who has decided that it's probably time to retire. Circumstances played into that decision that I'm going to have to adjust to as most of my objectives went unachieved. Those that were realistic originally, grew to be too idealistic as our country circles the drain and I've accepted that and am moving on. Originally, there was something I could have done, but not now so what follows leads up to what's next, after some background.

I'm a former businessman, political consultant, lobbyist and athlete with a neurological disease, Inherent Neuropathy: a progressive, debilitating disorder that in my case robs me of strength and balance but fortunately not my mental faculties or my sense of humor. On the serious side, unrelated to the disease, all my life I have always thought that the most beautiful word in the world was honor. I've always been a reader and historian and years ago I came across *American Caesar,* the biography of General Douglas MacArthur, my favorite American, and if it was good enough for him who am I to look further? It had great meaning in my life.

Over time I've been rewarded with a core group of many friends, most of whom remain close, and fewer enemies, one of whom has hastened my retirement. I feel sorry for him, nothing else, but he potentially cost millions of people their own lives in the future and that hurts me, as well as all the other victims of neurological diseases that would have benefited immediately. Because the window that allowed what I offer has closed. God will judge him for his lies and betrayals.

What's next is I'm going to have to adjust to that failure and truly accept it and that necessitates an alternative, which I hope comes to me as I'm writing this book. If it does I'll let you know. What I have excelled in along with my wife Becky is raising a fine son Logan, and it's to his sons, Pauly and Tommy, that I dedicate this work.

THE FIRST HALF

Chapter One

Getting Started

I was born to Floyd and Mabel Clevenger on August 6, 1941, in Kenton, Ohio, which was fitting as Kenton has a history of its own. It was named after frontiersman Simon Kenton, a truly legendary figure who, lore has it, capped his career when captured by Indians after a long battle, was tortured to his limit and scalped, with hot coals placed in the wound. Finally pissed, it was said that Mr. Kenton grabbed an axe, slaughtered all the Indians in the vicinity and ran off naked, head on fire, never to be found. It's not true, but that's lore for you. I doubt if I'll ever do anything that extreme, but it is inspirational and has been given consideration on several occasions in my middle years when things still mattered and I could do something about them.

We didn't live in Kenton but my Dad had a store there. My parents had recently moved to Tiffin, Ohio to open another store among the chain of Ladies Ready-to-Wear stores that he and his brother, Congressman Cliff Clevenger, developed throughout Western Ohio. Our doctors however were in Kenton, as well as many of their friends.

Floyd and Cliff were quite the entrepreneurs for that time, combining their chain Clevenger's Ready-to-Wear stores and a congressional seat largely in the same congressional district, which covered nine counties and was held for twenty-six years. They did well and got out at the right time, although Cliff retained his congressional seat well beyond. I remember at an early age the trips to Washington and meeting Presidents Truman and Eisenhower which even then I knew was special and made me curious.

My Dad essentially retired when I was born and basically bought the Tiffin store for my Mom to run. Floyd met Mabel on a buying trip to New York where she represented Macy's and the May Company. She became his second wife; his first wife had died prematurely of an ailment. I had a half-sister Shirley, now deceased, as well as two nieces and two nephews still alive and well, though we've drifted. We try to connect at Christmas via cards and occasional calls. I can recall early trips to New York to watch the Macy's Christmas Parade, staying at the Waldorf Astoria and watching from the Macy's Pavilion.

My Dad bought a horse farm outside of Tiffin, a town of 20,000 at that time. In my adolescent years in Tiffin it was accorded recognition as being the wealthiest town per capita in America, lots of business and industry. We split time between there and in an apartment above the store until his favorite horse Traveler died and it became time for me to start school. He was getting antsy, still in his 50s, and my Mom had the store rolling so he built a house in a nice area and rented out the apartment, having previously sold the farm.

My Dad and Uncle Cliff were naturally very close and we visited often, we to Washington, DC or Bryan, Ohio, Cliff's home base, or they to Tiffin. Cliff's wife Georgiana (Jo) and son

Jack always came along. I became Jack's project when in Washington and was probably thirty years younger but old enough to be curious and I became his "protégé." Jo was "all in" with the Washington thing (she called President Eisenhower "Ikie") and was a fart in a skillet driving my Mom nuts. But they got along because Mom kind of dug the Washington scene too. Jack was Cliff's "Executive Assistant," overseen by the secretaries, and a huge sports fan. He is why I got to know Washington so well.

Washington is an easy city to get around if you consult a map first. We would hit up the Senators and Redskins games regularly but Jack's big thing was pro wrestling. He was a big fan of "Gorgeous George"—famous wrestler George Raymond Wagner--and I got to meet him.

Retrospectively, I wouldn't change a thing about my youth except to say that virtually none of it could be lived now. Tiffin then was a sprawling upper middle-class community with the Sandusky River running through it but by no means dividing it and it was largely "always open" to its children. We had a public school system and a Catholic parochial system (at that time almost equal in size) and two colleges, Heidelberg and Tiffin University, all welcoming to everyone.

Take a few minutes and extrapolate the same time period of your youth to where you grew up compared to where you live now. Look at our country then and now. Sneaks up on you, doesn't it? Give your congressman a buzz, see if he'll pick up. Or return your call.

In Tiffin as kids matured, they either turned to sports (boys only, no girls' sports), cars or the opposite sex. There was generous opportunity for all. Or a kid could choose to smoke. I'll tell this story to make a point about myself that will become relevant later. Back then nearly everybody smoked and my Dad was a Camel man. By that time everybody knew smoking had to be bad for you but the cigarette people kept a lid on the data for as long as they could so as not to affect sales. Hell, when I was first allowed at the table (age 2?) I wouldn't eat if a cigarette was in evidence. My Dad used this to both our advantages by always making a point of putting a lit Camel on his coffee saucer at every meal until I'd ask him to put it out, which he'd do and we'd eat. As a result, to this day I've never had a puff of anything or ever tasted coffee. It worked for my Mom, a casual smoker, too. My Dad switched to cigars but not at the table. Cigars were considered okay back then. Go figure.

By junior high, most kids' choices were made and all our free time committed to that choice. Most of my favorite friends chose sports, but some other friendships were sustained since every group needed both a sheik and a wheelman to qualify as a well-rounded kid and those specialists needed jocks to boost their cred. Back then accommodations could be made to benefit the greater good. At the outset my group really had to settle when it came to a wheelman and my natural charm was put to the test many times. Once we found our groove we mastered the art.

About that time I started to go to Michigan football games. Uncle Cliff always had tickets to whatever he wanted and my sister Shirley had graduated from there by then and married an attorney classmate so it was a nice family outing several times a year.

On one such occasion at the first game of that year I had matured to the point that I really began to notice things and become aware of my surroundings. It just really hit me that day as I walked into the stadium. It wasn't the crowd; I'd grown used to the crowds. It was a player, number 87 for Michigan, and I just couldn't take my eyes off him. The poise, the carriage, the demeanor, moving from position to position during warmups, snapping passes out of the air, booming punts and place kicks, even taking snaps from center and firing bullets to receivers amid the roar. Little did I know at the time that Ron Kramer would become over the years one of my dearest friends or that I'd be the last person he would speak to in his life.

Chapter Two

The First Fate

The most significant thing that ever happened in my life also occurred at roughly the same time in Tiffin and life itself would certainly never have been as rewarding had it not. Back then it was commonplace for families to visit friends for dinner in their homes on weekends and one of our family's friends were the Talberts, Bon and Genevieve. Bon was a druggist in town and his son, Bon, Jr., was a senior and the football center for the public high school, Columbian. If memory serves I was about to enter Calvert, their parochial arch rival, so after the mandatory "Hi, how ya' doing," we had nothing to say to one another: he was a senior, man. They lived on Rebecca Street.

After about the second visit I noticed that the house across the street from Talberts had a couple boys in it that were about my age who looked familiar from one of the parks in town. Back then, kids, never known for their patience and with none of today's alternatives available to them, maxed focus out at about 30 seconds. I was hyper, so off the porch and across the street I went to meet the neighbors. They were represented by a little girl, two or three, dressed in a red and white dress. She had a scowl on her face and was sitting in a mud puddle on the sidewalk. It had rained that day and she was making mudpies. When she looked up the scowl turned to a big smile and she indicated the house for her brothers, one of which is still my brother-in-law. On August 27, 2021, Rebecca Schultz and I celebrated our 38th wedding anniversary.

    Things begin to matter more at this point in life and choices must be made wisely as prejudices from the outside begin to determine the future, especially in high school sports. It's an ugly thing. For me personally I had a lot to overcome. My family was wealthy by that time's standards and my Dad got bored again and bought some prime land and built five houses to sell to affluent friends and his brother, the now retired congressman, Cliff. When Cliff retired they moved across from us in Tiffin. I was old enough to be on the prowl and Jack had a Jeep that he would let me use to "hunt" out of season, which naturally I abused. It was my no-good friends that convinced me to see if it could traverse a creek in Hedges-Boyer Park. It could, but . . . . Those experiences would prepare me for later. My Mom sold the store to a friendly chain, Uhlman's, at a good profit. Besides her "big city" background was grating to some (many) and she was hard core Irish to boot. I probably take after her more than my Dad. Her brother, Dan Costello, was widely known as "the man who corrupted Babe Ruth," which was accurate. My Uncle Dan went to college at Mount St. Mary's in Maryland when Babe was in the orphanage there. Dan was later acclaimed the greatest athlete in the college's history in a ceremony at the Bishop's St. Joseph Cathedral here in Columbus, Ohio with Mom the featured guest, which made her later years thrilling. Dan starred for the Yankees and Pirates after graduation and Babe worshipped him. It didn't help either that Dan was a rounder and liked to pull a cork and eventually succumbed to it at age 35, weeks away from marrying a Dupont. I'm not certain if I'm happy or sad I didn't meet his standards.

It always helped if you were a long born local with a lineage. On our high school freshman football team the two top quarterback candidates were legally blind, but they had multiple big brothers who had been the quarterbacks for the varsity, so they were the quarterbacks. Thankfully one of them, the blindest, gained fifty pounds over the years and went on to become an all-state nose tackle, freeing things up for the less blind. Fortunately the ends were 6'4" and 6'6" basketball players forced to make dazzling catches. They received many college offers after their nerves settled.

I had some doubts to overcome too but I did so; I'm not going to belabor them and eventually chose basketball although I would have loved to have played both. This was an exceptional era for high school basketball in Tiffin as both schools were loaded at all positions, especially after our ends recovered. Lots of size and talent that didn't really need much coaching but unfortunately got some. Both schools made the best of it and underachieved for four years. As our skills improved we regressed as teams. But we survived, and each year a few of us went on to play collegiately. My best friend and teammate Paul Winterhalter, was the leading scorer in the state as a senior and was recruited by Michigan, my dream school. I was asked to accompany him on his visit. I was overwhelmed--a dream come true--but he chose Dayton instead. Fortunately a high school official from Tiffin, Mel Hoerig, a friend of the Michigan basketball staff, recommended they consider me based on potential and they later offered me an Academic Athletic

Scholarship to play basketball. It was good so long as I maintained a 2.5 grade average. Best news ever.

Socially things developed too and to many people's regrets I lost my naiveté and shyness around girls and began to enjoy them. It blew my mind how some people connected to others. I returned home after my freshman year at Michigan to see who had married whom in the interim. It shocked me. It seemed so many had just panicked and settled just as life was starting. That realization had a major impact on me as I was already seeing the same trend in new teammates at Michigan. In my entire high school period, I don't think I ever dated a girl from my class and not because there weren't options but because there were and I wanted to feel unfettered to pursue them all. I never liked gossip and in a town like Tiffin it's rampant. I've learned that to most others it was a second language. At least you are a topic, but strive for some accuracy.

When I got to Michigan in the fall of 1959 I was primed, never better. I'd worked all summer with other college players and had never had a debilitating injury. Our freshman team was loaded, widely acclaimed as our best ever and we started playing with the varsity, informally, from the first day in the intramural building. It soon became apparent that we were needed because we pounded the varsity with regularity. Their two best players were in pre-med and as I should have learned in the later years, many lab courses were required. Imagine—to be a doctor? Go figure. They were both guards, my position, and the captain was recovering from knee surgery. The other was our best player and he was _good_. Freshmen couldn't play varsity in those days so these scrimmages were the only competition we'd face all year. We later found out that the only chance the fans had to see us would be our pre-game basketball scrimmages with the football team. Since official practice hadn't started, we didn't even know who our coaches would be. Several prospective candidates, in our minds, would wander in and out from time to time but I don't even think the Head Coach, Bill Perigo, knew for sure, but they all knew we were for real. So did the varsity and they kept showing up to mix in even though back then organized practices couldn't be held until October 15. When they were, I was among the best all-around freshman guards and one of the team's leaders. Football Assistant Matt Patanelli was eventually selected to oversee our "progress."

When practice formally started in Yost Field House for the varsity and a handful of us and remaining in the IM Building for the rest, things started to sour. The freshman coaches selected had never seen us and those of us chosen had to practice with the varsity which rotated weekly. None of them could've coached a successful high school team. They were basically football graduate assistants assigned to freshman basketball to keep them busy, earn their credits.

Then too, recruiting favoritism took its toll. Of the fifteen original freshmen probably twelve of us could really play. With the exception of the two pre-med varsity returnees at least ten of us could outplay any of the other returnees on the varsity who awaited two or three athletes from the football team after their season concluded. Astonishingly there was a league rule that if football players wanted to play basketball they had to take two weeks off after the football season to rest up. In other words drink, eat and chase as much as possible and be ready to jump in. Fortunately all three were ends and like in high school could play, and before the Big Ten Conference season began in later December would be ready to contribute. When the two doctors got in shape the varsity would be able to field a competitive team if they kept practicing against us. Which of course, they didn't.

Once the legal practices started, alumni began drifting in to watch and none wanted to watch some freshmen beat their previous recruits senseless so they used us less and for the most part we returned to the IM Building to join our classmates who, justifiably, were fed up. All they ever did was scrimmage against each other with no plan and it was obvious that coaching favoritism figured heavily into who was selected to practice with the varsity originally, nowhere near the most deserving. I was very thankful that Coach Perigo liked me, but I did deserve it. So did some others.

When the varsity season began, we freshmen were an afterthought and the fun ended—with one exception. The coaches had scheduled one final scrimmage—with some alumni and some of us freshman, me included. It was supposed to start at 3:30 PM at Yost. Naturally it was a Wednesday and I had a 12-3 Chem Lab which I couldn't cut. I bolted at 2:50 PM and ran (no cars for freshmen) full blast to the arena, up the stairs, only glancing at the court where some fat guy appeared to be telling jokes at the foul line surrounded by the entire team, laughing hysterically.

Somewhat relaxed I walked over to the court (raised) and tried to blend in only to be targeted by the fat guy who said "Is this the freshman pimp that's been keeping me waiting?" As the laughter subsided and we formed layup lanes to warm up, the fat guy, about eight feet from the basket, pops into the air--and I mean pops, no steps, no crouching--and slams the ball into the basket. The ball bounces off the floor and hits the rim. All movement stops in silence. Hang on. Ron Kramer is here to scrimmage. So was George Lee, another alum and a high flyer himself who was then with the Philadelphia Warriors. Kramer was in mid-season with the Packers. But here they were. Different times.

I was his target for the day and I was overwhelmed. The scrimmage had a modified agenda as Kramer, the 6'3", 285-pound Packer tight end wanted to guard me, a 6'3", 190-pound freshman and although I'm sure that didn't fit Coach Perigo's original agenda, guess who was now in charge. Kramer was a basketball All American too in his Michigan days, still the greatest athlete we've ever had. But those days were past and he was in midseason and I was a cocky kid, not a pimp. He tried to guard me head-up at first on the perimeter, but I just fed our freshman big men and laughed at his insults because I didn't know what else to do. Then I faked some jumpers, getting him in the air and putting up some floaters that fell, always smiling at his insults but passing mostly, doing what a guard should do. Later he switched to center on our team to drill our varsity big men and I gave him some perfect feeds. After we finished he knew I could play and gave me a pat on the butt and called me a little pimp. Best compliment I ever got. Ron Kramer knew I could play. And it wasn't fat.

I've got to clarify that as I grew to know him Ron Kramer was larger than life and that was his style, especially if you needed it, and he was a great guy. We crossed paths over the years and became friends and finally business partners. He was immortal.

As the season started and the losses mounted, the varsity ended up 6-18, even at full strength. The best thing about being on the Freshman basketball team was getting to know the football players from our game day scrimmages. Like in high school most of the meager attempts at coaching us were wisely ignored until Bob Zuffalato came from Connecticut, I believe it was about mid-season and contributed for those still listening. But you could tell the "coaches" lost the team and many wouldn't be returning next season. Retrospectively, it's an impressionable age and the coaches have to make an impact and make the players feel wanted, especially when some of the best were being ignored. Back then you could have been a Billy goat from Illinois and gotten recruited by Michigan. Because our star player, John Tidwell, one of the doctors, was from Illinois, the recruiters seemed to feel that anybody from there would be the next answer. Just like high school in reverse.

After the season I had to get off my ass academically as I'd miscalculated on how many chem labs I'd have to grace and got a D. At the semester, I switched from Pre-Med to Phys Ed to improve my GPA and salvage my scholarship, figuring that Pre-Med and Phys Ed sounded enough alike that it might slide by the home front. Woops.

A friend of mine from Tiffin, Bill Leahy, was in Pre-Med at John Carroll and was going to summer school there. John

Carroll is a good Catholic School in Cleveland and happened to offer Economics I and II, back-to-back in summer school that Michigan would accept, an opportunity U of M didn't offer. Bill's father was our family doctor and good friend so it was an easy sell and really my only alternative. Their basketball coach gave me full access to their facilities and I only had 90 minutes of class every day in a major that I enjoyed and put to good use later. A friend of mine from high school, Larry Siegfried from Shelby, Ohio, was an opponent, then at Ohio State with a girlfriend nearby. She eventually married his OSU teammate John Havlicek. Sieg and I practiced together at John Carroll. This was beneficial to me and challenging.

We lived in a house across from the campus on the top floor above an elderly couple that only mildly objected when I brought in my weights. I was one of the first basketball players in the Big Ten ever to lift. It was something that became obviously beneficial to me. When I got to know the football players and watch them mature it became obvious to me how beneficial lifting weights could be. Back then not even many football players lifted and even fewer knew how to do so properly, but those who took the time and learned stood out and progressed. I, along with two freshman teammates and close friends, Don Petroff and Dave Kroll, both long deceased, took it up and had to lift clandestinely as it was strictly taboo with the coaches so we had to learn on our own. The secret is if you keep practicing your craft while lifting there's little downside. I've never stopped and it sustains me to this day.

On the humorous side, Bill and I had a roommate for summer school, an ultra-serious Italian named Joe who outworked a grave digger. He was also in Pre-Med and he resented me from the outset. This was going to be a perfect summer. We alternated going out for cheeseburgers most week nights and Joe absolutely detested mustard. He also figured that since I had ninety minutes of class a day and he and Bill twelve hours, to hear him talk, that I should get the cheeseburgers <u>every</u> night. He actually voiced that opinion—to ME. So, for the next three nights I made the trip and brought back the normal six cheeseburgers with everything, extra mustard. After that Joe made the time. Got him out, change of pace.

At any rate, the credits transferred, I had a new major, Economics, and sustained the scholarship probationally for another semester. But then I got in a wreck.

Chapter Three

Present Times

It's Christmas morning 2020 and Becky and I are celebrating alone in Upper Arlington. Fifteen minutes away in Westerville, another affluent Columbus suburb, our son Logan, his wife Laura and their children Pauly, three, and Tommy, six months, are celebrating too. Becky is doing a big prime rib that she will carve off half of and place in an appropriate container along with side dishes for Logan to pick up and take home to share separately later. Logan was in a wedding for one of his University of Toledo fraternity brothers the weekend before and one of the other guests came down with the Covid virus and alerted them and Laura later tested positive too. No symptoms, she felt fine as did the rest of both families, hers and ours. Somebody just tried to blow up Nashville. Just another Christmas.

Becky, Logan and I are more concerned with what's already in store for our country, probably to be determined in the next month. I am already resigned that whatever does I've done all I could have done to prevent it. That's not to say that in any way could I have actually prevented it, but I could have been a factor in influencing those who could have, had I not become afflicted with my neurological disease fifteen years ago. Because fifteen years ago people would have listened and you could get to them. Also, fifteen years ago we didn't know we had the problems and now nobody cares about what could have been done then. But you can get a lot done in fifteen years. Look at the Deep State. Now, if the Repubs don't keep the Senate and Trump isn't declared reelected, throw in the towel and stick it in the drain. I'm serious, I could have done a lot of good if I was mobile. Now, nobody takes phone calls and nobody reads emails, nobody tells the truth and nobody wants to rock the boat. And there's no honor anywhere to be found. God Bless America. You'll understand what I mean as you follow along.

Chapter Four

The Second Fate

Summer school at John Carroll ended in early August 1960 and I wanted to get back to Ann Arbor and reconnect. We had a new coach, Dave Strack, an assistant to Perigo when Winterhalter was recruited, and he somewhat remembered me. Dave was a taciturn man and had left for greener pastures in Arizona for a year, only to return to succeed Perigo. He had never seen me play and I was anxious for that opportunity, but I had some oats to sow and some friends to reconnect with. Most of the football guys were in town and already knew where the action was, so I joined in, got acclimated and went about finding an apartment.

About half of our original recruiting class returned. There were some critical losses, but they thinned the herd and we accepted it. Eventually I found a place on State Street about one hundred yards from the Athletic Department with teammates Don Petroff and Tommy Eveland, and cocky baseballer Jimmy Newman. It was about a mile from our classes, with a place for my car, a '59 Plymouth Fury, my graduation present from Calvert High School.

But first I had to screw things up. On my final night before returning home to pack and move up to Ann Arbor to register early and move in and attend the Basketball Welcome Back party the next weekend, I went into Detroit for a date, after which I planned to drive back to Tiffin from there. The date was worth the way to but not the way from, and I ended up attached to an abutment in the median halfway to Toledo. Demolished. Not me but the car. I was taking a nap and apparently lost focus and the steering column was bent over my left knee, which hurt.

Needless to say the next thirty-six hours were spent eating bucket after bucket of shit from Floyd and Mabel, deservedly so, and my punishment was having to settle for a '56 Chevy of some ungodly color to "represent the family" (I actually used that) back on campus. Our neighbor in Tiffin, Al Whitman, who had bought one of my Dad's houses, was the Chrysler Dealer in town and gave him a "good deal." I ended up making up the difference back on campus, as expected, but I could take as well as give. I told people it was "vintage."

What really bothered me was the ache and the swelling in my knee. I'd never been hurt before and this couldn't have come at a worse time. The door was wide open and I was primed. Then this, and Strack had never seen me play. What else could go wrong? I found out when I went to the IM Building to shoot after an unprecedented week off. I hadn't told anybody and after a few shots I remembered something Siegfried had told me earlier that summer: "You shoot with your legs, not your arms." He was spot on. I began making adjustments to compensate and lost my stroke as well as my speed, which I couldn't afford either.

I couldn't forget last year's captain who graduated to Med School, Terry Miller, and the year of misery he endured trying to come back from surgery my freshman year and that was just out. Nowadays for cartilage surgery it's six weeks and you're back, but then it was for the season, and if ligaments were involved, a year.

No sir. I kept quiet and waited for it to heal on its own, which it did to a point, at least I rationalized. But I lost my confidence and subconsciously changed my game. I finally told Dr. Denny Burke one of the team doctors and he diagnosed torn cartilage, the lesser of two evils that some people could play through, and I told him I preferred to try. Last year's wasted season was enough. He later told Strack, as was his job, but he also told him how well I'd played last year when Strack was elsewhere, and that helped. Dr. Burke was always a great guy and I appreciated that kindness. I played the preconference games as best I could and when the football guys came over and the conference games began I finally relented and had the surgery. We ended up 7-17. Progress. Seriously, improvement. Strack provided discipline and had a plan that I wanted to be part of. It all hinged on recruiting but things just felt better.

I've tried to interject some humor along the way to keep readers who've decided they didn't give a damn about my early history or me at all and I'll deal with that in separate chapters along the way, beginning with the next one. But stick with me for now because my life has been resplendent with larger-than-life characters throughout and some of them would join with me later in an attempt to save a huge portion of the world. But to appreciate that fully you've got to form an opinion about me, favorable or not, because I was the catalyst.

I haven't led a dull life at any point in it. Retrospectively, I think it was because I was certain from the outset that I had absolutely no intention of getting married until at least the direction of my life was pretty much determined and if that took a while, so be it. I knew I wanted to be a parent and I knew I wanted my wife to be younger than me, like my Mom and Dad. But until then I was going to enjoy the characters I encountered at Michigan and later in Detroit.

After the surgery and semester finals, Petroff, Newman and I decided we'd rush a fraternity like most of our friends that hadn't already. There was a handful or so of jock frats that would be interested when rush started with the new semester and one stood out to us because it was at the apex of Fraternity Row on campus: Phi Delta Theta, a huge house on a hill with plenty of parking for our (my) car; many of our friends were members. Eveland was too shy to join a frat but was all in for anything that would give him some peace. Besides that, because of my injury, and Petroff still playing the season and spring baseball for Newman, we figured the hazing couldn't be too bad.

An incident leading up to that begs to be recounted that occurred over semester break, if only for its absurdity and hilarity. As we awaited our grades and practices and rehabilitation continued, one cold and snowy day Petroff and I and teammate Dave Kroll were casually walking, me on crutches, from Yost Fieldhouse to the IM Building, about 200 yards. For some reason, Coach Strack drove up to Yost to an entrance opposite the one we'd just left. Now it must be said, for whatever reason, Michigan's Phys Ed curriculum featured only two truly difficult courses, Anatomy and Kinesiology, and both were recommended to be taken concurrently in the first semester of the sophomore year. By then I was back in LS & A with an Econ major and off the hook and Kroll was in the School of

Education. Kroll is a chapter in itself if it fit my purpose but it does only slightly here.

At any rate Coach sees us about 50 yards away, and we wave and keep moving as it was frigid, but then he calls out "Petroff, did you get your grades?" (meaning the big two), to which Pet responds, "Not yet." Strack counters with "How do you think you did?" Pet responds, "Pretty good." Strack "Do you know your scores?" Pet "I got an eighteen and a twenty-two." Strack, with a tinge of panic in his tone, "Out of how many?" Pet "One hundred and twenty, but I think they're grading on the curve."

Now I'm on crutches facing the IM Building and I can't move. Snot has just exploded out of both nostrils and I'm biting my lip to keep my head from exploding. Thankfully, Kroll is flat on his back in the snow, feet kicking, laughing uproariously, totally out of control. Big Pet is wondering what's so funny. When I finally turn around, Coach Strack is gone.

Now Petroff and Kroll are both about 6' 5", 225 lbs. and muscular, sneak lifters too. Pet had more talent; Kroll more style. Kroll was in our freshman class, but got married and had just returned for second semester, wife in tow. He'll soon replace Pet, who'll be ineligible. Kroll shaves his head and looks exactly like Mr. Clean. He carries a baseball bat around campus, class to class. He struts and beams at everybody. Fits right in. Right off the rack.

Every year at mid-term, some transfers appear and must be evaluated, by players as well as coaches. That year three appeared, all could play but had to wait until the following season to be eligible. Usually they were housed in an annex building (dormitory) next to the hockey arena across from the IM Building, close by. These three were all characters, which all my life I've seemed to attract. The first, Rod Linder, a 6' guard from Illinois, had been the state's leading scorer before starting out at Clemson. He labeled himself the "Original Hot Rod" at a time when, two years previously, West Virginia's Hot Rod Hundley had led the nation in scoring and was now a star with the Lakers. He had apparently minored in eating down south because he had now rounded out to a cute 220 lbs. and always joked that his famous behind the back dribble which he originated, was somewhat inhibited by the extra butt cheek he'd developed last semester. He was also already a Phi Delt and punctuated every statement most self-deprecatingly, with a silent giggle, which was infectious. He'd fit right in at the House, which he barely did. But he never could be squeezed onto the court.

The second, Danny Hoag, a 6' 1" guard from Flint, came from somewhere out west at a notorious outlaw school and was already a kept man, having latched onto a thirty something year old groupie named JoAnn while in high school who'd divorced well. JoAnn didn't accompany him to the annex. Hoagy cased the campus and welcomed the respite as long as the expense checks kept coming. He was a flat-out shooter and practiced the art, but apparently had never given much attention to convincing the opposition to let him take one. He too was a character. Every time you'd tell him something, he'd invariably respond with a quizzical "no it isn't" or "no you didn't" or "no you can't" and laugh uproariously. I'd agree that most of the information we'd impart in those days wasn't gospel but we tried to be helpful for the most part. He and JoAnn departed for greener pastures down south after a semester. She funded him a spring break trip to Florida with us before they left and even offered her convertible, which we declined.

The third, John Harris, really paid dividends and at first seemed the least likely. A lanky 6' 7" Black from Mississippi, BJ (for Big John) smiled all the time and had the most extreme southern accent I'd ever heard. We were the first teammates he'd met and I think he came from a junior college down there although none of us were ever sure. He'd visit a lot, as our apartment was close and we all liked him immediately. He had enormous potential, mostly yet to be developed, but seemed troubled.

For good reason. We finally got it out of him that his hometown Draft Board was after him full blown, even dispatching U.S. Marshalls to Michigan to drag him back. BJ was on the serious dodge. They were in the area and had visited the Annex, just missing him. He didn't know where to turn. But I did. And to this day BJ doesn't know what happened.

On my recruiting trip to Michigan at my Saturday morning final meeting with Coach Perigo before the football game as we were leaving his office down the hall, Athletic Director Fritz Crisler was preparing to leave his. Crisler was the ultimate Michigan Legend, an All Everything, All American, National Championship football coach, the later to be developed Basketball Arena's namesake and everything else. People questioned whether he looked like God or vice versa. He was the biggest name in the Big Ten Conference.

Perigo stops at his door and looks in waiting for acknowledgement and Crisler, standing behind his desk tidying up, glances up and nods, granting permission. Perigo ushers me in and introduces me and Crisler extends his hand and we shake. He then asks if I'm enjoying my weekend. I guess I must have answered in the affirmative because he then said "I'll see you in the fall." And it was an order.

So we knew each other and I figured now was the time to call in the chit. The next day I walked down to the Athletic Office and asked to see him and had to wait five minutes. He invited me in, asked me to sit and what could he do for me. Swear to God. Instead of saying "Well, Fritzy boy, where do I start?" I related to him John's situation to the best of my ability. He stood up, walked to the door and beckoned his secretary, asking her to get the Secretary of Defense on the phone, then turned to me, thanked me and wished me luck.

By the end of the week the Marshalls were gone and BJ could settle in. I never said a thing. But I knew. John Harris became an MVP and a lifelong friend. And, whenever we crossed paths, Fritz Crisler would nod.

Try that today.

Chapter Five

Maturity Beckons

By the end of second semester Pet had seen the handwriting on the wall and dropped out before finals so he could transfer to Western Michigan and be eligible to play there, as the curve hadn't been as steep as he'd hoped. Kroll's wife Sweet Pea had landed a job managing an eight story apartment building newly constructed on campus--a plumb get, so Big Dave was now a landlord. He and Eveland, as well as Tom Cole, a 6' 7" forward from Illinois, guard Joe Nameth, big Dana Baldwin and I were the only ones left from our class and I had rehabbed hard, never having been injured before. I'd missed some early games my senior year in high school with hepatitis but never before with an injury. Like I do everything, I overdid it. My grades were okay but not the 2.5 required overall so I lost my scholarship, but that worked out perfectly as I was working on a routine to justify summer school to the powers that be in Tiffin and it landed in my lap. From what I'd heard, summer school in Ann Arbor was a lot like life on the Washtenaw Riviera. And it was damn close.

There were several lakes in the immediate area and some guys always went together and rented a cottage or two for party purposes. Always plenty of girls. Athletic facilities were always open for workouts. The UM Golf Course nearby. And for those so inclined, a curriculum to choose from. The student counseling advised either take one hard course, usually a requirement, and a bunny or two (or three) if you needed the GPA. The student counseling knew of what they spoke and you could catch them in their offices in the Old Heidelberg Building (Fritz's) most evenings.

By this time, nearly all of the athletes from all sports knew each other and believe me there were some characters, many of whom would become my lifelong friends. During my tenure I've lived with, of course, basketball players, baseball players, football players (many), golfers, wrestlers, hockey players, tennis players, swimmers, trainers, gamblers and bartenders, among others: all wise men.

One summer evening with nothing planned a friend and I connected as we passed in our cars. He knew of a party just down the street on Sorority Row, so we stopped. It was an apartment party for one of their Kappa Kappa Gamma sisters who had just returned from New York where she'd been a Rockette at Radio City Music Hall--a big deal. This was an older crowd, graduates primarily, but that didn't matter to us. Apparently it did to one of their guests, drunk and leaning against the back storm door intent on denying our entrance. A pretty girl trying to get him to lighten up very nicely was told, "I don't know these assholes, Margaret," which always alters my response when we finally do meet. Margaret responded, "Neither do I but I'd like to and it's my party," which when translated means "Get away from the door and get out of my house," I'm pretty sure. Anyway, that's how I interpreted it and that's what finally did occur at the cost of a storm door. When I did enter I apologized about the storm door and she said, "That's okay, it's summer anyway." My kind of girl. We hit it off and talked until dawn. Margaret Hayes was special.

The Rockettes had just raised their height limit to 5' 9" for the next year; last I heard, maybe twenty years ago, it was 5' 10". Margaret was 5' 7" so she had come back to Michigan to get her Masters to teach dancing. She already had a job in Winnetka, Illinois, a Chicago suburb, for the year beginning in September and she would have one more summer school term after this. This was beginning to look like it was too good to be true. But I was smitten and we were together for three years. Nothing but good times, but with enough distance to allow the freedom my maturity level required.

We went dancing the next night at Centennial Terrace in Toledo and she made me feel like I could actually dance, teaching me in the process. This was Ballroom, Modern--her Major, and we had a ball.

Margaret was a funny girl and delightfully naive and beautiful. She never spoke ill of anyone but was a worrier and always worried about me. I never worried about anything. Later that would become an issue. For three years though we had a ball.

My first affair of the heart had occurred when I was a junior in high school with a girl named Carol. And I was smitten. She dumped me after close to a year and I took it hard and decided that was that for that. Until Margaret, nobody had that type of impact on me again, though I had lots of girlfriends, all fondly remembered. But by now I would never allow myself to be so affected again. I called it maturity. The way our relationship would end, however, showed my maturity needed some work.

But that's for later. We were just getting started and we had good times to have.

I had joined the football guys working out in a makeshift workout space above the locker rooms at Yost on a balcony where we had weights and benches. I had rehabbed all spring, got my shot back and joined the "crowd"--never more than ten-- to train, then shoot for an hour and run outside, then play if a game developed. The word was Strack had recruited well and I knew I was in danger of getting lost in the shuffle if I didn't start well. I wound up overtraining.

I had selected on sage advice an Astronomy course for my science and a Geography course, my bunny, for the summer semester taught by two Michigan icons, Dr. Hazel Losh and "The Chief," Ken McMurray, PhD. Astronomy was my science major so I knew Doc well. I'd heard about The Chief, a slight, elderly man who always carried a huge rollaway map over his shoulder and loved golf. His student graders were upper classman and good friends, baseballer Barry Marshall and footballer Ken Tureaud. Or you could buy him a dozen golf balls.

In Tiffin, neighbor Al had talked my Dad into buying me a brand-new white Plymouth convertible with stick shift. Back then on campus all parking meters were thirty-six minutes and all classes were fifty, which invited ingenuity. Everybody read the morning paper *The Detroit Free Press*. We had two evening papers too, *The Detroit News* and *The Detroit Times*, plus *The Ann Arbor News* and *The Michigan Daily*. In short order somebody discovered that if you wrapped a sliver of newspaper around a penny and inserted it into the meter it would jam the meter. After the first day every meter on campus was jammed. Michigan had justified its reputation as a research institution once again. I left the Chevy at the House for the wheelless brothers to share. It didn't require a key. Plus, I had met Ted Forbes and he would need it.

Nobody locked their doors in those days. There were usually four or five to an apartment and I don't even recall having a key for some of them. It seemed there was always somebody there, and even if there wasn't, it wouldn't have been prudent to risk getting caught pilfering, even if so inclined. It was a different age.

As summer school finals approached (I only had one, Geography, as Astro was a once a week night time lab course) the social life peaked. The Geo final was held in an Auditorium since the full contingent enrolled had to attend to actually take it. The Chief held court at a desk and chair on the stage as the tests were distributed. As we began, from backstage carrying a liter of Chief's preferred bourbon and two dozen golf balls, came Barry Marshall smiling, gifts held high, to a standing ovation. Most of us hadn't seen him since the night before when he'd distributed the answers. Barry was a Phi Delt.

The athletes enrolled for summer were freed up for three weeks, two for the footballers, to train, practice and party and determine fall roommates. I ended up with four brother Phi's: two footballers, John Walker and Skip Hildebrand; a tennis player John Wiley; a graduate student Rick Staelin; plus a gambler in Business Grad School.

We'd selected a full house equidistant from Ann Arbor and Ypsilanti, the Eastern Michigan Campus, five miles apart, so we could farm both schools. We all became great friends but I'll talk about the gambler here because I don't want to give the impression that we weren't well rounded culturally. Robin Perry was a self-styled man of mystery and a gambler. He called people "Charley Brown," after the Peanuts character, when he wanted to stress a point. He was a partier like the rest of us and we still talk frequently today, sixty years later. He had two friends, Tags Price and Burt Hutchins, both Business School graduate students themselves and great guys, also gamblers, who happened to be flat out geniuses. Tags had a younger brother Mike, who he claimed was far smarter than he but Mike was scary and stayed on the fringe. Tags and Burt would conclude long careers deeply imbedded in the CIA and later high up in its Administration. And they originally wanted us to protect them when Robin hosted their high roller card games with out of towners.

 I looked forward to fall semester and planned to take some time off from training to rest my legs and help Margaret get settled in Winnetka before classes started.

 I'd have to concede retrospectively what you have already concluded, that I'd led a pretty charmed life to this point and really hadn't been challenged beyond the normal bumps in the road; but then, between terms, my Dad had a heart attack. They were all serious back then and my Mom had him taken to the Cleveland Clinic for a complete work-up. It turned out to be a serious attack but they found other things to concern us too, namely cancer, a true cross section, in various stages. After several weeks they wanted to send him home to recover from the attack to come back to fight the cancer when stronger. Then I went off, with my Mom's support. "Fuck that. How in the hell is he supposed to get stronger lying in bed at home with cancer running unchecked through his body? He's here now, do what you have to!" What really convinced them to consider the alternative was, I don't believe, my outburst, but rather the glare of my Mom's stare after the dust settled. They didn't want to push that button. If you've ever seen Irish rage unleashed you would understand. I didn't have to say another word.

They stayed another six weeks (I didn't, as school was starting) and the doctors did what they could and the prognosis was treatment with drugs for as long as effective, but one of the cancers was pancreatic and, like today, there was no cure. Nor was there any estimate as to how long he had. Over the next year my Mom became a saint caring for him.

Chapter Six

Change of Focus

It was different for me for a while when school began in September but after some rationalization I concluded we'd made the right decision and Dad was in the best place and in good hands. Plus, Mom would be there to oversee things.

The time off hadn't helped my concern about my right Achilles tendon, however, and I saw Dr. Burke. I didn't recall injuring the area during summer work-outs and the two week rest hadn't helped. He did x-rays and saw no tear but did see some irritation that may signal some vertical shredding from overwork, so I knew that was it. He showed the x-ray to our surgeon Dr. Jerry O'Conner, who concurred. As the recovery time for Achilles Tendon surgery in those days was a year and out of the question, rest was the only option.

Strack had recruited well again. And his first class was eligible to play so I wouldn't be missed, but I was still in the system and wanted to see just how far back I could come. I followed Trainer Jim Hunt's instructions and focused on school and "campus life" as I rehabbed, visiting Margaret in Chicago about once a month. Same with Dad who was responding well to his new protocol for now and even visiting his card playing buddies at the Elks several times a week. That would soon change.

I enjoyed my Econ major and never missed a class, which is the key to college success. And we had the requisite connections to the right graduate assistants, as needed. One weekend in Chicago, Margaret and I ran into Kramer and Paul Hornung at Butch McGuire's, a U of M stronghold saloon, and we had a ball. They were in mid-season form in mid-season. Go figure. Those were the days. Butch made everybody from Michigan feel welcome and my buddies back home knew it well. By now home was Ann Arbor and Chicago was a frequent destination, as was Detroit. We were a cosmopolitan crew.

By semester break, both Strack and I knew it wasn't to be for me and after a failed attempt we made it official. He afforded me every opportunity and I could no longer measure up. His first recruiting class was now eligible. That was just the start and was providing the footballers, Scott Maentz and Bob Brown, two good friends and fierce competitors, some relief and support. John Harris and Tom Cole matured, Cole was in my class, and they became threats. And two little guards, Sophomores Doug Herner and Bobby Cantrell, great complements on the floor, would lead us to great heights when the next class arrived. That year we were 17 – 7. Hang on. The best was yet to come: Bill Buntin then Cazzie.

By then most of the athletes of that era that were ever going to know each other at that time did and I can't say I ever regretted meeting any of them. They were all characters on their own, and when appropriately teamed up, absolutely outrageous. If I gave even one example here, I'd be doing all of them an injustice and embarrass some of them. But not then. Most became very successful. I savor them all.

By Christmas, Dad's cancer had taken control. It was to be his last Christmas but not until eleven months later, November 4, 1962, when it would claim him after months of progressive suffering, shared by Mom, who discouraged my coming home to visit. By summer she couldn't even have food in the house for herself. The neighbors prepared her meals, which she ate in the garage. When I heard that I came home whenever possible to help out and watch him rot. On the morning of November 4th, a Monday, at 6:00 AM as I was asleep prior to heading back to school, she woke me up and said "Dan, I can't wake Daddy." My prayers were answered, he'd passed in the night, sixty-nine years lived. My idol. My Mom was both relieved and devastated. I don't remember a thing about his funeral, but I never respected anyone more.

Getting back to school helped as second semester began. By now most of my friends and all of my roommates were older than me and focused on the afterlife (after graduation), complete with jobs and marriage and, of course, the draft, which nobody wished to face. Viet Nam had broken out and that was a concern. I know that I didn't want to be drafted and probably wouldn't qualify because of my past injuries, but I didn't mind serving, so long as I had some say as to how and for how long. But marriage was not on my horizon. For some it was even a way out of the draft, which disgusted me.

My Dad was taken out of high school weeks before graduation to serve in The Great War, WWI, and never talked about it to me except to say he was an infantryman like most others. Up until now I hadn't given it much thought, but damn, it was time to grow up.

Then that spring a rash of marriages broke out. Some of Margaret's friends and even some of mine had made plans for that summer and Margaret would be coming back to Ann Arbor to finish her Masters, which I looked forward to, but for some reason I couldn't get the draft out of my mind. Most people thought I would probably get a deferment and Dr. Burke agreed. Like with most things, I filed it for now. I'd be in summer school too, taking more Econ to catch up.

My Mom had recovered from her grief and began traveling, first with a cruise to Alaska which did her a world of good, so summer school on the Washtenaw Riviera looked better than ever. I got an apartment with a pool with one of our "student" trainers and a character of immense proportions, Mackie Shilling, aka "The Shrew," in a new complex down the road from Fraser's Pub, a mile off campus and close to everything. The Shrew was a classic: a weightlifter, professional student and raconteur from Elyria, Ohio, one of the sons of an eccentric medical lawyer whose home featured an archery stand complete with two bales of hay supporting a target down the length of the main hallway. One had to be cautious when exiting the bathroom halfway down to listen for a "twit thunk" before exiting because you never knew when Ole' Ray would get the urge.

Our place quickly became the target of the athletes training at Yost and the weekend visitors, largely because of the pool and the Shrew who was down there every day, as was I. Margaret got an apartment on the other side of campus with Patti

Haas, an heiress and stand-alone character of her own, and our good friend and hockey player Jerry Kolb, who moved in with us for appearances sake. Who needed the lakes? Apparently we did, because several of our friends rented cottages for the summer at the prime ones. It was idyllic. Golfer Pete Passink's was our headquarters.

I got all my Econ requirements caught up, which was a relief. Margaret completed her Masters and I got back in shape. One more to go. I also switched back to Ed School to ditch the LS & A language requirement. My high school Latin had abandoned me.

We must have hit five or six weddings that summer and I could see where this was heading. All but one were Margaret's friends and they all urged her to catch the bouquet. I tried to head things off from the outset, cautioning them that I just turned twenty-one and Margaret, although twenty-four, had her Masters and a career and I had not yet graduated and was facing the draft with no clue as to a career. I had all the time in the world. Retrospectively I shouldn't have added that last but I, to this day, always overdo everything. But it sufficed at least until the next year, when it was my friends making plans.

Chapter Seven

Finishing Up

As fall semester of my senior year began Margaret and Patti took an apartment right across from the stadium so we would have ready access and parking for the football games and the downtown night life, which was always considerable on a bad day. The NFL-AFL war was just heating up and two of our friends, Joe O'Donnell and Tom Keating, both All Conference linemen, were prime prospects. The guys, about a dozen of us, selected two apartments in the same four-plex close to the athletic facilities, including Joe and Tom. It was the usual zoo with parking in the back with a single lane granting access for twelve cars so after about a week everybody just left their keys in their cars and the first guy out got the first car available. You might not get your own car until the weekend. By now Kroll had gotten lost in the basketball shuffle and became a delivery man for Fritz's Drive Thru to supplement his former landlord salary since he and Sweet Pea had divorced. With the utilities taken care of, it was time to buckle down and focus. I got off to a fast start and had everything lined up, when my counselor informed me that since I'd stayed in Ed School when I had changed majors from Phys-Ed to Econ, to graduate, I'd either have to student teach or take an Ed-Psych course this semester, if possible. It wasn't. After some finagling I convinced him to let me get in a course already underway at the UM-Dearborn campus, once a week. On my first trip, I found out it had been cancelled due to lack of students, so he let me audit it and take a test later. Best of both worlds.

Back then the bars downtown had begun to seek out the bigger rock bands on occasion and that fall the Flame Bar had snagged The Flames to perform: yes, James Brown and the Flames in their early days. This was the beginning of Motown in Detroit. We'd been seeing those people for years in the Detroit bars before they became rock stars.

A bunch of us went. And the Flame's dance floor was about the size of the free-throw lane on a basketball court. The place was packed. Most of us went to listen but Dave Glinka, our quarterback and a great dancer, got up as did Margaret, with me in tow. Before I realize it, Glinka and his date and Margaret and I are dancing with the cameras rolling--live TV, Detroit Station. And I was holding my own all because of Margaret. She made me feel so comfortable, giving me silent lessons as we moved. Dancing with her I never felt self-conscious at all.

Margaret, Masters in tow, got a job teaching Modern Dance to undergrads and Patti taught grade school. The football team was on the upswing and the NFL-AFL was already courting Tom and Joe big time; both would enjoy long AFL careers. Both were outrageous characters and played off each other beautifully and by season's end, scouts were in town courting them. Our apartments housed, besides five football players, basketball, hockey and tennis players; wrestlers; a trainer, a beer man and the occasional tenants (scouts). Kroll was kept hopping at Fritz's Drive Thru, run by Rolph, Fritz's Segundo, usually on the scouts' budget. The scouts, in constant competition, came to consider

Ann Arbor an oasis and eventually offered all of us try-out contracts to placate Joe and Tom, who played them like a symphony. The girl friends, with the exception of Margaret and Patti, both slightly older, were in and out in shifts. Wisely none of us took the scouts up on the try-out contracts. They were all former NFL stars playing hide and seek with their competing brethren and we became friends with most of them, even some of the ones who lost out.

It was a wild and wonderful semester and some of us graduated in December, only a month after President Kennedy's assassination. Eschewing the ceremony, roommates John Minko, another footballer, and Glinka and I decided to drive home with a stop at Glinka's in Toledo where the family always made us feel welcome. Then Minko and I drove to Tiffin and Mom, from where he would go home to Pennsylvania. Naturally we got overserved at Glinka's and stayed over and made it to Mom's about noon the next day. As I got out of the car Mom came out in an Irish rage. Apparently I had missed a carefully planned surprise graduation party the prior evening. Minko had taken about five steps from his car parked behind mine and wisely decided to exercise the option of proceeding on to McConnelsville where the temperature would be a lot warmer. I briefly thought about telling her how much I hate surprises but, showing my on-the-spot newfound maturity, held back and ate it. Hell, I love surprises. Mom, not so much. But, reconsidering the occasion, by dinnertime all was forgiven and we went out.

On the break I spent some time at Margaret's home in Saginaw and hit it off with her mom, who had been concerned about our age difference. Margaret had met my Mom the previous summer with the same concern in reverse. Plus, the draft was looming. Maentz had found an option that I didn't know existed, the Marine Reserves, and he recommended it. Six months of active duty and seven years of reserves, one weekend a month. Being a Marine held a lot more interest for me than getting deferred by the Army or going to Viet Nam, if only because of the superior training. I hadn't checked into my physical status but lots of guys got deferments with far less impairments, plus I was far from ready for a long-term commitment with Margaret, not at all because of her but because of me. Selfish? No, wise, as we had another batch of weddings to attend in the spring, this time my friends as well. And I wasn't going to start my life off with what some day may prove to be a mistake on the biggest decision I'd ever make.

I split the difference. I explained to Margaret that if my number came up, and it would with my name starting with a "C," and I passed the physical, I'd be in for two years, starting as a private. With the Marines, who were cash poor, it would be twelve weeks at Parris Island with far better training, four more at Camp LeJeune for Advanced Infantry Training, then the rest your option for specialization and out to Reserve Duty. We discussed it, condensed version, and I signed up in the Cleveland branch, which didn't deploy until June, giving me time to take that Ed Psych course and be around for the draft. It would be fun, and it would give me time to spend with Margaret and train for the Marines.

It was a great winter semester. I got the Ed Psych course in my wake to make graduation official and got ready for my June deployment to Parris Island. Margaret and I were together every night. Joe and Keats both went pro, Joe to Buffalo, Keats to Oakland. Both became stars. They both immediately got new cars--Joe a Corvette, Keats a sporty Pontiac--but we still had the same parking rotation so everybody made out. Our basketball team became a force with only better times ahead. The baseball team was coming off another great year after their National Championship of 1962 led by Dick Honig and Newman, among others, and great pitching. Their coaches, former Major Leaguers Don Lund, later Moby Benedict, had become my good friends. Moby had been our escort on my recruiting trip in 1959 and was a racquetball opponent over the years. He was a champion, a pure terrier, and I never came close to beating him. Don was always there for me for advice after college, as was our track coach, Don Canham, who would succeed the iconic Fritz Crisler as Athletic Director and would become the greatest of all time. I could only dream of making the contributions in my career, wherever it led, as they had in theirs. They were always an inspiration. Funny how things would work out.

    I went to Nassau in April to train and party and Margaret joined me over spring break. Back then Paradise Island was still largely Huntington Hartford's Estate, a mile away, largely undeveloped. I would swim over and train and get some sun, then take the ferry back about 4:00 PM to get ready to hit the haunts. I rented a top floor room just off the strip for $250.00 for the month. Besides Margaret, enough other friends joined us to make it the perfect vacation. I would return on several occasions over the years to come.

The weddings began soon after and Margaret began to see that ours was far from the planning stage. We loved each other but our agendas were polarized. She had her career by now in Suburban Detroit (Farmington) and I had never even had an interview, nor planned to until I completed my deployment. I knew it would start in Detroit though. We agreed to separate until my return and see. But I think we both knew.

Chapter Eight

A Change of Pace

On a whim on the day before I left for Parris Island, I called my first girlfriend Carol Stanford. She had just graduated from nursing school in Cincinnati and was back home in Toledo. I wanted to see if she would be interested in a bon voyage dinner to see me off. I think that's what sold her, the seeing me off part, but she had to be curious, so she agreed. We went up to Detroit to dine at the Whittier Hotel's Gold Cup Room, owned by the father of a friend, Ivar T. Quarnstrom, a wealthy and renowned Detroit businessman. His son, Bobby "Pee Wee" Quarnstrom, was a close friend to all of us and will be given his due in a more appropriate chapter, one that will be tough for me to write.

Anyway, Carol and I had a great time. It was cleansing for me because I had been carrying around a semi-torch for five years, since she dumped me back in high school. She would later marry a doctor and move to Kalamazoo, Michigan, have six kids, raise them to productivity, lose her husband to illness and become a prominent realtor in Kazoo and Naples, Florida, her winter home, still on the singles market. She is friends with Bob and Susan Brown. Busy girl.

I went to Parris Island with precisely the right attitude, resigned to the fact that I wasn't going to have a say in any decision for twelve weeks, and in great shape. Most of my platoon of eighty were either Blacks or Hispanics from the big cities or Whites from smaller towns. At almost twenty-three, I was one of the older ones and one of the biggest. Also as I was soon to find out, one of the few swimmers. There were no visible prejudices at all, at least among the recruits. The Drill Instructors, not so much. The key was you went along to get along and it took some guys more time than it should have. It was both funny and frustrating.

Back in early high school it was recognized that I had a mild vision problem and could use glasses, something nowhere on my original agenda. When I got to Michigan the coaches introduced me to contact lenses, new on the market, and I tried them, big suckers then but they worked and were comfortable enough. As I got used to them I found they made me shoot better and be quicker. But there was no place for them in Boot Camp so I put them away and quickly readjusted. I actually got out of shape in training but learned a lot and paid attention, laughing myself to sleep many nights. Time went quickly until we hit the Rifle Range and had to qualify. I barely was up until the final day when I wore the lenses and shot Expert, both pleasing and pissing off my Instructor and my D.I., who all along thought I was underperforming. I've always had great discipline when needed and my focus was to win this battle of wills and not let anything or anybody get to me. Some guys fought it every day and eventually washed out, but if you just go along and pay attention you get through. This was Boot Camp, designed to get everybody through, not Special Forces, which accepted only the elite, as I would soon find out.

The Boot Camp swimming tests were hilarious. If you could swim and were a natural floater, if you didn't panic, they were fun. You had to go up on the high board in full combat gear, jump in the pool and take everything off down to your skivvies, collect it, rifle included, and swim to the shallow end as fast as possible. That last part scared most people but the secret was to relax or you would drop stuff and have to start over. I came in first in my platoon out of the now seventy; only about a dozen passed.

After the twelve weeks and graduation we were deployed to Infantry Training Regiment (ITR) in Camp LeJeune in North Carolina for four weeks to determine our specialties, preferably infantry. One new option was Amphibious Reconnaissance, to be held at Camp Pendleton in Coronado, California. This would be their second class and of all the platoons stationed, only about twenty showed up to try and qualify. Of the eight from LeJeune selected, four were from my platoon, me included. Better the California ocean in late autumn than the Carolina mountains. Plus, the instructors at Pendleton were far superior to those at LeJeune with the same rank. I didn't want to be part of the herd headed for the Infantry. Besides we four--Harvey, Smitty, Bill and I--were good buddies from vastly different backgrounds. I'd made the right decision.

Coronado and Camp Pendleton in beautiful southern California was a step up from LeJeune, as were our Instructors, all Gunny Sergeants or above. We got right to work with a week of swim testing. Ultimately, you had to be able to hold your breath under water for three minutes. I knew the trick and managed four. You didn't hold your breath, you controlled it. Of our eight and Camp Pendleton's ten candidates, twelve made the final cut for training, all four from our platoon. The other six were granted deployments of their choice, not a bad deal when compared to what they left behind.

Now I was no more than a social swimmer--dive off the high board, swim to the side, preen for the girls and repeat--but I was a floater as were we all, and I was mature enough to think things through. This was to be distance swimming in a wetsuit, side stroke, carrying a backpack and a rifle that would float, thank God. Pacing, not racing, would be the key and the flippers were essential. No matter what, you couldn't panic and you had to stay together. We trained Mondays, Wednesdays and Fridays on the beach in Coronado, a mile away from the Navy Frogmen; on Tuesdays and Thursdays we had to swim ten miles as a group up and down horizontally past the surf zone around the Del Coronado Hotel up to San Diego Beach in the Pacific and back, under the supervision of an instructor. No cheating. You just resigned yourself to the task and stayed together. It never got easy, you just did it for eight weeks then onto a destroyer for war games in Hawaii against the Army.

If you learned in training war games were fun. If not, you were scared and alone. I made sure I could read a compass, as all our games were held at night when there was no moon, and we always deployed in either a straight out swim, a rubber boat, a speed boat, a submarine or a helicopter. On deployment you went in on an azimuth and returned on a back azimuth to your rendezvous point, never knowing how far to or from your target or pickup point. Unlike the Frogmen, we never wore tanks except for one day in training, and silence was critical as sound carries at sea. Also, going in to your target always on land, you can't hear the surf zone or sight your target. There's just a little lift in the surface when you hit the surf zone and when you feel that, hang on for the ride of your life and hope you are on target or you will crash on the shoals if you are a click off. Upon landing you have to control your giddiness, bury your rubber boat and/or wetsuits, pack up and head out on your mission, all the time aware that the Army is out there looking for you. Naturally, no talking. After your mission is complete, if you haven't been spotted it's your job to hole up and hide for the rest of the night and all of the next day with the Army in pursuit until it's time to return to your entry point. Then dig up your boat and wetsuit, time the surf zone so you know how much time you have to get through it without being washed back, and paddle, or swim, on a different back azimuth to the pickup rendezvous point miles away (you don't know until you are there) all the time wondering by which method the pickup will occur. Simple. Plus of course, prepare a critique of the results of your mission, which your superiors will already know.

On one of our ventures with me in charge and the Army in pursuit, I holed us up at a spot just below the horizon opposite the volcano to sleep—and hide. When we woke at dawn we found we had settled among a nest of sidewinders (baby rattlesnakes) that were apparently on the same schedule. We didn't exactly leave in formation. I could imagine us running atop the horizon, eight targets.

We did all five such "missions" on our two weeks at sea, all different. We were all amazed at our level of improvement with each one, a tribute solely to our training. On one we jumped out of a helicopter and swam in, on another we ejected from a submarine and were picked up by a speed boat to be dropped off to deploy, then had to swim out on a back azimuth to the ship. I was on point on that one and about three miles out in the middle of the ocean, I smashed my head, side stroke, remember, into the side of something. Panicked, I back peddled about ten yards, looked up at the sky and saw a thin line in the air where the lower part was a shade darker than the sky above. I had swum into the side of the ship. We gathered to settle and about fifteen yards from our position was a rope ladder. What a relief. There was not a sound to be heard nor a light to be seen until we opened a hatch and were blown away by bright lights, rock music and taunting chants as we entered. Breakfast at sea. I was proud of that compass read.

After our two-week deployment, it was pretty much over, with fine tuning occupying the majority of our final week. Smitty, Harvey and Bill, our original boot camp crew, were open to a night in Tijuana down in old Mexico. We were glad to be on land again and our exhaustion was put on hold. Since I was a Mexico veteran (Cancun) I led the way and we grabbed a bus to the border. Just across, we exited the bus and were assaulted by cabbies to take us to town and the "Hot Spots." This one, babbling all the way, took us on a circuitous route through side streets and back alleys just off the main drag, finally to pull up to the rear of a building that was completely dark. He parked and got out of the car and approached the back door. Obviously we smelled a rat, especially when he returned and waved us to follow and never asked for a fare. The man should get out more. What the hell, we were downtown.

He opened the back door for us and dissolved into the night as we were met by at least a dozen chiquitas, selling their wares, pulling us up a ramp to a different level and down a hallway with rooms on both sides and more girls. They tugged us into individual rooms, chatting away and had me at least, sit on a bed, then left. I assumed Harvey, Smitty and Bill received the same greeting. Just before I got up to check, the door opened and in came a huge Mexican, far bigger than I--but not me, at that time, especially after where I'd just come from--waving a switch blade and signaling me back on the bed. I sat and he motioned for me to take off my shoes, which were flimsy slip-on moccasins. After two weeks in flippers and boots they were a welcome relief. As I slipped out of them down the hall I heard a door smash open and American curses among the shrieks of the chiquitas. Harvey, I figured, from Texas, then another smash and more screams and curses. Smitty, another Ohio boy. By this time my big Mex had opened the door and was looking down the hall at the festivities. By now my moccasins were back on and I was enroute. As big boy turned around my foot slammed through his groin and he was down but I threw in a few butt drops on his head to be certain; my butt has always been my best feature. I could have taken his switch blade or I could have robbed him-- his roll was on the floor--but I hadn't heard Bill so I went out in the hall to check on Harvey and Wayne. They were under at least six Mexicans and several of the girls trying to rob them, so I headed the other way toward the street to find help, as on that route sailors and Marines would be up and down the busy streets. At my first turn out of the room around the corner were a half dozen or more of the girls ready to swarm me, but I popped the first one and she actually took flight into the others and I moved on, trying to find the way out. At the next turn was a ramp heading down, I hoped, to the street. As I headed down, building a head of steam, I noticed there was no door knob and I assumed it was locked, so hang on. It wasn't but there was a Mexican leaning against it guarding that entrance. He shot across the sidewalk, off a parking meter into a parked car and off that to another one of my running punches, right on the money and down and out. I looked up and down the street for help and there wasn't a serviceman in sight.

At the next storefront, however, was a tough looking little Italian guy, Mafia all the way--as they ran Tijuana--manning the storefront and watching what had just occurred. He'd been watching closely because he saw my dilemma and since servicemen are his bread and butter, offered to help. I didn't know how much value he'd have but he motioned inside and two goons came out and I could see the value they might bring, so I explained the situation and we reentered, the little guy still manning the storefront.

We ran up the ramp to complete silence and turned the corner to go down the hall and there was nobody there, empty. No sign except the blood and filth, unnoticed before. I thanked the goons and my benefactor and started up and down the street on a search of my own. On about the third pass I saw Bill across the street going in the opposite direction doing the same. He wasn't threatened by a Mexican and went right to work. He did hear the ruckus but figured it wasn't anything we couldn't handle and was almost finished anyway. By the time he did and the chiquita left, he'd just followed her down the ramp we'd originally entered on. He saw her climbing into one car as another was pulling away so just walked down the alley to the street to begin his search, probably just after the goons and I entered via the front ramp. We later would find out that Harvey and Wayne were in the front car.

Going to the Rurales (cops) was useless the goons said, so Bill and I resumed our search, going into the bars this time. Plus we were thirsty. It was easy to see why servicemen weren't in the streets: they were in the bars. Most of the rectangular bars had nude dancers in them. Sailors and Marines sat backwards on their bar stools leaning back with their mouths open waiting for a passing taste. The donors would squat down and comply. Tijuana culture.

We finally grabbed the last bus and returned, thinking Wayne and Harvey might have caught an earlier one--hoping really. They hadn't, and about 10:20 Saturday morning just before I was about to report the incident, they wandered through the gate, badly beaten and pissed at us. Even when we explained what transpired, they didn't speak to us until the next Friday's graduation. Saturday we were to head home.

That final week we were re-recruited by our various instructors, a very impressive group. One of the instructors from the Frogmen was there and tried to get several of us to consider a new group being developed to combine Amphibious Recon and them for a special focus team to be called the SEALS. We were flattered, especially Harvey and Smitty, who retrospectively should have considered it, but it was a six-year commitment and didn't fit my plans. I hadn't worn my contacts in twelve weeks except for weekends. We resisted and hit the Coronado bars that were flush with Navy wives with their husbands at sea. I was, however, successful in getting my monthly Reserve Commitment switched to Camp Pendleton because I wasn't trained for Advanced Infantry, the Detroit Reserves specialty, where I'd be living. A monthly flight to Coronado would be welcomed and it left the door open to reconsider the SEALS, or so I told them.

Harvey and Smitty disappeared that Friday night before departure back home. Michigan was in the Rose Bowl up at Pasadena with a lot of my friends playing the next week, but I wanted to be home for Christmas and take advantage of Mom being proud. Seriously, I didn't want her spending Christmas alone and I missed her. She would be happy too.

Harvey and Smitty reappeared shortly before takeoff on Saturday, their bags previously packed and loaded, and once we were airborne, showed Bill and me the Tijuana cabby's ear, freshly severed. I never found out which one got to keep it. Bad dudes. Haven't seen them since. Good old boys.

One other feature of the Coronado experience was toward the end: the Bills played the Chargers in San Diego so Joe and his roommate, Paul Costa, paid me an unannounced visit on the beach during training. Both monsters. I got new respect from our instructors, by now our buddies. We all went to the game Sunday and to the hotel afterwards. Semper Fi. All on the Bills' Owner, Ralph Wilson.

I was frequently asked about sharks on our forays over the years and I have to say that was never a consideration and never came up among us. We were too busy trying to meet our objectives and stay on course. The instructors assured us our "rifles" would be sufficient. Personally I never gave it a thought.

Chapter Nine

The Real World

After the 1965 New Year celebration with my old Tiffin buddies subsided and I checked back in at Ann Arbor for a few days of celebrating Michigan's win in the Rose Bowl, it was time to head for Detroit and launch a career—in something or other. I moved in with Jerry Kolb, the hockey player, who was living in Northwest Detroit with Downriver Davis among others, so named because all of his former roommates had left, wishing he'd gone back Down River, the Industrial Sector towards Toledo. His personality had never developed past the pouting stage, yet he was in insurance sales and getting by. Kolb was engaged to Patti who was living in Farmington with Margaret who by now was dating a doctor. Kroll lived just across the highway and was employed as a salesman/model for a clothing line, perfect as he still had the Mr. Clean look and was pondering a career with the Lions. He had become good friends with some and was smitten but his last football was at Alpena High, up north. Another good friend Gary Kane, a former Michigan football/basketball player from before my time but another former roommate, lived with his wife in nearby Plymouth. Also in sales, Gary was in Detroit every day. It would be sales for me.

Virtually half of the multitude of buddies I had at Michigan ended up in Detroit but it was the sales guys I always ended up running with. They were mostly still single and scattered throughout so we were connected with bars, gyms, girls and parties all over, plus we knew the city from our Ann Arbor days forty miles away nearly as well as any native we would encounter.

In my first week at Michigan in 1959, the basketballers had registered early and moved into their dorms to await their fellow classmates from all over the world. We had to live in dorms as freshmen, a wise mandate, so we all were looking forward to meeting our dormmates. At my Allen Ramsey House in West Quad, when the cars pulled in--Cadillacs and Lincolns with New York plates--the parents got out and strutted around like big city mayors or inspectors. Some had chauffeurs that emptied the son's luggage and brought it in to unpack then returned to be directed to assist the unfortunate chauffeurless fathers' sons' bags. The Jews were here. Of course, all took their sons out to dinner at Ann Arbor's finest and were reserved for the night in the grandest hostelry so we never got to meet any of them until the next day after the departure ceremony.

Back home our neighbors, the Max Berezins, were Jewish and owned a store that featured ladies ready to wear like ours used to be. The family included two foxy daughters and a son Alec, who would later make a name for himself as a Cleveland attorney. Fine family, but not these legendary New York Jews.

The New York Jews were standoffish at first, certainly not shy, but reticent until they found out we were athletes and had already registered. That made us special and things opened up. By the end of the day I found out that almost to a man they had already read their first semester's text books. Ours had been dropped off but laid unwrapped. Big Pet was not planning on opening an unwrapped text book so, figuring he had nothing in common with them, went on to bed. Why would anybody actually read a textbook? Pet could talk Anatomy and Kinesiology with anyone already.

At any rate, over the years the athletes and the Jews developed a fairly good relationship as a whole and an excellent one with our group. We kidded that when we finally joined the business world every one of us would have a Jew for when things got tough. And they kidded that they'd be proud to be our Jew, for a fee. Imagine that today.

In 1965, my very first interview was with Dun & Bradstreet, as I figured an Econ background would be attractive to them and D & B could advance my knowledge of the business world where I could actually use a Jew.

Dun & Bradstreet hired me and I moved downtown to an apartment, living alone for the first time. I went in with a good attitude, eager to learn and everything was great. They started me out compiling data on companies and clients from banks and courthouses, things I really needed, to be passed on to the evaluators to determine ratings, which were passed on to the client representatives to interact with their clients. Made sense and I soaked it up—for a while. I eventually learned that in the Detroit office it usually took five years to become an account executive, my objective, if everything went smoothly. That meant if I played the game I would be sucking up for the duration. Also, my background as an athlete and Recon Marine, initially an asset at hiring, became a liability and caused petty jealousies as things progressed. I got along with everybody but some lacked that gift, which resulted in pettiness, which I despise.

I had one final date with Margaret and she still looked super and we had restrained fun and a good talk. Patti and Jerry were getting married and her doctor was moving on and pressuring her so we left it as friends for life because I was no closer to that commitment. I was relieved but missed her for years. She taught me how to love.

Fortunately, after about ten months I got word of a new trucking company delivery service called United Parcel Service, recently opened and on the move. UPS was already stealing business from the Post Office daily and was the talk of the city. Its secret was simple: they had no place to store packages, only truck depots where they were transferred for immediate transport, pick-up and delivery, truck to truck to the destination, with no storage facilities to delay transport along the way. Nothing was lost or destroyed. Overnight service. Plus they had a policy of only promoting from within, making it a good place to start a career. Their offices were only several miles from D & B. I had to check.

Their Detroit boss, Jim Dorr, and I hit it off immediately and he invited me on an overnight run that weekend, Detroit to Pittsburgh, beginning at dawn at the headquarters in Detroit, where we loaded, to Toledo for a drop and pickup, to Dayton to Cleveland to Pittsburgh for the final drop and reload and return trip, back Saturday night to unload, reload and debark with a fresh driver. Impressive. My job would be to sell the service to Detroit businesses after a week's training at the local headquarters. Jim Dorr didn't mess around and neither did I. My only competition would be the Post Office. Talk about an easy lay-up.

And it was. UPS then currently focused on the major Midwest cities to get established and Detroit was the heart of the Midwest and the home of the Teamsters, with whom Jim was already dealing. I went from shipper to shipper every day and most were eager for the visit, being fed up with the Postal Service. I could usually charm those who weren't, especially if it was a receptionist. Things were looking good.

When I was in high school, there had been a Big Ten basketball game televised most Saturday afternoons. There were only three stations or networks: ABC, CBS, NBC. One game per week. It was the same in college for the first few years but, because of the budding NFL-AFL football war other channels began to spring up: new networks, the advent of Cablevision. One of my casual acquaintances from Ann Arbor, Tom Johnston, owned a radio station that featured as many Michigan sporting events as he could and he was thinking of trying television with his Interstate Broadcast Network. Good idea, ahead of his time. I ran into him one day in Detroit about this time, and he asked me if I'd be interested in joining his broadcast team. Hell yes. As a high schooler I had announced our football games over the P.A. System and what's to learn after that vast experience? Big Ten football and basketball, where Tom wanted to start, was the natural next step. So, I told him to keep me in mind. Things were falling in place.

Also, after extensive research, I'd whittled my favorite bars search down to two, Nemo's and the Lindell A.C., both downtown, about a mile apart and both legendary classics in Detroit. Nemo's for daytime/evening drinking; Lindell for nighttime post game activity. All the sports teams, Lions, Tigers, Pistons and Red Wings facilities were minutes apart then, ideally convenient. The characters that owned and inhabited both places deserve mention and constituted my Master's Degree in life. The good, the bad and the outrageous, as you will see. My night club research was still in progress.

I'd made a lot of my Detroit friends in Ann Arbor but many more on our forays into the city to see a game or hit a night spot featuring some of the up and coming Motown soul musicians such as the Supremes or the Temptations. Detroit's biggest star at the time was Dave DeBusschere, a local high school hero at Austin, an east side Catholic school, who played both basketball and baseball at an elite level and was a scratch golfer. Dave loved his beer. I first met him when his University of Detroit team came to scrimmage us in Ann Arbor in preseason and tore us a new one. Afterwards he came over to the Phi Delt House for a party carrying a case of Stroh's. He put it next to his chair and drank it, watching, laughing and chatting completely at home, until it was gone. Then he collected his teammates who had been drinking our beer and headed home. Class tomorrow.

Dave was with the Pistons now and pitched for the White Sox in the summer. I dated a girl who went to college at Marygrove, a Detroit based Catholic Girls College, for a short time and that was where Dave's girlfriend went, so we stayed in touch and became friends. Dave's picture was the first one you saw entering Nemo's.

After the pro games, whether it be Lions, Tigers, Pistons or Red Wings, those two bars—Nemo's and Lindell's—were the places to be, pre or postgame, if a good time was your intent. It was a different time then; the players were looking to blend as much as the fans. They weren't making any more than the next guy and needed off season jobs so they welcomed the interaction with fans, for the most part. There were the assholes on both sides, although not so much so at Nemo's, primarily a Union bar, but they soon were weeded out and by midseason pretty much everyone knew one another, at least by sight and recognition of acceptance.

As I said, Nemo's was primarily a Union bar. Unless there was a game, Nemo always tried to close down some time after 9:00 PM. It was usually Buttons' decision. Buttons, like so many others, deserves a page to himself, but I'm a handicapped man handwriting this with points to make. Nemo Springstead was a tough Irishman who ruled both sternly and benevolently. His son Pat runs it now, if they survive the Pandemic and Michigan's governor's absurd declarations, and I still check from time to time by phone and my name is familiar no matter who answers. You'll find out why in a later chapter.

Lindell's was owned by the Butsikaris brothers Jimmy and Johnny, two tough Greeks with Detroit Lions star Alex Karras, another Greek, holding a small piece. It was a dark, quieter bar with a completely different atmosphere, lots of confidential quiet discussions, deal making during the day, but wild and crazy at night, especially after games. Nearly every regular was shifty but I've always loved characters and I had listened in on many wild schemes at the Old A.C. It was a nighttime bar and I'd often stop in after a game of my own, or one of the Pistons'. I don't know if it still exists. So much has changed. All because of politics.

All that swimming in the ocean had completely ruined my hoops game but healed my Achilles so I could run forever but couldn't shoot, so I played as much as possible in whatever industrial league could accommodate me. I met a lot of characters there too, especially the Blacks. Some of them could really play and found that if they gave me the ball I could make it a lot easier for them. After a while I was in demand but by then my shot had come back and from thereon not so much so, as I would take the shot myself. But the teams that sustained interest began to win. I felt better about myself.

The decade before had seen the conclusion of most of the Union wars in Detroit, primarily between the Stevedores, the Longshoremen and the Teamsters along the Detroit River and with Jimmy Hoffa fully entrenched at the Teamsters. They were now pretty much unified and along with the Electricians and others became allies, leaving only the Mafia and public sector to deal with, at least until Bobby Kennedy came along. At Nemo's I got to know all those involved and I had to be careful. My strategy was to just never ask any questions. I was there several times a week and had a favorite stool on the front corner just down from Larry Brennan, who never sat with his back to the door, against the wall leading to the dining area. Nemo's had great food, cooked onsite, for two hours, 11:00 AM to 1:00 PM, then the kitchen closed down. Larry would soon be joined by Bobby Holmes, Jr. who would walk past me and sit at mid bar where drinks were delivered, me, among others, in between them. In later years they would come to be known as Number One and Number Two. Nemo held court behind the bar and Buttons made drinks and delivered.

Either already there or soon to come would be some of most outlandish characters ever conceived: Union bosses, of course, but also politicians, top business executives, hit men, athletes, doctors, lawyers, Indian Chiefs, secured ladies, police detectives, tourists (just for a moment), Santa Claus (in season) and those of us accepted as regular patrons. Naturally the back door admitted on a steady basis the usual coterie of Teamster toughs for security and intimidation purposes, as they mingled with the bosses and fellow unionistas.

Just as everything was looking good, Jim Dorr was reassigned to South Carolina to open up the southeast UPS. He wanted me to join him. If I stayed in Detroit with UPS, I'd be screwed because his successor insisted on daily extensive reports on every move you made and I was making lots of moves. He would rather know what was working instead of making sure it did on his end and we couldn't have made it work for long. I liked Chet Redpath but he only tolerated me and we would have clashed eventually. I was already their top salesman.

Besides, just that week in Nemo's I picked up a good tip that looked to be right down my alley. Sportservice was, maybe still is, a company out of New York that ran all of the concessions for all of the stadiums and arenas in professional, and some college, sports for years. They had recently opened another division to put together those sports franchises' game programs, including selling all the advertising. A friend from Nemo's, Joe

Gentile, the Lions and Tigers P.A. announcer, a Detroit Legend, had recommended me to Herm Goldman earlier that week so I gave him a call and on our interview he started out by giving me my supplies and an expense check and some Jewish wisdom: "Just sell." To hell with layups, this was a slam dunk. Joe G had some clout.

Sportservice's Detroit office was up north but my beat would be downtown, primarily at the teams' offices. The Pistons were ensconced in the Sheraton Cadillac Hotel, two short blocks from the Lindell, the Lions a mile up, across from Nemo's on Michigan Avenue, the Tigers a block from there in Tiger Stadium where the Lions also played. The Red Wings were in the Olympia Arena, another mile north. Also, a pro Soccer Team, the Cougars, would be debuting in the Spring. They all were anxious to get prime spots in their programs committed as soon as possible, almost as anxious as the returning and prospective sponsors were to commit. I got a salary plus commissions, free tickets to distribute as well as use and my time was my own. Representatives from most of the prospective sponsors would be at either Nemo's or Lindell's weekly and most of their offices were downtown or in the close suburbs.

To top things off I got a call from Tom Johnston saying that his network had a contract with the Big Ten's permission to broadcast a football and basketball game of the week on a delayed basis starting in the fall and wanted me to do the color. We'd be the only other game on after the major Network Game of the Week. He was trying to put together broadcasting an auto race at Jackson Speedway in the summer, something I'd never even been to, in the interim and wanted me to be a spotter there. Get the hang.

Now if all this sounds like it's too good to be true that anyone could be this lucky, it's not. It all happened, not without some self-made obstacles and poor decisions generously thrown in. But I learned from them all and came out a better person for the experiences. Just thank God I was single and still alive because it was a dangerous time ahead. Nothing like today, but relatively so. Through the process I began to suspect that I might just be an asshole, the title everyone sought to avoid. If that were the case, as it would prove to be, I subconsciously vowed that I was going to be the best asshole I could be because that was my style. To this day I just never could conform and to this day I have never intentionally tried to hurt anybody nor ever failed to help them if I could and I've encountered hundreds of bad assholes, hopefully with more to come. Ironically I learned all this at Nemo's, where they didn't tolerate bad assholes for long. I also learned the meaning of both loyalty and honor, to be true to your beliefs, whichever ones you chose. To be a man, just my kind.

By then I had moved in with Piston rookie Tom Van Arsdale. Half of the world's most famous twins, from Indiana. His brother Dick had gone to the Knicks and it was the first time they had ever been separated, so Tom was Dickless and needed a friend, and he ended up being my best. Both had it all and were two of the finest gentlemen I've ever met: although I've only met Dick a handful of times in nearly sixty years I still feel like I know him. Tom, I do, and consider him one of my two best friends along with Jere Carrick, from back home, who would be best man in my wedding seventeen years later.

Van had a little separation anxiety at first but once he knew he belonged, hang on. Dave DeBusschere was player-coach for the Pistons now and they blended well and we all hung out. We lived in a new four building sky rise complex, Lafayette Towers, overlooking the city. More to come. Dave's family had a bar, The Lycaste Tavern, not far away.

One of my good friends from Michigan days was "Pee Wee" Quarnstrom, a tough little guy from Grosse Pointe who was in for most anything and could see it through to its end. He came from money but didn't flash it and made friends easily but selectively. I was honored that he picked me. After Michigan, he went to the Detroit College of Law to become an attorney and married Karen Belanger, a super girl, and had two daughters and a son. Also, a plane. One year several of us flew to the Masters Golf Tournament in Augusta, and upon arrival were told that we would be on hold to land as there were other planes circling ahead of us. Pee Wee cut off the Traffic Controller with the message "Four-four Yankee, Quarnstrom, Detroit" and we were on the ground in five minutes, with attendants to slot the plane. Lots of good times for too few years.

One early winter weekend, Pee Wee and his Dad Ted, and their pilot were returning from Charlevoix in Upper Michigan, where they had a home, when a storm hit and the plane crashed, killing his Dad, and eventually the pilot. Pee Wee was badly burned and disfigured. I can still hear his agony when they changed his dressings. Burn units were primitive back then. He would recover but he was never the same. He eventually would perish in an auto accident in one of his cars, years later.

Chapter 10

Settling In

Detroit has always been a Democrat controlled city, as have most major cities, but in those days the chasm that exists between Republicans and Democrats today was non-existent. Both competed vigorously but once elections were over got along for the most part, stole as much as they could and were largely civil. Both also favored Nemo's and fit right in, blended even. All the regulars got "Get out of jail free cards" from the judges as drunken driving had become an actual charge, which was particularly helpful to Jackie Kelly, a union regular who loved the new north freeway with concrete walls that allowed him to bounce home at night.

I became good friends with Larry Brennan and Bobby Holmes whose fathers had been Hoffa allies, Owen Burt Brennan and Bobby Holmes, Sr., in the early days. Their successors nowadays work largely out of Washington at the National Headquarters. Larry, Bobby and Dick Fitzsimmons (another legacy), manned the Detroit local, the genesis site. Big Phil Lehner was the enforcer, as needed--6' 5", 260 lbs. You had to pay close attention if you were curious as to whether or not he had teeth since it's tough to scowl and smile at the same time. He always wore short sleeve shirts under his suit coat because his wrists were Popeyeish and couldn't be harnessed. Fit right in. Every once in a while, he was needed and had a prominent role in the aforementioned union wars. His best friend was Sam

Williams, a former Lions defensive end of long tenure who was always loud and ebullient with an outrageous cackle, another Nemo's regular. His picture was down from Dave's at the entrance.

But predominant in the Nemo Hall of Characters were Shorty and Norm (also pictured) and their "body guard," native "Newyawka" John Dooling. "Shahtty and Naum," as Dooling called them, were both 6' 8", next to 300 lbs. and former NBA centers from Detroit--Norm from U of D; Shorty, MSU, up the road. Dooling was a 5' 5" former boxer, always on, with a rapid-fire accented banter followed by a sneezy cackle, "zit, zit, zit, zit," punctuating whatever he said. Always hilarious. Still another package.

Shorty worked for the major liquor/wine distributorship in Detroit and Norm for Stroh's, the major brewery. Their jobs called for them to visit every vendor in the downtown Detroit area and push products. They took it to heart although by now they were legends. Anyone who didn't buy from them was ostracized until that changed and both brought crowds to the bars they serviced. Dooling trained fighters, having been one. I'll leave that to your imagination.

Most of the other regulars deserved attention on their own too, save it to say they were all perfect complements. For every Mutt there was a Jeff. Unless there was a ballgame, Nemo's was a week day bar filled with regulars who knew each other's agendas and old friends, sometimes closed by nine, but that was rare. I would be a regular my entire time in Detroit and an alumnus to this day.

One evening on a no-game late spring day after a workout and some racquetball at the South Y, Phil and I stopped in for a drink at about 8:30. It was still light out. Buttons was just tidying up to close as we entered the side door past those leaving. Buttons would always extend hours for Phil so we sat at mid-bar, totally alone, with Buttons serving. Buttons Mulcahy was a tough little Irishman and Nemo loyalist who had been with Nemo since opening years before and was distinguished by a stutter that was regulated by the situation at hand.

We hadn't finished our first beer when the phone rang. Nemo's had phones at both ends of the bar with long cords. Buttons answered and brought it to Phil and I swear to God something changed in the room. The look on Button's face belied it and he motioned me down a few barstools, stuttered something and went into the kitchen, where I could still see him, to another line. He began making calls. By now Phil was off his call and motioned me back and told me it would be best if I left now, right now. So, I did.

I walked right to my car in the lot out to Michigan Avenue (Nemo's is on Michigan & 8th) and drove around the block to the now closed Lion's offices. It was dark by then, and I sat in my car, directly across the street, to watch. Phil was sitting at the same stool sipping another Stroh's. There was no sign of Buttons, who I would later learn was well heeled and was quickly out of sight. After no more than ten minutes, six cars rolled in and surrounded the building, blocking off Michigan Avenue to westbound traffic, just like in Chicago P.D. As the drivers and passengers got out and approached Nemo's I could recognize them all. Good old boys.

The next day I came in for lunch. Phil wasn't there, but Buttons was serving and the place was packed as usual, with many of the car inhabitants at various tables. Nobody said a word about the night before so neither did I, ever. Years later I found out and suffice it to say it had something to do with the old union wars on the river years before. I wouldn't find out what for a generation and then by accident. I'll tell my grandchildren if they ask. Somebody wanted to settle a score years after the game was over.

In the summers on Fridays, a group of former area college players would gather to scrimmage at an East Side Gym, frequently Austin, and afterwards go to Joe Muer's for lunch. At that time, however, on Fridays at the popular seafood restaurant, a section was reserved until 4:00 PM for the remaining alumni of the old Purple Gang, the early Detroit Mafia. We were always welcome to join them and gorge ourselves on their ticket, if they had one. DeBusschere was their favorite son but he usually had White Sox or golf duty so they got to know and enjoy the rest of us. Mostly they envied our youth and regaled us with exaggerated, I hope, stories of their old wars. If I wouldn't disclose the background of the Teamster incident, I'm sure as hell not going to share theirs, even now. But it would prepare me for what was to come much later in Cleveland. They too had a code of honor and loyalty, however misguided, with severe penalties for any breaches.

Chapter 11

Let the Good Times Roll

When I moved in with Tom Van Arsdale in 1967 he was living with fellow rookie Paul Long out of Wake Forest, another keeper with all the skills but just one size short of being a star at 6' 2", 180 lbs. Van was 6' 5", 220 lbs. and could fly. Being from Indiana he wasn't shy about shooting either. When I was playing, Indiana would come out to warm up with each player carrying a ball and as soon as they stepped on the court they started to let fly at the hoop, like a bombing assault. This was Coach Branch McCracken's intimidation ploy and it worked because they could all shoot. All while we were still in our lay-up lanes, watching. It was effective, especially because no one else did it and they won, except when they played Ohio State who featured Jerry Lucas, Siegfried and Havlicek.

Our building in the Lafayette Towers Complex was Lafayette Plaissance, the plum, on the top floor of the twenty-floor tower facing downtown. A floor below us, also facing downtown but from a different angle, lived Detroit Lions rookies Wally Hilgenberg from Iowa and Texan Joe Don Looney, appropriately named. He reminded me of my old Marine buddy Harvey. Both were extroverts as opposed to Van and Paul. They had just completed their first season and were made men, eager to explore the community at their feet. We became fast friends and shared information on hot spots, their focus on Night Clubs, mine on bars, Paul's and Van's on both. We had it covered. Plus, the Stroh's plant was right next door, containing the Stroh-Haus where visitors indulged as guests and we were expected. Our doorman just assumed that any non-resident female entering the building would be headed to either the 20th or the 19th floor. There was plenty of free parking outside the building or down under, which would come in handy soon, as would our telescope, which so far we only used for recreational purposes and getting to know our neighbors in our sister buildings.

My Sportservice career went well and all the established patrons were automatic, with the Tigers' and Lions' programs expanding as both teams were improving. The Red Wings were a constant and with Gordie Howe's career winding down (there was a stud, I never saw a man hit a golf ball further or project a better image, which was genuine), and tenuous, I gave them a special focus. I also focused on the Pistons, who until that time offered only locals, Dave and Reggie Harding, Reggie a 7' cartoon character and to be rookie Dave Bing. The Cougars, the soccer team to come, would be a challenge.

I did my first auto race in Jackson as a tower spotter. My role was to climb a makeshift tower buffered by a stack of hay bales and fire trucks on the first curve of the 500-mile race and keep track of the leaders as they passed. There were two other spotters appropriately placed doing the same for the main broadcasting team at the start/finish line and at the midpoint. Easy at first, but thank God I had two lap counter veterans with me because it soon became a maze. I held my poise and did well according to Tom, who solidified my hire for the fall.

I still frequented Ann Arbor and got to know the next wave of athletes and to see the games. Football was on the way up and basketball was beginning a trend to the top under Strack, to be continued by his capable successors to this day. In my time, the only sport we had of the majors to be proud of was baseball, made up largely of my classmates who won the National Championship the year after their best player, Bill Freehan, left to join the Tigers for a stellar career. Bill is a friend to this day albeit severely disabled neurologically, and people reminisce that Freehan led them to their only title and that still bugs me because those guys were tough, had everything, and could flat out play, all peaking at just the right time.

I had to get familiar with the broadcast booth. Tom would do the play-by-play; I would do the color. More when that occurs.

As you see everywhere you look today, consecutive terms year after year of Democrat rule will put a state or a city squarely in the sewer. Retrospectively had I been concerned, I would have spotted it then because it became plain that everything was rigged. Detroit had become a union-run town with little government resistance. Hats off to Labor for its success, but it seemed like government willingly conceded to every demand and even suggested some. Labor was initially only interested in controlling its markets and its membership but Democrat governance enabled them beyond those original objectives and it was only starting. There were two mayors in my Detroit period and I knew and liked both of them but their terms begat the fall of Detroit. Their Democrat predecessors and successors just set it up and polished it off, like so many cities today. From the major cities it flows upward and outward to the states. Makes you wonder who's behind the Democrats, doesn't it? Years later Bing himself would bring it to a curb, far too late.

Since I mentioned his name earlier, I've got to tell you about Reggie Harding, another sideshow. When I first saw Reg I was still at Michigan, just heading out of Yost after some treatment, when he and another tiny Black youth, escorted by a Black coach type, came around the corner from a side entrance looking for Coach Strack. I hadn't seen him upstairs, so I told them and asked if they had checked his office next door. They said they had and were directed here, which told me this probably wasn't a planned recruiting trip. The feature kid was seven feet tall and had huge ears protruding sideways out of his shaved head. He reminded me of an undernourished baby elephant standing up to beg his mother for some bananas. By now the little guy piped up and proclaimed that he was I. W. Harper, that this was Reggie Harding and that was their coach, whose name I used to know but have forgotten. I had read about Reggie in all those newspapers we used to read to keep our parking meters plugged. Being the raconteur I had become; I wasn't about to forget I.W.'s name.

I took them back up the steps I'd just descended and introduced them to the trainers, figuring this would brighten their day. Trainers Jim Hunt and Lennie Paddock were great guys, great trainers and great friends to all the athletes and had been for generations. And they had great senses of humor which was why I had the idea. Plus, it was a slow day.

As soon as the introductions were completed I.W. took control, finally in his element, and laid out the deal. The coach turned his eyes to the wall, looked up and sighed, there was to be no turning back now. It was to be a package deal, he and Reg, here at Michigan to turn things around. This was going to go over <u>so</u> well with Strack. Table set, I left. The next day when they saw me coming, Lennie locked the door.

Turns out Reggie could play as well as he could gorge drugs and much better than he could read, so college wasn't the answer, but being a well-known local, several years later the Pistons thought he might be. DeBusschere, soon to become player/coach, was against it, but GM Ed Coil was desperate for a big man not already a fossil. I thought it was only better than trying to lure Norm out of retirement.

Reg didn't exactly have an era with the Pistons and one of the reasons may have been what occurred on a long road trip culminating in New York against the Knicks. Visiting teams stayed at the New Yorker Hotel across the street from Madison Square Garden. It was mid-winter and freezing but Reggie was low on his drug cache and needed a fix. He hadn't pooped in a week and was desperate. He hit the streets in the cold and apparently bought out the first pusher he saw. I think Reg was rooming with a much smaller guard, who like most people at the end of a road trip, was beat and wanted to sleep his afternoon away. When he saw Reg already strung out, he grabbed his game bag and suitcase and went to another room, staying away from Dave, who Reggie feared and was the coach by now. The Pistons would be heading home straight from the Garden after the game and wouldn't be going back to the New Yorker, probably a good idea because apparently by now Reg had passed out, the dam had broken and he had deposited the week's poop on his sheets. Without I.W.'s guidance, Reg had to think on his own and came up with a beauty, plain as the nose on your face. The only answer. Many hotels in those days didn't have screens on the windows high up and the New Yorker was one of them. Reg apparently stripped the bed, gathered the now scented sheets by their corners and prepared to throw them out the window of the ninth floor. But wait, think this through. What if they fell right below your room? No, that wouldn't do, throw them out in the street, where they wouldn't be noticed. Who is out on a Saturday night in New York?

Reg, apparently still with the sheets by their corners, winds up from mid-room and, after a few spins, hurls the now empty sheets to float out the window. He had redecorated the walls.

When I went to Metropolitan Airport to pick Van up early Sunday morning, Piston G.M. Ed Coil was there waiting for DeBusschere, who looked exhausted. Turns out the Pistons had been banned from the New Yorker on future trips. I.W. wasn't there to pick up Reg so he would have to scramble to placate Dave. Piston exec Billy Rodgers told me that story the next week. I embellished.

After his short NBA stint, Reg would go on to hold up his barber, wearing a Lone Ranger mask. The barber promptly shot him. A seven-foot Dumbo, Reg would later go down for the count when a drug debtor would walk up to him sitting on his front porch and do the same, this time for good. There are many other Reggie stories out there but this pretty much summarizes them.

In a trade that shocked us all Dave was traded to the Knicks for Walt Bellamy, the center they had been missing, and Butch Komives, a friend through Glinka from Toledo who played at Bowling Green. Butch was as tough as they came, a helluva a player and rounder to boot. We had met in college. Later, two other Knicks at the end of their careers, Len Chappell and Donnis Butcher, joined them. Leonard was playing out the string of a good career and Donnis soon became the coach, succeeding some makeshifts. Donnis was a thug on the court but a natural athlete. He would become a great friend and fellow Nemoite from around Harlen County in Kentucky (for all you "Justified" fans). He and Raylan and Boyd would have been thick. Dave would be free of his coaching burden and began to realize his Hall of Fame talent in The Big Apple.

Chapter 12

Racism in My Life

It's Inauguration Day, 2021, and as the Answer leaves for Florida, the Addled Puppet moves into the White House to oversee the reformation of our Republic. Racism will be a central theme, they will blame Trump for it, beginning with slavery, and explain how it can only be overcome by raising taxes and the minimum wage, which should be easy once they rid the country of the Pandemic and get the rest of those nasty small businesses shut down. If only Trump hadn't conspired with his Chinese friends to bring it on.

Here's my history of racism in my life. In my youth to my best recollection, there was only one black family in Tiffin, a town of 20,000, and I didn't know them and can't remember ever seeing them. But early on--and it was never even a topic of conversation in our house--two things bothered me instinctively. One, on a main thoroughfare in town, as Sycamore Street left the city limits, a sign turned it into "Niggertown Road." I saw it all the time as our doctor, Dr. Leahy, and his family lived on it a mile out of town and I was friends with his kids. Still am and two of them live in Upper Arlington. The other thing was after a while **why** had I never seen them? Like all other grade schoolers at that time, I was out and about all the time and you would have thought we would have at least crossed paths with the family. Of course I didn't go to grocery stores.

Naturally I heard the word "Nigger" occasionally on the street and knew it referred to the Negroes but I never could bring myself to include the word in my vocabulary. My Mom called them "Darkies," in no way disparagingly and my Dad, the Blacks, by way of description. Today's Dems would make those hanging offenses now. Of course there was the occasional jerk and naturally there was prejudice based mostly on ignorance, but it never affected me personally or any of my friends all through high school.

When I got to Michigan it was pretty much the same, since the Blacks had only recently been fully integrated into our athletic programs as it became apparent that they were the answer. Largely the only issues were competitions for positions on the various teams. Personally I found most of the Blacks to be quiet and respectful individually, more raucous and outgoing amongst themselves and sometimes funny as hell. If there was any prejudice it was between coach and players, as the coaches had alumni to answer to, but they also had to win. Fortunately I never had to compete directly with one for a position. Imagine that now.

When we went to Detroit, the "Jungle" as it was I guess disrespectfully referred to, to hear the to-be Motown Bands, there was never a problem. Maybe it was because we were athletes and came as a group; maybe it was because the Blacks welcomed us and were proud of their performers, or just didn't care. We really never gave it a thought. That was also the case later, although we went less frequently after graduation, often with a group of visiting pros in for a game and some Motown. Wilt Chamberlain loved the place.

There must have been some undercurrent going on progressively all along because the Riots of 1967 came as a surprise and had an impact. Things went bad overnight, then to worse. Van and I watched it from our telescope as a curfew, then a lockdown, were ordered, the city totally unprepared. Finally the National Guard was deployed as the city burned. We could see the looters going from store to store and the police positioning themselves to arrest them.

We brought our cars into the garage beneath the Towers and hit the small grocery/liquor store on the main floor for supplies and settled in. I don't recall if Paul Long was still living with us or if Jim Fox, a 6' 10" swingman from South Carolina, had joined us but they were both great characters and players who live in Phoenix near the Vans now and my story wouldn't be complete without them. The riots were nothing like today but a forerunner of things to come. This was the start.

I have just watched Biden's Inaugural Address targeting the slow learner element of middle schoolers and am coming down from a shudder. Biden got nominated for three reasons: he was completely malleable, the only one with **any** name recognition, and a Catholic to further placate the Illuminati element of the Deep State, having already gotten their Pope. Don't get me wrong, while the Dems are bottom dwellers, the Repubs are far worse because they know better and are doing it on their own by choice, with little programming required, focused on inaction. I have just gone from being one to declaring myself a Conservative. I was never possessed by greed. More than enough was always enough for me. I have sometimes fallen short but I have never compromised and my word has always had value. Misplaced trust, however, had always been my weakness.

Inauguration Day started out peacefully, then sloped out of control after the ceremony to a rampage that night, all carefully orchestrated by the Dems and Deep State to set up Trump for another impeachment, which would set the table for the Repubs, who will amp up their standard defense, protracted whining. Let things fester until it's too late and play the blame game until Trump makes his play, then watch him. Without Trump they have no leadership.

Chapter 13

Tigers to the Rescue

I had become friends with Ted Williams, a former Michigan State pivot man whom I met at our Ann Arbor Y at a shoot-around the next spring. Ted was living in Ann Arbor for work and still had the urge so I introduced him around to games in AA and then Detroit and our Friday noon games and rendezvous at Joe Muer's with the Old Gentlemen. We also played on a Grosse Pointe team, East Warren Lanes, in the Detroit City League. Stiff competition.

One of our games was against the Lions, by now led by Ron Kramer, who had negotiated a trade from the Packers to attend to personal problems at home, including his son Kurt's eye problems. Before the game he took me aside and asked me to be sure to kick quarterback Milt Plum's ass. Plum had come over from the Browns in a trade and nobody could stand him. They were steadfast behind the incumbent. Plum thought he could play and couldn't and thought he would have the refs on his side and didn't. I did, and Kramer "accidently" provided some screens for me to run Uncle Miltie into, as did some other Lions, most of whom I knew. I'd forgotten, however, to introduce Ron to Ted, whom he didn't know, and they gave each other all they had all evening. We won. Ted was amazed by Ron's athleticism. Plum left bitching at the officials, who laughed.

In the summers, Van and I would go out to the University of Detroit to play occasionally. Their coach, Bob Callihan, was a friend, and Tom Villamuer, who played with Dave, his assistant, would join in. Dick Vitale was to come. We would go one-on-one, alternating for hours. Officially I am here to tell you what set Tom and his brother Dick apart from the NBA competition they faced through the years was Tom's SPEED. No moves to speak of, but a great jump shooter on the move, and fast, especially off the ball. His next stop would be to a place with someone that could put those qualities to good use.

I did a couple more races in Jackson and some more football games were scheduled for the fall--no basketball yet. There was some competition on the horizon with the advent of cablevision, apparently generously financed. We had done four games in the prior year--two in Ann Arbor, one each in East Lansing (MSU) and South Bend (Notre Dame)--and I had the hang of it. As long as you didn't curse there were few restrictions on what you could say but we were on tape delay so I kept Tom (Johnston) on his toes. He had plans for a weekly show in the winter featuring me, Joe Gentile and Dan Currie, the old Packer linebacker, native Detroiter and good friend from Nemo's. One of the first sports talk shows.

Van got married that summer to Jeannie Klise from Kocomo, Indiana and I moved to a hotel until I could latch on elsewhere. He also got traded to Cincinnati where the great Oscar Robertson awaited in search of a small forward who could move without the ball to join him and Jerry Lucas, Adrian Smith and Connie Dierking in their pursuit of the Celtics, whose aging lineup in a rapidly expanding league was thought vulnerable. Not quite yet.

While still at Michigan I'd updated my contact lenses to a newer, smaller model that worked wonders, comfort wise. The reason I mention this is they wouldn't later and that's significant.

One summer in undergrad my roommate John Walker, a football MVP, was working at a mental institution toward Milan and one Sunday his job was to escort six inmates to a Tiger game and a meal afterwards. He asked me to help him out. Our friend Bill Freehan, also a footballer, was the Tiger Catcher so we got there early so we could visit with Bill. We left about nine to load his charges and arrived at and were in the stadium by 11:00. The seats, hospital purchased, were the worst purchasable, just short of the roof, but the guys were happy as clams so we went down to the field where Bill was tossing a football with pitcher Joe Sparma, a former Ohio State quarterback. We hadn't chatted for three minutes when John looked up to check on his charges and they were gone. Not really gone, just down on the field chasing Tigers, who couldn't figure out what to make of it. These were grown men, chasing the players. Bill and Joe were laughing uproariously until they saw the look on John's face. John saw the humor in it for a nanosecond but they were his charges, now out of control, but having the time of their lives. Anybody who hurt them in rounding them up, Tiger or not, would need to deal with John, on the spot. Plus, John had that look about him and Bill knew it too, from football. Sobering would be the mildest adjective. So, we got out on the field and joined the roundup. When we had them corralled, they were laughing uproariously and as they giggled away their situation dawned on us all. These people weren't inmates, they were patients, locked up because nobody cared, out for a day at a ballgame. We commandeered a box near the dugout and stayed to the end. On the way back we stopped at the restaurant the hospital had selected for dinner. A grease pit. We loaded them up and went to a place we knew to get them a decent meal, on us. If I remember, John quit that job the next week. We exchange Christmas cards each year, see each other occasionally at a game. I can't go anymore.

That summer, 1968, the riots quelled and things were back to normal and beyond since the Tigers were headed to the World Series. One sunny day Van and I decided to take in a game with the Yankees in town. Tiger thirty-game winner Denny McClain on the mound for Micky Mantle's last hurrah. We chatted with Bill Freehan beforehand and he told us to be sure to stay until the end, so we went out to the centerfield bleachers where we could spread out, unsurrounded, to get some sun. The Tigers jumped out to a modest lead and the Yankees were largely phoning it in but in about the seventh inning, Mantle was due up for what could be his last at bat in Tiger Stadium. McClain struck out Roger Maris and up strode the Mick. Bill went out to the mound to talk to Denny and it dawned on me—they were going to serve one up. I saw Bill say something to Mantle, then the pitch, the swing, and a baseball bouncing between us headed higher up in the bleachers: number 568, his last.

Another Mantle story told by Billy Martin, his former teammate, in later years, involved an incident at the Sheraton, where the Yankees stayed when in Detroit. Martin and Mantle would room together on the road and one of their running partners had picked up a groupie at The Lindell, a block away. They were lodged on the seventh floor, again no screens, and, of course, drunk. So, it only made sense to crawl out on the ledge and edge next door to watch for technique, but the shade was drawn and the window locked. Fuck. Martin was crawling point, Mickey at sweeper or last. Now Mickey was terrified of heights, a fact momentarily misplaced in his memory, until Billy told him to back up to their room window ten feet away and reenter. No way. Now it made no sense to knock on the teammate's window inches away, since he was occupied, so the only recourse was to crawl forward to the next window or the next, whatever, so long as they could find one open. Relieved by his mentor's strategy, Mick found he could advance once again so long as he didn't have to turn around, but a corner loomed ahead. With Mantle panicking again at the thought of what may be at hand, Martin knocked at the last window and was taking off he shoes to smash it in, not relishing the thought of cornering himself, when it opened and there stood Ralph Houk, the Yankee Manager. Billy told a few of us that story himself a few years later after he was Tiger manager, at his bar across from the stadium. Again, I embellished.

After I had judiciously distributed the World Series tickets to the program sponsors that fall, I had about fifty left over and the home games would be played in midweek, perfect for me because I had to broadcast both weekends. The Teamsters rented the ninth floor of the Sheraton for the duration and I was living in a hotel nearby. All the bars, particularly Nemo's and Lindell, would be swarming. Detroit would be playing the St.

Louis Cardinals and their ace, Bob Gibson. What a scenario. I had asked several friends from Tiffin to spend the week and they were blown away. The city was swarming, just what Detroit needed after the riots at just the right time. I knew that almost all the Metro airport stewardesses stayed at the Sheraton, with the limos bringing a load every forty minutes, so I went down to make sure that they were all invited at check in to the Teamster Open House on nine. I spotted Joe DiMaggio sitting across from check in, reading a paper, apparently trolling himself, and said "Hey Clipper, Teamster Open House on Nine." He got up and followed me to the elevator where Dizzy Dean, the former Cardinal pitcher who was in to broadcast, awaited. We all went up together.

    The Teamsters know how to get it right and a lot of unique characters came from all over. Notorious people. All day, all night, Tuesday, Wednesday, Thursday, ten bars, the entire floor. Some people never left, stews in and out, eating it up. My Tiffin buddies were blown away. I didn't sell one ticket, took what I needed, gave the rest away—to deserving people. The Tigers won in seven, clinching in St. Louis as I was calling football. When I returned about 6:00 PM, the place was a madhouse. As I entered Nemo's, Aretha Franklin was dancing on the bar singing "Sock it to Me" or whatever that tune was called, the riots put on hold. She was headed for Lindell's next.

    My Tiffin buddies were welcomed at Nemo's and that would be significant for what was to come.

Chapter 14

In a Groove

I had always stayed close to my single Michigan buddies, especially former football captain George Mans and other players/roommates Bill Hooth and Tom Watters, and I moved in with Tom, who taught at Grosse Pointe High, across from Hooth's house. Bill was an attorney and eventually would help me get a business started. George's family owned a lumberyard downriver in Trenton and he and his cousin John, a Phi Delt brother, would eventually take it over. They had a family yacht in the Detroit River which offered us that option and Grosse Pointe was one target. The Pointe also offered great night life just up from Tom's apartment, on the river, side-by-side, Sindbad's, a restaurant/bar, and The Roostertail, a restaurant/nightclub, which featured top flight entertainment. A young Wayne Newton headlined my first visit and he stuck.

With Dave and Van gone, while I was still a Nemo's regular during the days, more time was spent out east in G.P. or up north at Coral Gables, a bar/night club owned by Pat Burke, an old Spartan footballer who had expanded his Lansing holding (Coral Gables) to Detroit. Pat knew what it took to "pack 'em in"--dynamite help--and CG always had it. One night after the Royals visited the Pistons and a friend from Tiffin, Pat Leahy, was in from Columbus, we went out to the Gables after several warmup spots after the game with Van and Jerry Lucas, his now teammate, and an old friend. Since both are still living I'll skip the details but suffice it to say it was a hilarious evening and as he often did, Luke completely belied his image.

As I have said, the unique thing about Nemo's was that for the regulars unless there was a special game, it was pretty much a weekday bar with the regulars heading home after "cocktail hour," usually around 8:00 PM. A different crew came in on game nights. Most of the daytime crew pretty much led double lives, with two families, Nemo's and home with all that that entailed. Those that didn't fit soon knew it. The place just had characters and not everybody fit. Not necessarily good character in many cases, but in a serious conversation--and I would have many over the years--you could take a man at his word and there would be lots of secrets.

I've got to fit this story in someplace and there hasn't been a spot so here goes, as it's a classic. Just out of the Marines, I had a job interview in Dallas, a city that then was completely polarized from Detroit and in which racial prejudice was rampant, disgusting even. I knew going in it was a waste of time. Maybe it helps explain the riots. It was a Friday-Sunday interview and I had impressed but I wasn't about to decline until I was back on home soil. I had a layover between flights in Indianapolis on a late Sunday night and had an hour to kill in the airport. I swear the only other person in the airport other than the employees was Dick the Bruiser, the wrestler. You have got to be old enough to remember him or this story will fall flat.

I walked up to Dick and asked him if he wasn't afraid, being alone in an airport at night and asked him if he wanted some company. He rasped, which meant "sure" and I sat down and introduced myself. I chatted and he rasped for a while and if I've properly broken the code, he lived in Indianapolis, his flight had left without him, so he was waiting for the next flight, an hour away, same as mine. I wondered if the pilot panicked. Dick was off on a Tour after some time at home.

Dick was currently World Champion and had taken a break to recover. He had a yacht in his backyard, up on blocks because of his busy schedule and, after lifting all morning, he'd spent the week drinking beer on his boat, still on blocks, and throwing the empties out on the lawn for his kids to retrieve, then trying to run down his wife for an aperitif. As soon as he found out I was from Detroit the talk turned to Alex Karras. Dick despised Alex, I think because the Lions preferred him to Dick who had played, I believe at Minnesota, at a try-out.

I told him that a new Lindell A.C. was opening about a block away from the original soon and that I'd heard Alex had a piece of it. That was pretty much the end of our encounter as our flights came and we parted. Not long after, reports began to surface that Alex and Dick had a feud to settle and Dick wanted to settle it in the ring and offered an open challenge in Detroit at Alex's convenience.

Now I had met Alex before at the old Lindell but didn't really "know him" at all. The times I had been around him he seemed always "ON," playing the "Alex" role, trying to be funny but too hard. Any serious seeming conversations were usually at the end of the bar with the Butsikarises or other Greeks and all non-footballers were outsiders, or at least so it seemed. It also seemed that Alex thought all The Bruiser's taunts were just typical hype for a desired match, and I knew it wasn't. Dick apparently was working up a lather or maybe it was just a routine. I had spoken to him more than to Alex and I liked Dick, not so much Alex.

About a week later in mid-summer, I was with a couple friends about to enter the old Lindell about 10:30 PM when Kramer, then still a Packer, and Tom Tracy, the Lions running back, came barging out of it laughing hysterically, telling us to go elsewhere because Dick was in there mopping the floor with Alex and destroying the soon to be vacated insides and all the memorabilia. Dick was on a rampage. We got the best of our curiosity and went elsewhere, as sirens were approaching. About two weeks later the match was booked at Cobo Hall, by now fully hyped. The Bruiser won in a decision--packed house--a few months later just before football season began. Had our conversation in the airport in Indianapolis sparked a thought?

A lot had happened in both the sports world and the cultural world in the late 60s that dawned on me when I got to Detroit from my deployment. I had only been gone six months completely out of touch, but what had been a gradual progression seemed like a bolt from the blue. In the sports world, both football and basketball had expanded rapidly, the NFL and AFL had merged and we had a Super Bowl. In basketball, the NBA was now coast-to-coast and just getting started. The lesson for today is if you don't pay attention a lot can pass you by and you can see the result of that in today's America. People hate what is going on unchecked but feel there's nothing they can do about it, largely because of the corrupted media, so they either resign themselves to it or ignore it, deserving what they get. And the opposition, whose meager efforts to fight back go unmentioned or denigrated by that same media, only exacerbates that impression. Factor that occurring over a number of years, unchecked.

In the cultural world was the full-blown emergence of the Sexual Revolution. I didn't particularly think it was needed but it sure as hell was upon us by the time I got to Detroit. Suffice it to say that when I went to Michigan's first football game that fall a drugged out hippy couple, apparently students, stripped down and got to it in the stands, on about the forty-yard line ten rows in front of us. People parted and cheered them on. And we had just won the Rose Bowl.

On many Friday afternoons, George Mans and I would meet up with Larry Hughes, a former teammate of Dave's at U of D on Bob Callihan's great teams of the early 60s, at a fertile Dearborn bar, Anderson's Gardens, for Happy Hour. The stewardesses from Metro that didn't stay downtown at the Sheraton stayed at the Dearborn Holiday Inn, which was close to the airport. If each of us found a fit we would go to George's boat a few miles downriver in Trenton and take it upriver, through Detroit to Sindbad's in Grosse Pointe for dinner and drinks. That soon got around and we became even bigger targets than we already were in Dearborn. So, we had downtown, north, east and west Detroit covered and had George's boat downriver, or south, a boxed compass. George Mans, by the way, would later become Mayor of Trenton.

With football's and basketball's expansion, minor league teams sprang up, then leagues. The Detroit based football team

Pontiac Arrows drew Bill Dougall, Jim Ward, Bill Hooth and Tom Watters from Michigan, all close friends. They played the home games at U of D. Some MSU friends played too. They had a ball and drew decently well but had no NFL-AFL affiliation and were insufficiently organized at that time.

The Continental League emerged for basketball, with close by teams in Toledo, Port Huron and Lansing. I filled in for all three as needed and Ted Williams was a mainstay in Lansing for the Capitols, at least at first. What always astounded me about that entire league was that it was meant to be a development league to get guys with potential prepared to play. It ended up like in high school. All these guys could score so they thought that to outscore their teammates would get them a call-up. At the start, they would practice twice a week and have two games. The players all had jobs to work around. What I offered was that I wasn't a threat to them, knew some of them and only tried to complement their efforts, not compete with them. Plus, they knew I had some affiliation with the Pistons, even if it was only selling ads in their programs. Larry Hughes hopped around too. Ted quickly got fed up but stuck it out.

I had remained in contact with Ann Arbor as well. An old townie friend Jimmy Morrison, a local contractor, always sponsored teams in all the city league sports, most of which featured himself as the star. Now Jimmy could play the hell out of fast pitch softball and fielded a great team year after year. I played one game. I hadn't played baseball since little league and wasn't asked to return. But he had asked me if I wanted to play on his basketball team. I had seen them play and they sucked. I agreed if I could bring some friends, which he reluctantly okayed.

He hoped to be the point guard but was in his forties so I had to convince him to be player/coach, like Donnis Butcher now was with the Pistons. Thank God or Jimmy wouldn't have bought it. I brought in Dave Kroll, Ted Williams, Gary Kane and John Tidwell, now in residency at U of M Hospital and his friend, Dr. Dave Middleton, a former Lion receiver. Scott Maentz, who I infrequently saw at the Marine Reserve Meetings in Detroit (the Detroit branch and the Coronado branch yet to resolve my transfer) and who was now a serious stockbroker living in Ypsilanti, recently married to Ashley Mulholland, joined in as he could. None of us could make every game but enough of us did to make us a force and we were undefeated halfway through the season but the rest of the roster, many of which constituted the softball team, felt left out and threatened to quit. We understood and parted company graciously. Jimmy resumed his point guard role with enough games left to miss the playoffs but retain his team.

He repaid the courtesy by asking me to join his "All Star" softball team to face the King and His Court, a traveling phenomenal Professional Team that toured the country playing the cities' best all-stars of their own. Back in Ohio I'd seen Rip Riley's similar team play a local group and Rip's pitching right arm hung six inches lower that his left. No one got a hit but some did hit it so I fully expected to be totally embarrassed by the King.

The deal was everyone got an at bat. Mine came in the third inning. Only one player had laid wood and that was a dribbler in front of the catcher. I'd seen, or rather observed, maybe five pitches, the others I heard, smashing into the catcher's glove. The catcher was part of a routine as well, his role returning the ball to King before the batter's swing was complete. I just decided to swing when I best judged the ball to be advancing since I didn't expect to see it. At the peak of his wind-up, I started to swing and heard the ball smack into his glove. King's glove. I had hit it; he had caught it. Off my bat. I got a round of applause. I had shown him. His right arm really was six inches longer too. No one else did much better. Things were good.

Chapter 15

Trouble Afoot

At Sportservice, Herm Goldman, in poor health and heavy, had retired. We had a great relationship as I did all the legwork and P.R. and he, like the good Jew he was, did the books. He had absolutely loved my tale about my first day at the dorm when the influx hit. He told me he would be my Jew anytime, especially after the success the teams had that year. He told me finally to be on my guard of his successor. His best recommendation, which I had, wouldn't mean anything.

Herm always understated everything but I wasn't prepared for this. His successor was Sid something or other--I've repressed it for years--his boss's son in his mid-thirties who knew at the very least everything, plus most things yet to be realized. His first "request" of me was to take him down to meet the teams' executives to let them know with whom they would be dealing from now on. Ah, a vote of confidence.

Herm had dealt with them through me and I dealt with their secretaries. I got to know the Execs by being the guy who always brought in sponsors or interviewed their players for Interstate. They got to know me and I got to know them and we got to be friends so, fuck Sid. I knew that one of the reasons they didn't do what I did themselves was that I was already doing it, and <u>they</u> weren't paying me. Sportservice was, I could do it better than anyone else could and Sportservice was providing the game snacks already. That's <u>four</u> reasons. Then I told Sid he should stay in his cubby and handle the art work and billing, as Herm had done and we'd get along fine.

From then on Sid and I never seemed to get along but I know he was trying to undermine me in New York, as Herm called me and we laughed as I recounted our first meeting. I figured all along that if the teams took it on in-house there was a good chance they'd hire me to do it, as I already did and was good at it. Sid would not have made a good first impression on them either. Herm passed shortly thereafter. He could be my Jew anytime.

Back in Tiffin, Mom wasn't feeling well and I went back more often. She was seventy now and wanted to go on another trip, this time to Rome the next summer for the Canonization of Mother Seton as a Catholic saint. After my Uncle Dan graduated from Mount Saint Mary's, Mom entered Seton Hill, its sister school around Baltimore, both founded by Mother Seton, a Catholic nun. It would be later in the summer and would I take her. Hell yes. It would be in August just before football responsibilities. I'd never been to Europe, let alone Rome. What better place to start? The Bishop of Baltimore was arranging the trip and all we had to do was buy tickets and meet up in New York for the flight. She made the plans.

After the DeBusschere trade to the Knicks, Nemo's sponsored a weekend flight to New York several times to catch a game and do the town. I went twice. Shorty led the way, familiar from his time in the league with all the spots to hit. He was as big a force there as he was in Detroit. We'd stay at the New Yorker, usually about a dozen of us. Of all the stories I could tell

I will tell the one about after the game. Dave DeBusschere was supposed to meet us at Toots Shor's, the famous saloon of the stars. Shorty was holding court to a packed house recanting tales and exchanging insults with Toots when Dave walked in with two guests in tow, Dustin Hoffman and Robert Redford. Shorty spotted him and broke away and gave him a big hug and extended his hand to his guests. Dave introduces them and Shorty, after shaking hands, asks, "What do you guys do?" This was shortly after *Butch and Sundance*. Shorty, as always, was in a world of his own.

Mom's illness, while a concern, wasn't yet alarming but I advised her to get an appointment at the Cleveland Clinic as soon as possible and I would take her up to make sure. She remained active with her friends and got around well and ate out a lot. All good signs. They were gossip friends and I often wondered how I was portrayed since she rarely asked me about my "career," such as it was, which I considered a blessing. She never inquired about my personal life either, for which I was grateful, but it was just weird.

Now I never thought I had won my confrontation with Sid, only delayed the inevitable, because I had joined the Press Club at Joe Gentile's insistence, one of the best pieces of advice I had ever gotten. For those of you to whom that name is unfamiliar suffice it to say that Joe, just behind Yankee Stadium's immortal Bob Sheppard and right up with pro-football's John Facenda, was the greatest Public Address Announcer that ever lived. Tiger Stadium froze when he spoke. I always got chills. The game was at hand. Especially the World Series.

One day soon after, at the Broadcaster's Luncheon at the Press Club, Joe and I shared a table with Tom Johnston, Jim Brown and Roone Arledge of ABC. ABC local broadcaster Dave Diles, a late arrival, also wedged his way in next to Roone, who, along with Jim, were our guest speakers. I sat on one side of Roone with Joe next to me on the other and across from Brown, who had the largest head I had ever seen. We ate lunch and chatted while Diles sucked up. One time as Roone glanced my way, I winked at him and he rolled his eyes. Brown bantered pleasantly and watched the show. He smiled at my win. After they spoke and we mingled, Roone gave me his card and told me to call if I was ever in New York or Los Angeles. Joe had seen everything and thought I'd handled things beautifully. Like an idiot I never did call because I didn't want to live in New York or LA. Who is playing in this year's Super Bowl? Oh yeah, Tampa and Kansas City.

Every year another "Club" in town, the "Good Sports," always held a raucous golf tournament in Motown at a tolerant club up north with all the barmaid talent and the in Clubs anxious to attend and provide service. I'd grab a cart and load up with booze and girls and tour around. It always paid to follow either Shorty or Donnis around because their foursomes were the biggest crowd pleasers in a gifted field, Shorty for his banter, Donnis for his game. Donnis was a natural athlete and while only an average NBA player, he was an NBA veteran of ten years. The only other natural athletes I had ever met besides Butch were Kramer and Hornung, DeBusschere (who played in the Good Sports when he could) and Scottie Maentz, who also played tennis at Michigan. Anyway, Donnis would bet on every hole while either playing it with his putter or the club of his opponent's choice against the opponent's full bag, chattering all the time. He always won at the end of the day. Donnis could con with the best. And he was a fantastic softball player.

By then full carts of girls were dispensed and were serving drinks and everything was getting out of hand, as designed. I could continue with the stories and the people involved but I'll leave that to your imagination. Suffice it to say everybody involved had to be a "good sport."

I had played golf as a youth at Mohawk Country Club in Tiffin with other kids my age but not in my group of friends that were members' sons and they all cheated. None of my crew played but I never grew to like any of the cheaters so maybe I credit that initial impression with why I only rarely golfed. I had a shooting court in my backyard and always was an early riser so while my contemporaries were either sleeping in or golfing, I was shooting baskets. That paid off for me more than golfing or sleeping ever did for any of them, so I have always equated golf time with workout options. But I could golf a little and could get into the mid-high eighties on occasion, when pressed. I have never enjoyed a round in my life. I mention this now because I used to host a golf tournament, which will become a critical point of discussion in a later chapter.

Chapter 16

Obstacles To Come

I am writing this on recall, not research. Any research will come from my wife's computer skills. My disability allows me to scratch out about a chapter an hour on a tablet, double spaced. I find the more I write the more I remember and I try not to disparage anybody still living. I was able to do the things I did and didn't do largely because I was single. I never got married until I was forty-two and never regretted the wait. I couldn't have a better wife or better family. My wife types this as she can. She will be canonized, too.

I was never right off the rack either and it worked for me. I have some great friends and some nasty enemies and am very emotional about both. My Inherent Neuropathy, a progressive, degenerative disease, has disabled me for over fifteen years and has just about maxed out. There is no cure and none of the "remedies" work on me so I fight it by working out six days a week in my home on a Rogue Echo Bike and a rower to retain what strength I have left. That's the best I feel all day, except when the grandsons come.

I have some regrets but only one I can't live with and it looks like I'll have to. That is what I am leading up to. The most productive years of my life were taken from me, but that only changed the challenge, and in the end my true friends came through for me and my faux friends allowed the world's greatest scourge to rage on, unchecked. God will square things for me. He always does.

Chapter 17

Change Afoot

There was a rare number of con men in Nemo's but they knew to leave their game in the car. I have seen several "newbies" given the Bums Rush over the years, yup, nape of the neck, seat of the pants, through both doors and into the street by Buttons or one of Nemo's sons, Pat or Mike, naturally, who also bartended. Pat did the books. Both sons to be proud of but polar opposites, personality-wise. Pat was all business while Mike was still searching for his niche. Both great guys. Lying wasn't approved of and an outright liar wasn't tolerated for long but bull-shitting was rampant, even expected. There was an understood difference. There was never a time I entered Nemo's when there wasn't a topic in play; interjections were welcome, unless the topic was business. You could always tell and you just moved down the aisle to another group or empty (not for long) seat. You didn't want to know about the "business" anyway. As I mentioned earlier, the best way to get accepted at Nemo's was to never ask questions. That was how you learned.

Sid had interjected himself into the teams above my back--not behind, because I knew it would happen--and quickly became a pain in their respective asses, so I stayed away. I could see what was coming. Football, basketball and baseball were taking off, concurrent with Cablevision and over-the-top advertising would be needed to keep up. Tom Johnston's TV niche was seriously threatened too. I needed to know where I stood. I doubted the teams would allow Sportservice, with or without me, to lead that marketing campaign. Programs would become incidentals. And Tom wasn't savvy enough or cash rich enough to compete with the big Cable networks.

Plus, there was the question about Mom's health and lately my eyes had been bothering me more and more. On sunny mornings I wouldn't even put my contacts in because the glare blinded me as I drove. At night or on cloudy days I could tolerate it but I couldn't count on that for long. My Ann Arbor optometrist had both retired and died so he probably couldn't help. I had given thought to actually calling Roone Arledge, but not like this and it would only be worse in the winter with the snow glare. I doubted if anybody at Nemo's could recommend a good eye doctor.

On the times I went to Tiffin to see Mom, I would also hook up with an old high school buddy (Columbian) Paul Assenheimer, who was an elementary school principal. His school, Clinton, out in the country, had a small gym where we would go shoot around, go one on one, or get up a game. One of his old friends, Dr. Bob Ross, was an optometrist, a good one in his judgment, which I trusted. Besides I was getting desperate and was due to see Mom anyway. So, I called for an appointment.

On previous trips to Tiffin, I would usually spend the weekend and hit the spots at night, a couple of them owned by high school friends. There was also a golf course just past where Dad's old farm was a couple miles out, part-owned by another high school acquaintance from a county school. I checked that out and liked it—Seneca Hills.

When I was in high school there were two athletic divisions in the state for schools, A and AA. City and town schools were A; village and country (county) schools were AA. Currently there are eight divisions. We never played each other in games, but frequently crossed paths in the summer and they could play. And boy did they want to. Against us. When I was in school, we would have kicked the shit out of them, both Calvert and Columbian, but other years, they would have been close games. It seemed that the former county studs all hung out at Seneca Hills and still played too, in the winter. It was golf now and hell raising year around. Jere Carrick from nearby New Riegel was co-owner with Bob Eilert from further north and Wayne Hoover. Fritz Smith from Upper Sandusky, Jack Wickert from Old Fort, Bob Oder, the golf pro, Dick Taylor and Dal Critchet were the other hoopers with Skip Bozarth, who played briefly for OSU. All tough guys and good players, used to winning. I got to know them on my visits.

I don't know if it was on my first visit to Doc Ross that I found out I had Keratoconus—a disorder of the eye that results in the thinning of the cornea--but we made progress. He was a genius when it came to eyes and whatever he gave me as a stopgap provided instant relief. But I needed a solution and he thought he had one but would need to check things out and have me back. He also had three cute girls in his employ so I didn't mind returning. One went to Columbian when I went to Calvert: Georgia whom I knew. Kathie, a blonde, and Becky, a brunette, were both younger and in their first jobs. I always checked these things out. On my next visit I would find out that Becky's last name had been Schultz and that she was married, out of the mud puddle and all grown up. She'd done a damn good job of it too.

Now I don't want to say she ran right out and filed or she'll stop typing this, but on my next visit she was separated and <u>very</u> attractive. It had been uncomfortable for a while and she decided it wasn't a fit. Like so many, just too soon. She'd gone to Tiffin University and landed at Doc's where she would get all the education she would ever need. Doc was a beauty. Since Doc has children and the old "leave it to your imagination" clause would fall short, I'll just leave it at that. But the man was a master of his craft, ahead of his time.

He prescribed a soft lens on the eye surface with a hard lens over it, piggyback he called it and it was very effective and easier to get used to than I had anticipated, but the surface could change so we would need to keep an eye on things. In the years to come the same thing was combined in a single lens and that was the answer. Doc became a good friend.

I still had problems to solve in Detroit.

Chapter 18

The Next Step

Everything was still in place in Detroit but dramatic change was inevitable and soon. Sid had ruined the Sportservice label with the teams by his demeanor and they wanted to explore doing their own thing. My name never came up, nor did I inquire. Tom was adjusting to compete for his niche, whatever that turned out to be, and still had Joe, Dan Currie and me, along with his regulars, for whatever he landed. He was small but well connected, especially in Ann Arbor and East Lansing. I for sure didn't want to start up fresh and all the team broadcasting jobs were locked up by veterans better than me, and established.

We (Mom) had one of the storefront buildings the she owned on Washington Street, the main drag, open and when my eyes were bothering me I thought casually that it would be a great place to open a health club. They were popping up in Detroit and the only other options were the Ys, same with Tiffin. When I took Mom to the Cleveland Clinic, they first thought she had cancer, but after further examining her at my insistence (what's this "thought" shit?) found it to be Black Lung Disease from her youth in Jessup, Pennsylvania, outside Scranton. Not fatal but requiring medical monitoring. Mom had grown up in a house on a hill just off the main drag with a large porch all around it on top of an abandoned coal mine. It was close to the top of the hill and you could look down on the town from the porches. Lift a trapdoor in the basement and there was the mine, should you choose to go exploring. Mom was one of nine, three boys and six girls, and her Dad, Ed, owned property all around, and a saloon. He had long passed when I arrived, as was the case with Dad's family, so I never had grandparents, one of the reasons I'm writing this book. The cross streets that intersected Main were avenues; one through eight, starting from the top. Theirs was 408 First Avenue, a grand home.

They all went to college--Papa Ed insisted--and were strong people. Of the nine children, two became teachers in the high school--Ruth the matriarch and Ida--lived in the Jessup family home and maintained things. Ruth also maintained things for the rest of the town, at least until Mom visited, then just the town. Mom's brother Dan (I am his namesake) we've accounted for. Both Gerald and Donald had government jobs in Washington and Philadelphia respectively. Evangeline was a nurse in New York; Florence had died in childhood; and the tough one, Genevieve, was Reverend Mother Agnes of Jesus, the Head of the Carmelite Nuns in America, consultant to Cardinals and Bishops. She built monasteries across the east and the Midwest and was heading up Chicago when she passed. I was glad Becky got to meet her. She NEVER raised her voice, just spoke softly and ruled. She died peacefully in her Carmelite Monastery in Chicago and is on the canonization list. Years later, when Logan was young, we attended Becky's niece's wedding in New York and passed through Jessup on the way home to see the house. The family that bought it had removed all of the porch. Had I been alone, I would have burned down the house for that.

We visited Dad's family when I was young on our summer trips to show me the country, forty-seven of the forty-eight states, omitting only Maine. They were scattered all over by now and, while nice people, I was too young to remember them. Uncle Cliff left an impression for the family, he and Dad, who never spoke of the war. But he knew his business, as did Mom.

Rejuvenated, with confidence restored with the vision, I returned to Detroit with a plan. I went out and re-signed all of the program sponsors in all five sports, Tigers, Lions, Pistons, Red Wings and Cougars, for the next (1970) season. They had heard rumors too, but I reminded them that if things did change, as we all foresaw, the contracts would either have to be honored or voided, with no loss to them, only potential gain. The main client, Gil Mains' Truck City, a huge truck stop on the I-94 exit to Chicago and beyond, was owned by former Lions Middle Guard Gil Mains, a great guy and very influential. He always had the "main" spot in the middle margin of the scorekeeping page. A Nemo's guy and very vocal, Gil touted my strategy among the teams, which probably both helped and hurt me because I never heard directly from any of them, but the contracts were ultimately honored. The networks had far grander plans for the teams and the leagues and had their people in place. I still never called Roone, because truth be told, I never aspired to be a corporate guy in anything. Too much going along with the plan, no individuality allowed. I would wait to see while I looked around, mainly out of curiosity.

Also, a lot of my guys were getting married. George, Hughes, Hooth, and a couple of fringe guys. Ted was transferred to Virginia. Tom Watters was thinking of moving back to

Pennsylvania. George was tired of co-running the lumberyard and hired on as an assistant coach at Michigan, which was right for him. Life with Tom Watters was okay when it was his place but it sure as hell wasn't going to be mine. This was a Grosse Pointe man, you had to have you some digs. Tom remains a great friend.

Before we got to the next phase of my saga, I have got to fit two stories in that I still smile about to this day. One Sunday evening in the summer when I was living with Van in the Towers, we decided to walk about a mile to Jefferson Avenue, which ran east along the river from downtown to Grosse Point and St. Claire Shores. The Playboy Club was on Jefferson across from the end of our street, Lafayette. The Detroit version, and many others, had never taken off like Chicago's original, but it was first class and a little slow on Sundays.

The entertainment for that weekend was Professor Irwin Corey, "The World's Foremost Authority," a scraggly older "gentleman" that specialized in double talk. He had to be seventy. Now Van and I were in a mood where his blather was just what we wanted to hear at that time and since it was slow, we asked a couple Bunnies to join us. After his act, the Professor did, too. So, there we sat, the five of us, no one else, at 11:00 PM, two and a half hours before closing. Van and I got up, prepared to settle up and leave, and then, so did the Bunnies, to join us. Hmm. But then, so did the Professor, to further join us. He suggested we stop at the "White" something or other, let's go with "Castle," across the street for a bite. So, we agreed to that, too. We ordered and ate, then Van and I both "had to pee" so we retired to the Men's Room to strategize how we were going to free ourselves of the Professor. We were surprised he didn't have to pee, too.

No, the Professor didn't have to pee; he had to flee—with the Bunnies—leaving us the tab, about $20.00. The employees were smiling when we came out, then we all had a good laugh. We were going to go back and give them some shit but the Prof had closed out and was on to his next gig. I saw him again years later at the Roostertail and he bought me a drink.

The other story I will have to qualify as to accuracy chronologically because it's really two stories that I think occurred together, but both did occur, and one won't matter to the reader unless they're Tiffinites.

Most of you basketball fans will remember when the Lakers, with Wilt, hired former Celtic great Bill Sharman, a strict disciplinarian, to be their coach. I can't recall with certainty if they still had Baylor and/or West (and this is not a research book), but they were underachieving in management's eyes. Thus one of Sharman's first decrees was that on road trips there would be a mandatory shootaround at 11:00 AM at the home team's arena. Sharman was a phenomenal shooter--opposite Bob Cousy on Boston's legendary run of championships--and all business. He had hired Al Attles, a no-nonsense guard and Chamberlain's former roommate at Philadelphia as his assistant, largely to motivate Wilt. I had interviewed Attles before and I liked him.

L.A. opened the season winning two home games and then came to Detroit. At the start of the season there were usually only three games a week, giving them time to gel. I had seen Wilt out the night before at a Motown Bar with two girls, one of whom looked familiar. We waved, Wilt and I, as I had been out with him before, and it was who I thought it was, a girl from my high school (not my class), Miss Goodie Two Shoes herself. I left soon after to meet somebody. The next day around noon, I entered the Sheraton to go to the Pistons' Office to drop something off and coming down the escalator with the two girls, Goodie still one of them, was Wilt. We waved again; Goodie looked away.

Now I am almost certain that that was also the day when at 10:00 AM the team manager was assigned to call all the players to remind them to assemble downstairs to go over to Cobo for the shootaround, the inaugural one. He had gotten through to everyone but Wilt after many attempts. Wilt must have been a heavy sleeper. So, as I heard, the manager, in desperation, went to Attles, wisely avoiding Sharman, to see if he could help. One way or another Attles got through and reminded Wilt of Sharman's decree. It was the first Wilt had heard of it, but after careful consideration he advised "You tell Sharman I'm coming over there <u>once</u> today." Now that's an old story by now but it makes this literature. The one and only.

The final story I will relate for now is to show how well rounded I am. Often when I was living alone I would go out to Baker's Keyboard, a jazz place on Livernois, up north, on a Sunday night. It was slow there too, which I liked. On this night, George Shearing, the blind jazz pianist, was featured, at the end of his gig, too. He was on a break and sitting alone at a remote table with his head in his hands, looking deeply forlorn. I left the bar and went over and sat down. He said "Don't bother me." To which I responded "You're not bothering me; I love your music." (me being the noted jazz critic that I am). He looked up, for whatever good that did, and smiled, and we talked throughout his break. He rose and felt his way to the piano and dedicated his final segment to "the young man at my table." I sat through to the end and we shook hands as I thanked him. His last words to me were "No, thank you." Stuck with me. There's a lesson there.

    I still don't know a thing about jazz, just enjoy it now and then. Only hearing Jimmy Durante at the Roostertail tops that night. Love the Classics.

Chapter 19

Circling The Drain

Gotta' jump ahead here because of what is happening around me. It is January 31, 2021 and Biden has been in office for ten days. By the two-week mark he will have implemented at least fifty Executive Orders, more than all modern day presidents, all of them designed specifically to destroy the America we know. And the Republicans are powerless, with the real president facing a second bogus impeachment and the majority of the others wildly scrambling to salvage what is left of their aborted careers.

The Republican that can be counted with certainty, Ohio Congressman Jim Jordan--whom I should know well, but that introduction was denied me by one of the pimps that betrayed me later--must rally the troops, who, if they continue to deny Trump as their sole hope, will buckle under. Some of them are pure traitors.

I had thought it would take the "Take their Guns" phase to put the Good Old Boys over the top and start a rebellion but if something doesn't happen soon we will buckle and succumb. Then I won't be able to get this published. See, you knew there had to be a selfish motive in there somewhere.

You might ask "Who the hell is a bar hopping ex playboy" to advise me on my country's future? But you have to concede "the boy had a few salient points to make." Read on and you will see just how qualified I would become in the interim.

Chapter 20

Home Again

By late 1969 I moved back to Tiffin, but kept both hands in Ann Arbor and Detroit as well. Mom was feeling better once she knew it wasn't cancer but after a short time I noticed she had begun losing track of things, not bad, just unusual. I had started seeing a girl I met at Seneca Hills who lived in Fostoria, twelve miles away: Phyllis, short, perky and cute, recently divorced with two kids.

My college experiences had caused me to make a vow to myself and some of you may think it confirms what I have already admitted to, that I am an asshole. In the balance of my story, I will relate dozens of experiences with them, if not hundreds, and by way of clarification right now there are Good Assholes (GAH) and Bad Assholes (BAH). You don't get anything worthwhile or substantive done without them. Ask yourselves. I like to think of myself as a "GAH." Anyway, my vow to myself: I would never marry anyone older than me, tiny, with children, a confirmed smoker, or a chronic worrier. This vow was made long before I had anybody in mind or any prospects, so that justifies it for me. I have already owned up.

I knew I wanted to get married and have children, at least one, no more than two (go for a boy), but not till after I was established career wise. I had hoped my wife would have a career too. I'd seen too many of my peers rush into what I knew would be a doomed relationship and limit their own and their spouses' careers in the process. Starting out behind the eight ball. Not for me. You might call it selfish; I call it sensible.

I began making plans for the health club, as Mom thought it was a good idea. It would be on Washington Street, the main drag, across from the theater, near the river and just down from a pool hall/bookie joint called The Stag, owned by two good friends, Bill Stoner and Monte Watters, two collectables themselves. There were five apartments upstairs with off and on tenants. I also knew "The Downtown Athletic Club" (no we didn't award the Heisman Trophy) would ultimately <u>not</u> be my career, just another experience.

I hung around with guys at Seneca Hills. On weekends my political friend from Columbus, Pat Leahy, Executive Director of the Ohio Democratic Party, would come home and rally his buddies, Denny Bridinger, a one-time Cleveland Brown turned school teacher, and Don Miller, a high school principal from Bucyrus, both original Tiffinites and "originals." Mills was/is a chameleon and is still kicking at eighty-six, having outlived all the evidence but me. I'll keep it clean. He'll be safe. And I'll be challenged.

It took a while for all of us to blend, and to the degree that it eventually did, I'll take credit. All the hopping bars in town were owned by friends of ours and as we bonded we trafficked them more. Most of the Seneca Hills crowd were either married or divorced or in the process. Only one, Fritz Smith, had an ideal marriage and he has sustained it to this day, becoming a successful businessman and father in Tiffin. Most of that crew ultimately moved on and did the same, mostly down south.

Not that we lacked for characters, but they were available and soon Larry Watson, a former Bowling Green football center, now mason, and Russ Mook, his high school teammate at Columbian and a Tiffin University graduate with the most dangerous looking smile I have ever seen, joined the pile. Collectively, we were quite a package.

By then it was basketball season and I had finished my football television commitments, so I joined my golf course buddies' basketball team. It was fun, because I only strived to complement their efforts, thus we bonded quickly. Jere Carrick had blown out both knees in previous action, so he was coach. All the guys could play, but we only had a local schedule, while neighboring towns and cities abounded with leagues to join. Instead of a dozen games, why not fifty? It would give us some competition as well as some time to gel; add some pieces.

Soon we were playing up to forty to fifty games a year in various leagues and winning most of them, even the Toledo League, which had former and disenfranchised pros on their rosters. The Toledo League's Commissioner, Herman Kander, who had been my coach with the Toledo Twisters of the Continental League a couple years before, told me, as we warmed up for the first game, that we were outclassed. We lost a few but won in the playoffs, got our pictures up at Tony Packo's Saloon, a Jamie Farr (Mash) hangout. Add Toledo to the list.

Our group collectively was indirectly responsible for a renaissance in the Tiffin bar scene. The originals flourished, new ones sprung up--good ones, bringing the people out and creating competition and we were catalysts. A lot of the guys now in the flow--girls too--would have just settled and let life pass them by. Our group was raucous and had wins to celebrate and we knew how to do both.

The sexual revolution was in full bloom in Tiffin, less inconspicuously than before and everybody that was out was in. Very few secrets survived. The Seneca Hills crew had bought another golf course in Fostoria. Phyllis was working there now and intimating things about our future. The Theis Brothers, fellow Calverteers and now contractors who hung out at Seneca Hills, did some work for Jere and he recommended them to build my health club, which they did (on their own schedule). If I ever hear "one of these first days" one more time, I'll explode. Turned out great. The Downtown Athletic Club (DAC) had one of those big Universal Gyms, abundant free weights, a large sauna and whirlpool with carpeting throughout and a flashing sign out front. I had a plush office and a huge cooler filled with beer. There was also a pop machine in the back. Hours were nine until noon, Monday through Saturday for women, noon until six for men with alternating evenings, six to nine. I hired a special girl, Joyce Schmidutz, to train women. She was a real find who was looking for such an opportunity. A real looker in great shape. The Seneca Hills crews' wives prepared me a great "Open House," which was well-attended. I got a nice write-up in the Advertiser-Tribune, a fine launch. Jere found me a nice big fountain for the front window, lavishly carpeted too. A good start.

At first the women were slow but not the guys. Joyce soon got her friends in the door but since by now I knew so many girls, I thought they would be interested, at least. Not so. I never really did capture the girls I'd see out at night. Too self-conscious, I imagined. Not at night in a saloon but never in daylight. Go figure. On the upside I did get girls in that I would otherwise never see and they were open to what Joyce provided. Some were gorgeous and in play within their group, you could tell, inconspicuously, but for public consumption? Sure. Soon after, Heidelberg College got a Universal Gym similar to mine for their football team. Jim Getz, their Athletic Director, was a great friend and hoped I didn't mind. Hell no, I didn't want a <u>team</u> in here anyway. I got a lot of players though, individually.

Tom Johnston's Interstate Broadcast Network had been squeezed into a niche role to survive cablevision and Joe and I understood that he had to stick to his original broadcast staff. We had had a lot of fun on our run. Good experience, great memories. I bought four M Club season tickets to the football games and would have them for forty years. I could always get basketball tickets but the winter drives from Ohio were always problematical so I only went to special games. I always stayed in touch with both sports since George was on the football staff. I would later recommend two Columbian players, Chuck Heater, a running back and Steve King, a tackle, two great guys that visited the club, to George and they became stalwarts, with Heater still in college coaching at a high level on some championship teams and King, after years with the New York Jets, now living in the Columbus area. We remain in contact. Almost immediately after my recommendations to U of M, George got the head job at Eastern Michigan down the road. I would feed him some club members soon after. Keepers too.

By now I had become a regular visitor at Doc Ross's office for Wednesday lunches when we would grill steaks and drink and "enjoy life." I would get to see Becky, who was rapidly becoming special. She was 5' 6", 125, now single with no kids. She took things as they happened. Phyl was special too and deserved far better than she ultimately got from me but my parameters would ultimately prevail. I know that sounds terribly cold but to have judged otherwise would have been both unfair and a mistake for all parties involved. I would never meet two finer ladies than Margaret Hayes and Phyllis Van Aelst. I would love them forever but I was falling in love with Becky Schultz. As with Margaret, I couldn't stand to hurt people and would make a mess of calling things off with Phyllis.

I would go over to Seiberling Gym at Heidelberg most mornings when the women trained at my place to run and shoot baskets or play some one-on-one. Jim gave me a key to the gym and I began to draw some "Bergers" or students to join me. Also, some coaches. Soon every morning featured full court games, something totally foreign to Tiffin; before long, Tiffin University players joined in. They began learning what I instinctively knew: you became a "player" in the summer. Fritz, Dal Critchet and Jack Wickert were former Tiffin University stars and they would join in occasionally, something formerly against their nature.

Becky and Kathie Sutter lived across the street from Seiberling, renters in a Heidelberg owned house. There was a track right across the street from them and I got Becky to run occasionally. There were no girls' sports at Calvert or Columbian when I was in school and only tennis for Becky's class. She half tried cheerleading but that wasn't her calling. Being an asshole, it was my nature to force feed an idea, but I really thought it was her niche so I would just let her watch me train. Ultimately it worked. She used to smoke, too, but knew I couldn't stand it so she quit without my asking. We were bonding. Becky liked to party though and Kathie was non-stop. The only time Kathie ran was from party to party. We had some grand old times in that house. That's where Becky and I got Cuddles, our first dog.

Jere had become a coach/teacher at New Riegel High School in the Seneca (Tiffin) County League prior to the golf clubs, as was Bob Eilert at Hopewell Louden. Jere's last team was a great one and several of his players joined our team, strengthening us further. Great kids, young legs. Paul Gnepper, Larry Gase, Jeff Underwood and Steve Lucius, all just out of playing college ball, who knew their roles and played them. Jere's knee problems cost him a pro baseball career of his own.

One of my proudest projects was Tom Bogner, a tough as nails guard from Columbian, whom I was able to help get a scholarship at Eastern Michigan from their coach, Jim Dutcher, an old friend. The reason for my pride was he came from a good family and was willing to listen, watch and learn, but mostly because he left nothing in his tank, every time, and was nasty. And his favorite target always seemed to be me. He would join us in time, too. I would later be best man in his wedding with Terry Addis, his high school flame. That wouldn't last, but our friendship has, and he would later join Jere at his golf course in Florida. I would like to someday meet his new wife.

Chapter 21

Staying in Touch

I would go to Detroit often to maintain my connections and check in at Nemo's. It still felt like home, like nothing had changed. I would talk with Jere about a golf outing similar to the Good Sports, at Seneca Hills. Jere could organize a clusterfuck and make it seem like training a puppy. He was in, so one time I floated it to Nemo. I explained that we had a motel on the river, cleverly named the Riverview Inn, first class, just out of town (no police) about two miles from the golf course, which Jere and his partners owned. The Riverview Inn's owner, John Egbert, another friend who could use the traffic, had a great bar overlooking a nice pool, overlooking the Sandusky River. He didn't realize what he would be in for, but John was no field mouse himself and once he saw the way they spent with nothing broken and with both the celebrity and notoriety they brought, he couldn't complain. He even tolerated the nude swimming in the pool just outside of the bar. Nemo liked the idea, then in came Shorty and Bobby Holmes and Nemo told them. Why not? Shorty even thought he would bring Sweet Lips, which was not a pet name for his wife. Those were the only three I needed to sell. All we needed was a date.

I went out to the Roostertail that night. The Rat Pack was there. Frank, Dean, Sammy, Peter and Joey performing, then next door to Sindbad's to drink. I thought about it but, nah, they were probably booked. You would never see a Nemo's guy at the

Roostertail unless Rodney Dangerfield was booked—or Don Rickles. Not even then. I think the first New Riegel Open was 1971. They wouldn't let me down.

I would also go to Cincinnati to visit Van from time to time and we would do the town. He and Jeannie had a nice house up north with a pool. The Royals had Oscar Robertson, Lucas, Connie Dierking and Adrian Smith with him as starters and Bob Cousy as player/coach, which fouled things up. Cousy could no longer play and when paired with Oscar neither could he, to his level. It was obvious to everybody but Cousy. Even with Cousy at his peak it wouldn't have worked and it affected everyone, especially Oscar. Cousy might have been the greatest point guard ever to play at one time but Oscar was the greatest <u>player</u> ever to play for years to come and their pairing was the best chance the opponents had. You could tell it by watching Oscar's demeanor at practice. You could tell Luke was fed up and everybody was underachieving collectively. We still had some grand times downtown or at Connie's Bowling Alley or at one of Johnny Bench's parties on the Hill. Van was a commitment for the New Riegel Open, too.

Back in high school nearly everybody went up to Lake Erie in the summers, to Cedar Point or Put-In-Bay or hopping targets in between. It was where rival athletes from the various towns or cities got to know one another on neutral ground. One of the best places was Gem Beach, where I first met Siegfried and his Shelby group. Earlier in high school, my sophomore year, come tournament time we had to play the second game of a scheduled double-header in the Marion Coliseum while Shelby played the first. Sieg was lighting it up when we went down to dress at halftime and when we came out to warm up for our game the PA announcer was reading off the previous game's stats. "And, for Shelby, the leading scorer with sixteen of sixteen from the floor and sixteen of sixteen from the foul line, forty-eight points, Larry Siegfried." The boy could play and later did so for the Buckeyes and the Celtics in their glory years.

My first high school trip to Put-In-Bay had been with Fearless Farley and Turk McCrory, both high school friends a year ahead of me, grizzled veterans. Fearless (6' 6") was one of the two tall receivers that also played basketball that I alluded to earlier--Dan Moran was the other (6' 4")--and Turk was the fullback on the football team, both tough guys (more later) who looked upon me as a protégé. We took the ferry over and hit the hot spots. By then I was a junior. They got in fights, so far so good, and I got sleepy. It was supposed to be 3.2 beer, what's this? I wobbled over to the little two-story hotel next door and while the clerk wasn't looking took a vacant room for a snooze. A while later two inconsiderate bastards came in saying that they had been assigned this room, my room. The clerk came in and made me leave. I was still tired so I walked around to the back of the hotel, climbed up in an overhang and waited for them to leave, figuring they would head for the Strip, after check-in. I was right and also figured they would be gone for a while and since we were friends they wouldn't mind if I resumed my snooze so I jimmied the window and got back into bed. The next time the clerk brought the constable, who banned me for life from the Island. Where's a sense of humor when you need it? I had missed the last ferry to the homeland so I had to wait until morning to be escorted to the docks for the ferry, in a cell. I should have just started there. When he dropped me off, we were buddies. He had only been pissed because he had to break up a fight and had to kick two guys off the island the night before. I figured my ride was gone. Had to hitch-hike home. I should have jumped in the fight.

Anyway, being the Open's hosts, we knew the surrounding areas well and could get the word out in plenty of time to salt the tournament in the manner of the Good Sports. We wanted an impressive debut so the event would endure. We could never imagine the Grand Finale five years later.

I alluded to Tiffin police earlier and I was referring to only one member of the force that I won't mention by name but I was a freshman when he was a senior and a former bully. He had it in for me from day one. He looked upon me as an arrogant prick but just because he could spot 'em didn't give him the right to wait for his moment. I probably figured on him becoming a cop and when I didn't return immediately after college he probably got hives. But here I was now, a prominent business man in Tiffin. Where does he start? He started by tailing me around at night. But most of my nights started at the Golf Course, out of his jurisdiction, then Fostoria or a basketball game, or at Becky's. If I hit the bars, I usually stayed until after midnight, when his shift ended. Patience, Gerry, patience. He finally got me one night around 10:00 PM after I had just left my Club after a sauna. I always drank beers in the sauna but I also sweat like a pig so I wondered, should I risk it? Naw, I refused the breathalyzer, which in those days meant it immediately went to a trial.

Art Graham was a local attorney, a former Heidelberg footballer and a fellow arrogant prick that I liked. He was of the County Club set--good guys with families and reputations to protect--hence, Mohawk. Golf, dinner, cards and discretion in a small town. Prerequisites. Art took my case and with no warrant review or visible preparation of any kind, proceeded to remove Gerry's underwear in front of golfing partner, Judge Bon Talbert, Jr. Frontier justice.

I didn't know how officer Gerry took a joke but for his own sake I didn't want him harassing any of the Nemo's crew at our Inaugural Event. What if he pulled over Phil, or Tom Starling, or Sam, or the Candy Man? It just wasn't done. Surely not George Patterson. Wait and see.

I did a lot of other things too. Russ Mook was taking a real estate course at Tiffin University and I joined him. I was a good test taker, even without studying in advance, and I would have all my licenses before I was through. I did own property--Mom's--and would have to sell it sometime, as I sure as hell wasn't a career Tiffin guy. I'd still be in Detroit since my eyes were fixed if it weren't for Mom and Becky. And all this fun.

Chapter 22

Arf

I'm going to do a chapter on dogs now. I always planned to at some point but today is Groundhog Day and that will do for an excuse. The reason is every day I detest people more and more and realize that ultimately it's all because of technology. You can slit a person's throat with a computer without ever having to get out of bed. Technology in itself is our future and its developers are heroes but it always seems to end up in the hands of the Devil and his minions and nobody currently in office can ably defend us, or cares to.

Every day as I write this I am listening to Fox on TV, which is as close to truthful objectivity as you will get. I had hoped to get this book done before the rebellion but we are living in a land currently "governed" by a retarded puppet and the world's dams are about to burst. Next week our only hope goes on trial, probably for treason. So, I'll talk about dogs now before there's a bounty on them.

I think dogs are God's gifts when they are born and the more you love them the more grace they dispense, they are your best friends if you let them and if you do, angels when they pass. No one should ever harm a dog in my presence, even now.

Woof! My first dog was Duke, an Irish Setter already in my parents' possession on the horse farm. Duke wouldn't leave me alone and apparently I didn't mind, but Mom did and Duke was banished to the barn with the horses for a while. Later I wouldn't leave Duke alone. When we eventually sold the farm and the lone horse left, I was told Duke went with him. Ultimately I think Duke bought the farm but my parents couldn't tell me. In college my frat house had a mascot, Devil, who pretty much came and went as he chose. Thank God for Phil Craig, the good one, who always looked after him. One year a group of us got a dog from the pound in Ann Arbor when we shouldn't have and he had to be put down. I'm still ashamed of that.

Phyllis and I had a dog, a black Cocker we named "Chopper," which Phyllis got for her kids, Tammy and Timmy. Chopper was phenomenal, a mauler and a lover. When we parted, it was Chopper I missed the most, but she had a great family to give her love and care.

Becky and I soon got "Cuddles," a little black mix of poodle and terrier that was all rascal. We had Cuddles for fifteen years. Becky's Mom, Helen, got the runt of that litter, Sparky, who made it to twenty-one. Then it was Ebony Snow, "Ebbie," a black and white Cocker Spaniel for fourteen years and, until recently, Digger, our beagle, who we would have for fourteen and a half years. Our angels, Digger especially, still look after us from above.

When I first went to Michigan I found out nearly everybody hunted. Opening season was a ritual. People hunted in Ohio, but nobody I knew ever went. We just knew it went on. Other than to know it wasn't for me, I just primarily blocked it out. But in Michigan it was considered a heroic deed, especially among the country guys. Not so in Ohio. To this day, the thought of killing an animal sickens me, even household pests. If you are a hunter, fine, just keep it to yourself around me and we will be fine. I am reduced to naming the squirrels and chipmunks on my patio and playing with the dogs I encounter on my electric scooter rides around the park next door, wearing my MAGA hat. Once in a while I run across Shemy Schembechler and his family who live nearby. They have a son, Bo IV, thirteen, who is a replica of Bo. Shemy is a pro scout, GES Advisory. They have a dog, too.

Put a BAH in my sights, with feasible deniability, however, that's another story. Pop! Pop! Pop! Take a nap.

Chapter 23

A Satisfying Time

The summer of 1972 was a big one starting with the Inaugural New Riegel Open in mid-June and my trip with Mom to Rome in late July. A lot went on, both before and in between, at the Downtown Athletic Club. A lot that I am proud of. First, one day Russ and I were sitting in my Club sipping beers among the clients when in walked this mountainous kid that immediately reminded us of Baby Huey, from the cartoons. David Hoover, hereafter to be known as Hoovy, was a to-be junior at Calvert who wanted to get into weightlifting. Hoovy was a "Diamond in the Rough": 6' 2", 230 lbs. and totally untrained, not a defined muscle in his body. But they were there, popping out. A signature piece, unspoiled. I knew how Michelangelo must have felt. If only he would listen.

He listened. I started him on the Universal to get the soreness out, then right to the free weight flow motion exercises, the cleans, clean and jerks, hang cleans, front and back squats, dead lifts, high pulls, leg presses and finally the bench press, the least critical, yet critical, core exercises. Later I would put in this regimen for Michigan trainer Lindsay McClain for Coach Johnny Orr's basketball team. Their current weight trainer, Jon Sanderson, still deploys the same principles today, with modern modifications, for Coach Juwan Howard.

You had to practice these motions, get 'em down, or you would hurt yourself. You didn't necessarily need light weights to begin, but rather enough weight to make your body flow fluidly with the motion. Hoovy listened and learned and, ironically, so did Russ. Russ's playing days were pretty much in his wake, but man, he took to it and after six months was clean and jerking 220 lbs. seven times. Old "Roosky," he had to have a target in mind, being loosely wrapped. I hoped it wasn't me. Another tribute to Hoovy, he was a far better athlete than I had given him credit for and was a helluva baseball player to boot.

I was always big on rope jumping, too, and Hoovy, inept at first, soon was a master. If only all my members were like him. Over the summer he dropped that baby fat and got up to 250 lbs. When the season started he kept coming. After the season I would call George.

Word got around and the athletes started to come. Two especially, the Gase brothers, Art, the eldest, and Bill, previously Calverteers but out for a while and wondering what their college shots were now. Chuck Heater and Steve King had begun their Michigan careers and word was getting around. Art and Bill were polar opposites, with the exception that both had been lineman. Art was a medium; Bill "The Grape Ape," after the cartoon character, a large. Art relied on technique; Bill on bulldozing. Both needed work but both listened and put in the work. More Michigan assistants that I knew were getting Mid-Am head coaching opportunities like George but I wanted to be sure so I wouldn't blow my contacts. Currently I was living on Heater and King. There were others too, who came and didn't listen, the vast majority, and they dropped by the wayside. But it was always a kick to get one who listened. I was getting more and more

Heidelbergers too and the rumor was that Tiffin University, a basketball powerhouse, was taking up football as well. One of my best clients, later a close friend, Robin Farris and another, Jim Huss, with whom I remain close today, both TU standout cagers, trained here and later joined our traveling team, mostly TU alumni. I later would get Robin hooked up in Europe for a few years. He now coaches the women at Indiana/Louisville, last I heard. It was gratifying that they listened, even more so when I would hear from them later, which I would from one especially. Stay tuned.

The New Riegel Open was upon us and we were ready. By noon on Friday the cars with Michigan plates began arriving at the Riverview, about fifteen of them, for the Inaugural. Tom Starling's huge Lincoln with his train engine horn at full force, terrifying the lunch crowd. Van had come in Thursday and was staying with me. By 3:00 PM most had arrived and got started on the "Hospitality." Ultimately, the most surprising thing about those outings, gratifying even, was how the locals bonded with the visitors, at least at the golf course. Out on the town with all the bars welcoming our stops you would encounter the occasional drunk jerk who felt left out and would mouth off challengingly, only to get tossed by the owners who were in this with us. The bars would be salted by 10:00 PM. Hang on!

For three straight days Seneca Hills was packed. On Sunday morning most of the Detroit crowd, instead of hightailing it back to Detroit, returned to the course to say thanks and reminisce. We had us a memorable debut. I went up to Detroit the next week and those that missed the first committed for the second. Also, DeBusschere was getting married to Gerri, a great girl from Garden City, Long Island, and an epic bachelor party was planned. So much to do; so little time.

Next up, The Eternal City. Mom and I flew to New York, had dinner at one of Mom's old favorites and met up with the Bishop's contingent the next morning at Idlewild for the Charter to Rome. Before we took off Mom had met up with two of her old classmates. I started to giggle. Cary Grant in Rome, free to roam. On the flight, they noticed another one, accompanied by her daughter Margi, a cute redhead who was playing the same role I was, but freshly married. She smiled at me, rolled her eyes and sighed.

We both left and arrived on Friday and stayed at a legendary old Roman hotel, which name I can't recall. Hopefully it will come to me and I'll interject it. On Saturday and Sunday tours were planned all day, busses with stops and guides, the way to see Rome for the beginner, with dinners afterward, and of course, services. It blew my mind. Incomprehensible. The majesty of it all, and it never ends. As the bus moved along, no one spoke except the guide and every eye was out the windows. I am not going to elaborate further until the Canonization Ceremony the next Sunday, simply because I would be doing such a disservice to its majesty. But for God's sake if you ever go anywhere, go to Rome and take your time.

At Sunday night's dinner with Mom and her buddies, Margi's Mom suggested that Margi and I should feel free to go on tours of our own, on foot, which is really the way it should be done if you have a plan, while she and the others stayed with the group. Now I had never indicated such inclination to Mom either way. This was her trip. But then she agreed and I about had another one of those Petroff moments. It had been Margi's idea. I wouldn't have voiced it until the next morning.

So, we blended, about half and half, and really did it up. I was dazzled and vowed that Rome would be my honeymoon site. More about Rome in that section. The one special thing I wouldn't be able to replicate was the night Margi and I listened to old Louis Armstrong songs at Harry's Bar on the Via Veneto, just after he died. Three all-time legends in one setting. I had previously heard Armstrong live, at the Roostertail. Also, post passing, in the audience was Bogart (Harry's was Bogie's favorite bar), plus Princess Caroline of Monaco and her buddies, live.

The Canonization Ceremony was held outside at the Vatican because there would be over 1,000,000 people in attendance from all over the world. Pilgrims, home to worship. Again, I can't do it justice. Our seats couldn't have been any better. The Pope blessed us all individually, probably 300 in total from various points of the globe; the others, just the faithful, here to welcome a saint. Nothing further need be said. Screams of "Ile Papa!" was all you could hear. For hours. That's all I can write.

Chapter 24

Fate Strikes Again

A side effect of the Open was it seemed to galvanize a lot of old friends that had moved away and settled in to what greener pastures offered. This brought them back more frequently and it was good to see. I would go to Columbus to see Pat. He was Executive Director of the Ohio Democratic Party, serving under Chairman Paul Tipps, a wealthy businessman and a great guy. Pat was essentially his enforcer, keeping Paul pristine, and it was meant for him. Back then it was far more civilized than now, opponents either worked things out or they perished. Of course, there were no computers or technology of any impact. Relationships mattered and despite his over-the-top style, Pat was good at developing them. He was also a man of his word. Pat was a far bigger GAH than me and, then, a great friend.

At the DAC, Stan Wilson, a townie, had joined and really got into it. He had been a lifter looking for just what I offered and became a regular. He would look after things in my absence willingly so I comped him and he became a friend I could count on. Art Gase and the Grape Ape worked almost like Hoovy, but with less potential, so I would see what I could do for them, too, if they kept it up through the winter. Then Becky's brother came in, Mike, a hard hitting defensive back from Calvert, after the season ended. He jumped in, worked hard and progressed but seemed never to be in school. He picked up the workout protocol well and gave the required effort and progressed but seemed to lack the attitude to achieve at the next level, which was his stated objective. College included classes.

Becky came from a great family and I knew and liked them all but Mike was on the fringe. One time I came in the back door after running an errand to find him shining his shoes with one of my towels, polish and all. Ordinarily I would have given him the Nemo's Bum's Rush out the front but held back because of Becky. But that set the tone.

Ultimately I recommended Mike to Bowling Green as a preferred walk-on, only because of Becky. He started all ten games on special teams as a freshman, was a gunner on kick-offs and, as we found out later, had never attended a class. He returned to Tiffin, wisely stayed clear of me and jumped in to the local drug scene. With his attitude, that, too, would be a short-lived career choice. Not to speak ill of the dead, Mike had one saving grace, he loved his dog Sparky, the runt of the Cuddles litter, until the day she died at twenty-one. Sparky was her Mom's, Helen's dog, really, but Mike was living at home and working as a painter. Once home, he couldn't put her down.

So, things progressed. I sold George on Art Gase for Eastern Michigan and Hoovy had made a favorable debut and was starting as an offensive tackle for him so he vouched for my judgment to the Toledo coach, another U of M aide with George, of Bill, the Grape Ape, who quickly made their team. All eventually graduated and made favorable contributions. Everything went on as usual but I never was destined for a small town life. I loved and missed Detroit, was energized by my Columbus trips and Pat offered connectivity at the highest level there, and I knew Becky as the one for me forever, but not here. I couldn't be married and live here. There was no growth potential. For me, in Tiffin, I was always at the top level.

The New Riegel Open grew each year and was looked forward to at both ends and 1975's was on the horizon, scheduled for mid-June. I made a couple trips to check in and all was well, with some new blood scheduled. Dave had gotten married and stayed in New York to advantage himself of all the opportunities that were offered as the Knicks started to gel. Van had gotten traded again, first to Philly, then Atlanta, and was living in Phoenix near Dick, his identical twin, now with the Suns. He had divorced Jeannie, who stayed in Cincinnati. We always stayed in touch, always.

The Big Weekend came and we had a banner turnout. More people than ever, especially Teamster Execs. Brennan, Holmes, even Fitzsimmons, for the first time. More Detroit ladies too. A wild reunion type atmosphere by now, with new blood. Everything as before although more so. Those who brought their ladies would retire about midnight to hit the Riverview bar and pool, away from the carousing downtown, to join Nemo and his cronies.

As usual, most returned to Seneca Hills on Sunday morning for a checkout brunch and to relate tales about the night before and say goodbye. We sat around most of the afternoon unwinding and relaxing.

Until about four, as I recall, when whatever we were watching on TV was interrupted by a news flash: Teamster President James R. Hoffa had gone missing.

Chapter 25

National Impact

On Tuesday morning, June 27, 1975, at the DAC, after I just got off the phone with Nemo, in walked the FBI. Nemo hadn't known anything more about it than me and I had made plans to go to Detroit on Wednesday. The word was it was a hit, of course, but by whom, on whose order, was the big question. Of course, the FBI had been there too, and they got the same from me. The truth. The Open was an annual event, just ask Riverview owner John Egbert. The crowd from Nemo's always stayed at his place; John would love the notoriety and probably delay the FBI long enough for me to get to Jere if they hadn't already been there. We didn't need any creativity here and, forewarned, Jere could have them thinking of an excuse for their own whereabouts.

When I walked into Nemo's the next day everything was like nothing had occurred, except that from time to time one of the "Old Gentlemen" from the Union Wars, now residing in Walled Lake, would walk in, take a seat and inquire of Buttons as to "what the fuck happened?" They were ready to roll, just point them. Buttons would stutter out instructions, I think, and they would leave with a "let me know" order. Buttons would, when allowed.

On that trip I tried to put together what I knew and the only concern was why was there such a large contingent of union officials at our golf tournament on the weekend? Elmore Leonard, my favorite author, whom I had met there before, was there again, but we didn't talk. Not to an author, not today. As the day went on things fell into place. Chuckie O'Brien had driven Hoffa to a roadhouse for a meeting and went in to make a phone call and when he came out Hoffa was gone, was the story. But since that had originated from Chuckie himself, no one believed it. Other stories developed that made it a Mafia hit with Hoffa becoming manburger in a Detroit Meat Packing House, just to start. My own thoughts told me that Chucky probably was telling segments of the truth or he wouldn't be alive but not the whole truth because he wasn't choking. Things were just developing. My own thoughts today are that recent TV adaptations probably came close, especially the DeNiro version, but in those days I can't believe the body ever left Detroit, when there was still a body anyway. Nobody from Nemo's ever talked to me about it to this day, after that day, nor did I inquire. Suffice it to say that was the last New Riegel Open but it remains lore in Tiffin.

Chapter 26

Time to Wake Up

It has always been my style, if you will, to break things down to their simplest form to make a judgment, to try to never make things harder than they have to be. More and more people today are such connivers that they cloud their intent in useless rhetoric, never more in evidence than when you are forced to read prospective legislation. Bills are written with the intent that you won't read them. Just pass them. The Master of this Art is the Asshole, the BAH himself, usually a Democrat, not always. See, I'm breaking things down to make my points without making this a boring read.

Most, not all, of the Democrats you hear from today are BAHs and active conspirators to bring our America to its knees. Republican patriots such as Mike Lindell ("Absolute Proof") are hot on their heels with proof of their misdeeds, but many more in and out of office need to step up, singularly and collectively, now. Without their media support the Dems are no match for the Repubs, either intellectually or governance content wise. But they do have the media. And the media is even dumber and more devious than they are.

The only hope for the Republicans remains Donald Trump. He's the only Republican with a set, along with Jim Jordan, to stand up to and challenge the media that they can't resist covering. And we need that to happen because their counter to his claims will be so absurd and off target that our message will get through to the extent that other options, hopefully substantive, will follow. The Republicans can prevail if they follow their leader. Only if they can get the word out.

The only other thing on their side is that, left to proceed at this current pace, the Dems weaken our country to the point where we are forced to defend ourselves militarily at about the same time they make their attempt to take our guns and the Good Old Boys step up.

There you have it in three short paragraphs.

I would like to compare and contrast two GAHs for you to make sure you are clear on my perspective on people. Both have my utmost respect. Hoffa and Trump. First, both were nondrinkers and driven for power for good causes, Hoffa for his members, Trump for his country. Both utilized unorthodox methods to get and keep it, Hoffa the Mafia; Trump, our leaching allies and our arch-enemies. He called them out. Both were cheated out of power by the people they saved. Hoffa was assassinated; Trump is a target, even more so after this absurd impeachment ploy is put to rest.

I had met Hoffa on good reference and had spoken to him on several substantive occasions. I had never wasted his time. I liked everything about him but would never have sought his responsibilities. His son, James, Jr. went to U of M Law School with my roommate, Don Corriere, several years before and we had met.

I had talked to Trump once before and I forget where I was but it was before cell phones, probably the DAC. Kramer and Hornung were in the Trump Hotel in Atlantic City, in Regis

Philbin's room with Trump, when Kramer called to introduce me to both out of the blue. Regis first, asked how it benefitted him to talk to me and I told him I had a cure for shortness, best I could do off the cuff; then Trump, who was laughing, having listened in, told me to get my ass out there to spend some money since he was comping Ron and Paul and they were emptying his reserve of booze. I think I told him it was a cheap price to pay if it kept them away from his girls, to which I heard Kramer say "they're next."

When I was a sophomore in high school, Hornung had just won the Heisman Trophy at Notre Dame, narrowly defeating Kramer in the balloting, when he came to Calvert with Coach Moose Krause to speak at our Athletic Banquet. Of course, as always, I wasn't up for any of the awards but I did shake his hand. Years later, when together in public, I introduced Paul as someone who had always wanted to meet me. Sought me out, even. He would just roll his eyes.

Kramer, Hornung and Regis were all GAHs, as well as Trump.

Big day for Michigan yesterday. Tom Brady just won his seventh Super Bowl and Charles Woodson was elected to the NFL Hall of Fame. Both would figure in my plans later.

Chapter 27

Time for a Change

It began dawning on me shortly after the final New Riegel Open that I was in a rut. People around me were growing and progressing and moving, largely because of me, and Mom needed my attention more and more, even though she still went on her trips, in groups, and had her friends. I had gotten four season M Club tickets for Michigan's football games earlier and increased it to six to include my friends and got a prime parking pass behind the press box for easy access and egress. We would go up early and party all day, then come back late, usually in an SUV. Then my old friend from school, Bill Laskey, retired from the NFL wars and joined his family business, Laskey Ford in Milan, right on the way, where Joe O'Donnell, also recently retired, would join us in Bill's motor home. Over the course of the season, we would see everybody, both visiting us and in the M Club Lot in front of the tunnel where the band and team would enter, which was nearly impossible to get out of after a game with all the tailgaters and their elaborate presentations. Our spot offered placement and mobility.

Everybody I would see from the old days had families, either beside them or at home, and it had changed them ever so slightly. I was the same old me, perhaps more so. I had never lacked confidence in myself, sometimes to the point of arrogance, internally, I had hoped. But the problem with my eyes sobered me up, lesson learned. Arrogance never brought you anything but more problems and enemies. I would see the old bunch, meet both our predecessors and successors at the games and forge relationships to be sustained to this day. Thank God for them. They were a lot of why I am me. It all goes back to Michigan; then, not now.

I had also made inroads in Columbus through Pat, both socially and politically, at the top. Attorney John Connor, who at that time specialized in liquor cases but took on anything because of his connections, was a hellraiser and the Catholic Diocese attorney. Jim Cardi, a former Heidelberger with Pat and football teammate of Denny at Heidelberg, was a Schmidt's Beer distributor, took care of those problems. Dick Slavens was an ex-cop, now a thug, and his former partner, Phil, was a beat cop/fixer. Playing racquetball at the Y, I had met Mike Burke and Roger Marshall, both Swat cops. We would play at 6:00 AM, right after their shift ended and they were surging with adrenalin. We had some classic matches. Between them all, they knew all the spots, had all the connections. Unlimited opportunity.

Phyllis and Becky knew of each other and it wasn't a comfortable situation for any of us but my mind was made up. Neither ever mentioned the other but Becky just had more of what I needed and wasn't a worrier. She was a tough German who stood up for herself, with vastly more potential and someone I felt I could count on, forever. Plus, Becky was seven years younger than Phyllis and looked forward to starting a family. Nothing against Phyllis, a fine lady, but Becky was my one true love, then, and now. Even more so I am looking towards our futures together, whatever that brings. It has already brought a fine son Logan (Indian for Wolverine), his wonderful wife Laura and two fine grandsons, Paul and Tom.

Soon Pat came to me with the opportunity of a lifetime, out of the blue. Ohio Attorney General Bill Brown, a Democrat, announced his intention to run for governor against the legendary Jim Rhodes, a three time incumbent Republican, heretofore thought to be unbeatable. His own Lieutenant Governor, Democrat Dick Celeste, a voracious campaigner, was also challenging, so it would be Brown v. Celeste in the primary to face off against Rhodes in the general election. Pat had suggested me to be Brown's Administrative Assistant, the one to accompany him on the road throughout his campaign, day after day. I would be in charge of him, theoretically, whenever out of the office on campaign matters. With no experience, besides being a Republican. Okay, that sounds like me, fully trained and all. Bring it on. It would be up to Brown. See if we got along.

Now in those days Dems and Repubs were opponents, not enemies, like today. The difference wasn't as polarized as it appears now. After all, Democrat Celeste was Republican Governor Rhodes' Lt. Governor, yet they were running against one another now. To win, Brown had to defeat both, consecutively, and I was the answer? His front man, riding point. Now it was beginning to make sense. Who else?

Brown was a shorter (5' 6") more compact version of me, not quite as handsome or humble but our personalities were identical, two GAHs, that could almost read each other's thoughts. I would be his driver, keep him on schedule and safe, relay and send message to the Headquarters and advise him, as appropriate. I was to start as soon as I could free myself of my Tiffin responsibilities.

There was no way I could maintain the DAC and be out front with a candidate for the Governor's office but, with Stan's help we did so until school started, after Labor Day. Stan collected all the keys from "special members" and kept one for himself as payment until I could close up formally. I had a lot of disappointed members but no conceivable alternatives and everybody eventually understood. I would ultimately give the Universal Gym to Tiffin University, now into football. Lots of good memories.

I got an apartment in Pat's complex close to downtown and the newly constructed Rhodes State Office Tower, which was, at 40 stories, the tallest building in a city of 350,000 (now close to 1,000,000). When Becky would come down to visit there was <u>one</u> stoplight between Tiffin and my place; now when we go back to visit Tiffin from Upper Arlington, a northern, closer suburb, there are forty. Data. You gotta love it. There was a nice pool right out of my patio door.

My office was on the 17th floor, right next to Bill's and his scheduler, Geoff Littlehale, also new. He would prove to be an invaluable ally, both competent and loyal. We were surrounded by Bill's top executives and his first order to me was to go around and introduce myself, which I promptly did. It was 8:00 AM on the Tuesday after Memorial Day and they all were just settling in, apparently available. So, I would knock and walk in, extend my hand, smile and state my name to which I would get a puzzled, annoyed look, a more efficient way of saying "who the fuck are you?" My first test. Brown had not apprised them of my hire.

Now this was right up my alley, from my days in Detroit. I would stand there, smile at them and patiently explain to them "I'm Dan Clevenger, Bill's Administrative Assistant for the Campaign. I'll be your liaison to him on the road." At least I passed my test.

None of them passed theirs. I had never seen "haughty" like this before. As I found out later, they had all either hoped to be chosen themselves or to select who was. Now I'm going to teach a course here on running political campaigns that Pat already knew and I think Bill did, too. The critical part of my job and why I was chosen was because I wasn't a "yes man," too close to the campaign and the candidate to be objective. Not everything was going to be "great" and if things weren't, the worse thing I could do was to sugarcoat things and imply otherwise. This was a world of AHs, G and B. I had to keep being a G.

I would find out later that this was a test that Pat and Bill had set me up for, and I had passed, but we were on the road right out of the chute and the only person at the office I would talk to was Geoff, who was learning too. Bill, Geoff and I established a good rapport the first week and neither Geoff nor I felt any need to apprise the Execs of how things were going. One of them in particular could challenge Professor Corey for his crown, with less style. Let Bill do as he chose. Before long they sought us out and a rapport was developed, albeit with me it was tenuous. Geoff was with them every day.

From now on I am going to have to consolidate because a lot of crazy things occurred as I matured into my role and unlike Detroit, for the most part, Cleveland was active duty. So was

Youngstown. You have got a leg up if you have seen "Kill the Irishman."

Floyd Clevenger (my Dad)

Mabel Clevenger (my Mom)

Shirley Clevenger Schroeder (my Half-Sister)

Congressman Cliff Clevenger (my Uncle)

Rev Mother Agnes of Jesus (my Aunt Genevieve Costello)

Dad & Traveler

Duke & Dan

The Costello Home in Jessup, PA

Becky Clevenger (circa 1953)

THE SECOND HALF

Chapter 28

Taking Charge

I am a principled person, and first impressions have always meant a lot to me. Usually they have proven out in my favor but not always and I have paid the price. I wouldn't change if I could, besides now it's too late so this chapter is for my contemporaries. See if it hits home.

It is February 11, 2021 and my horoscope for the day is as follows: LEO (July 23-August 22) "One benefit of living a principled life is that the rules can simplify your thought process by eliminating dozens of small decisions in the way that 'no wheat' or 'no meat' eliminates an entire category of options."

I only glance at the "scopes" because they are at the bottom of the comics in the liberal rag, *The Columbus Dispatch*, which I only read to fuel my day but this hit home. Hell, that's me. The Execs were never going to be on my side, no matter what. If Bill Brown won the election it would be because of them; if he lost it would be because of me. That would be fine with me. I would know.

Let's all go back in time and briefly reminisce. When we were growing up, what dominated our front page news? Wars and Organized Crime, Wars and Organized Crime, day after day.

Today there are no "big wars," only small ones that eliminate the "insignificants" because of the threat of Nuclear Weapons. And there is no mention of Organized Crime either. Why is that? Could it be that it was absorbed by or even absorbed for itself, the Deep State? Look at the Catholic Church. Becky and I are lifelong Catholics and will remain so because of its Doctrine but when you go to Mass you get the same pap they fed us and feed their grade schoolers while our government's main objective is to discredit them. It would be to eliminate them were it not for the Illuminati, a Deep State critical element that has already taken control of the Vatican and could use us as a tool for their mission. I am not handy with tools; I could get downright pissed being one.

In Detroit I was around Union guys every day, hence the occasional wise guy, but I never had to deal with either. It was purely social. We were bar friends in a neutral venue, Nemo's. His rules prevailed because they were respected, even revered by both parties and by us innocents. No pardons for deviants. If I had been called upon to testify before the FBI (before it too became part of the Deep State) when Hoffa disappeared, there was nothing I could have told them other than to provide alibis for our guests.

In Ohio, even today, but much more so when I debuted, all political campaigns ran through Cleveland. It was then a Mafia stronghold run by the branch that extended from Buffalo through Pittsburgh, then Youngstown to Cleveland, and they ruled the Unions. To win, the Dems had to completely dominate the Union vote. That had to be Bill's objective and I had to be prepared to be looked upon as his protector. That's how they would see it.

There are other things you have to know about campaigning too and of course I had to learn them on my own. First, there are Capitol Politics and Outstate Politics; Cleveland especially then, not now. It's relatively equal now. Second, it is all about relationships and every contact has value and should be maxed out. Every contact you make must be substantive, have the purpose to gain a commitment, which hardly ever will be kept. Every person you are scheduled to meet has an agenda of their own, which they expect you to prioritize if elected, and Rhodes and Celeste both outranked Brown then.

Geoff Littlehale would prove to be a phenomenal scheduler and I would be a good administrative assistant because I always insisted we adhere to it. After a while Bill knew better than to resist me because he knew I'd persist and eventually challenge him, so we would leave and move on. I always planned for that every meeting. If a person doesn't respect your schedule he won't respect your agenda or his commitment.

Brown had what it took with the Execs and Youngstown crew as both he and his executive assistant Mike DeAngelo, who was from there, went to OSU Law School with Eddie DeBartolo, Carmen Policy, Eddie Flask and Danny Thomas, all connected Y-Towners and ardent Brown advocates. Together they were a hoot, barging in and taking over the other Execs' offices at will, feet on the desks, making phone calls. Their frequent visits lightened everything up; even DeAngelo loosened up. All the Execs turned out to be okay guys and I could understand their initial reticence toward me, an ex-Michigan jock from Detroit coming in unannounced on a reference from Pat, whom they feared but didn't respect--he wasn't an attorney-- without notice from Bill. That was a lot to overcome.

In our debriefing meetings they would read my reports, which they should have beforehand, and then ask Littlehale questions. Now I could write the shit out of a report and I was proud of them and Geoff relied on them for future schedules. Once, fed up, he said to them "Didn't you read Dan's report? He's the one who was there." That was my last debriefing meeting; they'd showed me.

On our many trips Brown and I became close. Initially I didn't have an underground parking spot and had to park my car by the YMCA, then go get his, (theoretically) underground, and go on our trip. Ordinarily I would pick him up at his home which was on the way to most places, but there were times when I was inconvenienced so I bugged him about it until he folded. His was an assigned car by the Office and mine was a sporty sedan and I would get mileage, but still, the Execs had them and what the hell did they do?

Bill was a Camel chain smoker and I would always have my window open so he would have to yell to converse as we drove. When he would speak I would put it up then down when he finished, up, down, up, down, until he would go off and either shut up or quit smoking. We compromised. In the cold he would smoke less, in the summer, my option.

My background was perfect for this job, no one intimidated me and I had the ideal temperament: feature and support the candidate and record (remember) his conversations and commitments in a summary paragraph and write his thank you notes. His secretary, Jean Mayhew, thought I was great at that. I would remember the smallest essential details to personalize them.

A year and a half would be a long haul, always busy but largely boring to what I hope becomes my audience for this book. But we had our moments, mostly in Cleveland, which I will recount now, and back in Columbus, which I'll describe later. I was fully into it and my best would be required.

First it must be noted that forty some years ago, Cleveland was by far Ohio's largest city, two and a half times larger than Columbus. Cincinnati was second, Toledo third. Today Columbus is larger than Cleveland, Cincinnati and Toledo combined at just under one million. Demographics change. So don't mistake today's for back then. Also, like Detroit, today's Cleveland had radically changed. Today's Ohio is Red (Republican) but its cities are Blue (Democrat) except for Cincinnati. Michigan is all Blue. What I alluded to earlier is now full blown and the Union members are on the verge of rebellion. Dave Bing's best efforts fell short. They are in the desperate stage.

Some Cleveland Parameters: William J. Brown was the Attorney General of Ohio, the Chief Law Enforcement officer in the State, and he was running for Governor. To win, he needed the Unions. I was his Administrative Assistant, the only other person representing both his office and his objectives to the Union officials he needed to support his agenda. We were both up to it because of our pasts.

Shondor Birns was a Cleveland "Restaurateur," the owner of the 10-11 Club on 1011 Chester, right downtown. His clientele included Tony Salerno, John Nardi, Ray Ferritto, Jack Licavoli, Mike Frato, Louis "Lips" Maceri and Frank Brancato, all of whom "dabbled" in Unions too. Add the rebellious Irishman Danny Green, who dined elsewhere, and you pretty much had the roster we would need to win over, besides the elected Union officials.

Now I knew people like that in Detroit but never had to deal with them on business, nor was I representing the state's top cop. Bill had been AG a while; he was in his second term and was in tight with the Youngstown boys and the DeBartolos, clean, but connected. We would deal with the Union officials and let them deal with the 10-11 bunch and we would dine elsewhere, usually at Swingos' further uptown, where we would also overnight on occasion. Jim Swingos was a connected ally on both ends.

Try as we might, we would cross paths, hopefully unobserved by the media, and made the best of it, laughing, joking, back slapping, often alluding to business but anytime anything turned devious I would have to step in to somehow divert and it had to be good. Honest to God, one time when Bill was getting buttonholed in the middle of a meal in one of Cleveland's riverfront restaurants and I was grasping, Jim Brown walked by and smiled and waved. All attention diverted. I became the focus. "Oh yeah, JB and I go way back" (to the Detroit Press Club).

Relatively, this happened a lot and our mission was to generate support and <u>not</u> alienate anybody and never show weakness or vulnerability. We won hands down and the Youngstown bunch confirmed it. They accepted me as an ally to the cause and let Columbus know it. Twice, however, when we were in meetings in downtown Cleveland, we heard explosions close by--car bombs, both deadly, to people we had dealt with. No matter how comfortable you got with that bunch you would have to remember that, come to it, they would kill you without hesitation and you would probably hesitate.

One thing I felt confident of months later was we had done well in Cleveland, Celeste's hometown and that bode well of the Democratic Primary. While Celeste probably took Cleveland for granted initially, he was all over the rest of the state, way ahead of us in the outlying areas and some other cities. He would frequently travel alone on his own schedule. I added a lot to the Brown package and Celeste, solo, did the same for his; he had a lot of groupie types that worshipped him all over.

Bill was always good in cities, not so much outstate, which favored the Rhodes Republicans. Celeste was a big guy, bigger than me, but not intimidating, which in itself, left an impression. Rhodes stayed in Columbus, cutting up pies with Democrat House Speaker Vern Riffe, the two most powerful people in the state, whom I got to know. This was just the primary. The Governor sat tight.

Back in Columbus the Execs now spoke only to Brown, who gave me my due—and a raise, richly deserved. He would call me into his office more and more to confer. I told him what I thought. What the hell are the Execs doing to help out? Geoff would tell me that the executives, who oversaw section chiefs for every conceivable legal matter in the state, would just strut and pontificate, belittle me and confer with committed allies, then take long lunches with lobbyists. All of a sudden Bill wondered the same and brought it up to the execs. Naturally that incriminated Geoff and me. So different from what I had grown used to in Detroit. Of course I was in an entirely different role. Geoff wouldn't put up with as much shit as I would. He would go on to excel in Washington later.

Chapter 29

Folding the Tent

Bill would usually travel with me three or four days a week, one or two evenings, substantive calls, well-selected. He never treated me as an aide but as an ally. We really liked each other and I had his respect because, no matter what, I would never take any shit. From anyone. Even when I should. The only person from the office I would ever mention was Geoff. There were two really sharp attorneys who stood out, Dick Walinski from Toledo, a smart, savvy, great guy whom I'd played against in high school and Bruce Rakay, a slick self-server from southeast Ohio coal country. Bill was from Cádiz, down there, that was also the birthplace of George Armstrong Custer and Clark Gable, who looked just like my Dad, sans mustache. Walinsky was a legal scholar; Rakay was ruthless ambition. Trust one, beware of the other (of the attorneys, the latter was the only threat).

Sometimes I had to get gas right out of the chute, the first few times he would ask me why I didn't fill up before I picked him up but I would always have to stop to let him get a pack of Camels anyway, because of his wife Cheryl, and he couldn't wait. Once in a while coming from his home for a trip Bill would get in the car, take out a pistol (.45) and slap it in the glove compartment (when he could get it passed Cheryl), then glance at me. I would show no reaction. At one of these gas stops, he took it out and palmed it and asked me if I thought I could handle "this baby." I didn't say a word, just took it and field stripped it then snapped it together and handed it back. That was the gun we trained with at LeJeune. I didn't mention that nor say another word.

Celeste, Bill's primary opponent, usually traveled four or five days, three or four evenings, and had his brother Ted minding his office. He usually had a driver but met alone for two reasons: he knew his stuff and he was an imposing presence, especially relative to his groupie drivers. I added to Bill's package, a complement; Dick's drivers detracted from his, truth be told. Midway through, Celeste was getting to more people, was running for Governor and was already Lieutenant Governor. I thought we had some ground to make up. I told that to Bill and Geoff. I didn't want to be on the road any more than necessary but I thought it was necessary that we were. We would see how that flew.

During the week, whenever possible, and it usually was, I would get up at 5:00 AM, lift, then go to the YMCA to play racquetball with Mike Blake, one of the Swat cops, before heading out. I might as well be traveling, because as far as I could see, doing more of what we did was the only chance we had. I wasn't aware of and didn't care what the Execs thought except through Geoff, who agreed with me but thought it was Cheryl who put a cap on Bill's travel and had let the Execs know it. Rakay went with us once to coal country, his home base, and was impressed with our presentation but agreed we had to get it into more "theaters," so to speak. On the way home Bill confessed, it was Cheryl. His brother Tom, President of Lazarus, our largest department store, was already up her ass about it. Bill was a newlywed and Cheryl should have "known the job was dangerous when she took it," if Tom was one to quote from Super Chicken, according to Bill. He got the quote from me. I still use it. My choice was to let things work themselves out. Stay out of it.

Cheryl also liked Bill to be home for dinner by 8:00 PM on days we traveled, which eliminated cocktail hours with our targets when most deals are made and frowned on all overnight trips. Were we allowed recess? It would have to be up to Tom to make her see the light since Bill's performance was directly proportional to the climate on the home front and to start out behind the eight ball at the outset was nothing but a wasted, negative day. I shared that thought with Bill and he agreed, was appreciative even. Still nothing changed. With all that on the table, at least the Execs lost their scapegoat, me. For a while.

At the Y and on my time with Pat and the crew I met almost all the shooters in town, the critical people, and developed relationships that lasted until my illness hit shortly after the turn of the century. Treat 'em right and they will stay. The key is to never lie so you can't get caught up in one and don't have to remember everything. They are all dead now but we were just getting started then.

Many were attorneys representing the big firms, and I was shocked to see that virtually none of them had been contacted by the Brown campaign. Celeste's, yes. I was astounded as was Pat and he got all over DeAngelo about it, which was just what was needed but was the last thing I needed. Then he went to Bill which then was the last thing _he_ needed. Others were stockbrokers, same thing. Now lawyers and brokers have clients who vote. They are also credible to those clients, influence peddlers all over town, in this case the Capitol, if not the state. And I was the one who needed to learn the game?

Today all that stuff has to be locked in before a prospective candidate even considers a run for city council, let alone Governor. Only nowadays it ultimately wouldn't matter because no one's commitment has any meaning. No value at all.

Anyway, shortly thereafter, Bill pulled the plug. Weeks before the Primary, he announced he would be running for reelection as AG. Celeste had a clear field to ultimately lose to Rhodes in November. The Execs couldn't blame me and I had held up my end, even gotten a reputation. Celeste himself congratulated me. Opportunity awaited.

Chapter 30

Choices

I could stay with the AG's office as long as I wanted with no assigned role. I would be expected to assume one after the General Election in November, with Bill assured of being reelected, but that wasn't an option for me, or Geoff, who had eyes on Washington. It was time to sort out my private life.

Phyllis had moved back to Muskegon, Michigan her hometown, and put her kids in school, close to her family. She had a tough time believing I was gone so much on the campaign, but I was, and all her calls went unanswered because I wasn't there, not avoiding her, but I was. I didn't do break-ups well, as you have learned. That would be my last.

Becky was willing to talk to Bill about a job in his office, came down to interview, and was hired on the executive floor, down from Bill in the Court of Claims Section. Thirty-one years later she retired, having served under nine Attorneys General, having several different executive positions, the last fifteen as a fiscal officer in the Finance Section. Doc Ross would miss her but was happy for us. I had to see him again as I made the transition to the new "soft/hard lens in one" model I was told about before and, as before, it was the answer. Good to go.

We found a nice apartment: two bedrooms on the other but close side of town with a good safe place for Cuddles to romp. My lease at my apartment ran out that summer when the pool closed and I moved in with Becky. It was good to have Cuddles with us both again. Cuddie had a little second floor balcony she could safely spend her time on when we were working. Nothing changed socially: when the guys went out we would join them. Soon they brought girls; everybody was welcome. Pat still lived at Tivoli so we still had access. On previous trips Becky had met Marlys Brown, a flamboyant free spirit living down from Pat and they became good friends. Marlys would eventually be her maid of honor in our wedding.

Even during the campaign I was able to make most of the Michigan games. I would go home Friday night, see Mom, then pick up Becky and whomever were in the entourage for the Ann Arbor trip, leave the next morning at 6:00 AM, go to Milan and pick up Laskey and Joe and head in to Bill's spot down from mine in the motor home by 10:00 AM, see the game and the guys, wait until the lot emptied afterward and head home, partying all the way. What a release.

Chapter 31

Priorities and Commitment

It was past time for me to grow up and face up to my responsibilities in life and quit coasting. I was approaching forty and had learned a lot without really being responsible for much. Mom was in her 80s and weakening, both physically and mentally, and I had a lot of family responsibilities with the properties. I would be getting married. Becky was excelling in her role at the AG's office, which was gratifying, because up until now, despite her Tiffin University courses, her only real experience was with Doc Ross, where she could assist in everything and was an experience in itself. She really blossomed with all the responsibility and would advance rapidly. I was really proud of her but felt it was about time to be proud of, not just satisfied with, myself.

Thus far everything had come easy to me and after some self-examination I realized that in my career I had never rally <u>asked</u> anybody for anything, but rather just <u>offered</u> something, usually something they wanted already. People just tend to tolerate people who don't always <u>want</u> something from them, money and support, for which he would be then indebted to them. In a campaign back then, no one was going to give anything to anyone other than the candidates, especially if he was a challenger for Governor as an Attorney General and the underdog to boot. Should the Execs follow up to collect? I questioned that.

Bill and Tom Brown came from a well-to-do family in Cadiz coal country, and were two undersized tough guys only slightly older than me. One was CEO of Lazarus, the largest department store chain based in Ohio at that time. Two forceful guys, very personable, but every time you encountered them you felt like they wanted something from you. Bill was the youngest Attorney General ever and he <u>did</u> always want something from you, from me my best, which he got every day.

Pat always got me tickets to all the Democrat fundraisers in Columbus and after a few everybody knew who I was and welcomed my handshake, especially Celeste. We would run across each other occasionally on the road and he would always make it a big deal with the intent of course to place doubt in the Execs as to my loyalty. I became friends with John Glenn, then Senator Glenn, the Astronaut, in a strange way. One of the fundraisers had a country theme and John played it up big, not this horse, and came in dressed right off-the-rack bib overalls, a flannel shirt and a straw hat. I was standing next to him at a urinal and as were shaking it off, I casually mentioned to him "Jesus Christ John, you've got to break that shit in!" It must have hit him just right because he broke out in a giggle and actually stumbled away. We were friends. His top aide, a <u>very</u> possessive Dale Butland, also a friend, next in line of course, would later ask me "What did you say to him, he was giggling all night?" I told Dale I told him to make sure he didn't get it caught in his zipper, to which Dale just sighed.

Speaker of the Ohio House Vern Riffe ruled the Democratic Party and was legend even then. He would serve as speaker for twenty years, unheard of before and since. The biggest fundraiser of the year was always his birthday party, to which I wrote my own check. He and Republican Governor Jim Rhodes, who I also knew slightly, would cut up the pie at the end of the year, after the election. Rhodes would be governor for nearly twenty years too and after the upcoming term would retire and Celeste would <u>then</u> become his successor, not this time. Even when he wasn't, Rhodes was always referred to as "The Governor," which always irked Dick. Retrospectively, even if Cheryl had come around, Bill couldn't have won the gubernatorial race, but for me it was a great experience and I was to make the most of it from then on. I was about to bring something of mine, on my own, experience.

As I mentioned before, I had always wanted to learn the investment world and get all my licenses for my own benefit and to not have to rely on someone I didn't know to advise me. There was an insurance company not far from where Pat and I lived, The Clegg Group, that was well respected and hired former athletes. Another friend, Dave Tingley, a former OSU defensive back who worked there and prospered just by targeting former Buckeyes, recommended me. Frank Clegg, the owner, and his sons Cap and Skip, ran the place and we hit it off. My pitch to them was that I was well connected politically, having just come off a gubernatorial campaign. Therefore, all the major law firms and brokerage firms would allow me access once I became proficient, which I fully intended to become, to apprise the respective firms' estate planning attorneys of the best insurance options for their wealthy clients. Back then Phoenix Mutual Insurance Company had the best investment managers in the business and they sponsored Clegg. Years later Phoenix became a stock company, no longer a mutual, and all the tax advantages that came with a mutual status went down the drain but that was then, this was now. Let it grow tax deferred, take it out as a tax free loan, as needed. But the growth had to be realized by the policy holder, not the provider.

Frank talked it over with the boys and they liked it. They had a gift for me. One of his salesmen, Randy Osborne, a former wrestler and a great guy, not yet thirty, knew his products stone cold and all the laws down pat but was totally unconnected. We should team up. Boy was that a Godsend. After a few weeks together while I was still on the AG's ticket and was learning the rudiments of estate planning, we tested the waters with attorney Ed Hertenstein and Stockbroker Randy Rogers, both with huge prominent firms. When educated thoroughly by Randy, they liked it, "good to know." I left them with "Better for your clients to know. What I want to know is it a better option than you are advising now?" Yes or no? We were here to do business. "If no, show us because we are here to help you, and for you to help us. We are just getting started." Then I would just sit there, waiting for a commitment. With a lawyer if you don't get a commitment, you have just wasted your time. Sometimes they were lies but I would always get one.

Randy was always picking up on my clues on how to max out meetings and was always prepared. That was also the way I learned best and truth be told in those days there weren't that many options for life insurance in estate planning. They were good ones, but few. I have no idea now. We made several more such contacts to good reviews and established ourselves. Everybody was pleased and we made some money, fifty-fifty split.

I got all my licenses with good scores with Frank's and Randy Roger's firms' sponsorship. Frank was always, in a good way, pressuring everybody to do more, always more. One time he hired one of those traveling lunatics that mass called, usually at dinnertime, to sell life insurance to "give us another option" and requested "mandatory attendance," at 5:00 PM. Most of us had to hear this so, at the end of day, we struggled in to humor him and get a good laugh.

The guy was a monster, your typical "Art Fern" of Johnny Carson fame who went a quick 0-2 on his first calls. He let his audience pick which numbers to call from the phone book, so he was legit. On the third call he got some lady fixing dinner and she tried every conceivable civil way to get him off the phone, with no luck. Nothing even fazed him. Finally, she said "Oh, alright, my husband is here, I gotta go!" to which he responded "Can I drop by after dinner?" and she again said "My husband is here, I got to go!" and hung up. He took a bow. Yet another Petroff moment. Frank thanked him and bid him adieu. Tingley was crying.

The next morning the guy showed up with a signed contract for a $25,000 whole life policy. Frank was preening again. You couldn't write this shit but I am. All of it's true.

Chapter 32

Inevitability

Mom called one day and asked me to ride with her out to the county garage to get her driver's license renewed, an odd request because she usually just drove herself out to and took the test. I supposed it was just an age thing but I was glad to go. Most of my visits were pass through, so we could make a day of it. As we exited Orchard Park, our little cabal, to South Washington Street to begin our short journey, I sensed adventure afoot. Stop lights and stop signs were invisible to her, not even an option, and direction was on its own. I asked her to pull over before we got to any real traffic and asked if she realized what she had just done, the signs she had missed and she teared up and started to cry. I just held her. How had I missed this? Hell, I hadn't been around.

I drove us home and calmed her down and we talked. I later took her to lunch at T.J. Willies, a nice place owned by a friend of mine that she had never visited and she enjoyed it. I think she had forgotten about that morning, not a good thing, but good for now. I went next door to the Aubrey's, our neighbors since my Dad had built the compound, now both retired. I told them of the problem, which was no surprise. They had been meaning to call me. They shouldn't have had to, I should've known. They came over and we talked and I slipped them her car keys after they agreed to look in on her several times a day until I could hire a daily part-timer to start. She was healthy and mobile and safe. No "homes," only hers.

Back in Columbus I called two girls who had worked for me at my club, both trustworthy and competent. Both had moved on to new employment but the latest thought she had just the girl, her neighbor with two kids in school full time and looking. She was right. After just one week I made the best hire of my life: Linda Schreiner. They got along, no easy feat, and became friends. Mom cleaned every day, not necessarily in sequence, and bathed, and so long as she wasn't alone and ate and had someone there, her wanderlust was dormant. Personally, I couldn't get it out of my mind. Things would only get worse and she was my responsibility. There was nothing I could do to solve her problem then, but later there would be for others, and it would be stolen from me.

Our Columbus crew (not our current soccer team) was a special group, well connected, always up for a good time, always available. John Connor was an attorney with connections in all the right places, especially the Catholic Diocese and the bars, all of them. Whenever he could, he would join me for my early morning workouts at the Y and he would work hard but just wasn't an athlete. Also, no matter how hard he would work in the morning it was no match for how hard he worked in the evening to cancel out the benefits. And he was a spender, a very serious one. When a bunch of us would go to a restaurant only one check would be delivered, always to him. And there would be no argument.

One day the Bishop called him to ask if he would take Bob Cousy over to the Y for a game of racquetball, knowing John played, but not how well. Cousy was in town for some Catholic Event and wanted some exercise. This would be the same Bishop who would soon host the event for Mom that honored her brother and my namesake, previously mentioned. John called me and I filled in having met Cousy before. He was in his sixties and could still play but I was still me. We had a great time and then lunch. He spoke really well of Van.

Another good fit was Dick Schafrath, a friend of Pat's and a former Buckeye and offensive tackle for thirteen seasons with the Browns, a classic. Schaf was a Republican like me, and loved to goad Pat into political discourse, which I knew better than to do. He did a lot of work for the Repubs and ran a canoe livery in the summer in his home town up north, Wooster. He was one of Woody's favorites, Hayes being a staunch Republican supporter. He did a lot for his state senator, Tom Van Meter, of whom I was instinctively suspect. We would all go canoeing at Schaf's often. What a story this was.

Since the involved parties are no longer in place I can tell this story and it's a classic. Schaf's best running buddy was Andy Russell, the Steeler linebacker during their glory years. Cleveland to Pittsburgh was a short jaunt so they would get together often, much to the consternation of Schaf's then wife. On one particular occasion, faced with inclement weather, Russell decided to fly up instead of drive but it cleared up just after Schaf left to pick him up at the airport. Remember, there were few cell phones back then but Russell figured he would see that he had either missed the flight or decided not to come and go back home. No. Schaf figured he had missed the flight and would be on the next one, in two hours. Plus, there was a bar in the airport and it was open. A sign. Inside the bar were two girls. Another. Let's put this together now. A bar, open, two girls alone, Russell in route. Hmmm.

At any rate, Schaf got home about false dawn and his wife was already up and seemed put out. But he covered. He and Russell ran into former teammates downtown and were reminiscing about the old days and time got away from them. Everything was very carefully detailed, down pat. Then he had dropped Russell off at the airport for his return flight and came home.

But after hearing him out, Schaf's wife countered with "Russell called just after you left and had decided since the weather had cleared, he would just drive up as originally planned and meet him at Schaf's home, where he would logically return to when Russell wasn't on his flight. They stayed up and talked until midnight, then Russell drove back." To which Schaf responded "Who are going to believe, me or a liar like Russell?" He had her there.

I would later have the honor of sponsoring Schaf for the NFL Hall of Fame up the road in Canton. He just missed the cut, a travesty. Oh, there would be more of those with the Hall and me. Schaf never knew of my intervention. He missed out because there were "too many Browns already."

Another of note was one of the SWAT cops, Mike Blake, who became a great friend and early morning racquetball opponent. Coming off a shift of midnight to 6:00 AM he would be so wired he would bounce off the walls like the ball and we would have to play three games just to unwind him. He could play but never won and that only frustrated him further, especially because he would blow as many games as I would win. Then the weights. Finally, by 8:00 AM after a shower, he would be housebroken. His partner, Roger Marshall, took everything in stride. Back then they had to pull their guns two or three times a week, a heavy load. I have no idea what the ratio is now.

Becky and I bought a gun from Mike, a .38 revolver five shot the we still have and he took us to the SWAT Range to familiarize Becky with the fine points. She was a fine pupil. We still keep it here today, albeit unloaded because of the grandchildren. My trigger finger is so distended and lumpy that I can't get it through the trigger guard so if we are attacked it's her show. Mike retired at his first opportunity and I haven't seen him since. If anyone deserved a fine retirement, it was Mike, but I could only be hopeful.

That only sets the table for what is to come--defines the parameters. Lots of other people figured in, more bad than good, but I made a point to stay close to the powerful and that started with the Speaker. Also, to stay close to my past.

The last person from my past that I will touch on before focusing on the second half of my life in which he would factor as a true friend, was Charley Wachtelhausen. I first ran across Charley soon after he graduated from Bowling Green and was teaching school at Mohawk High School, a county school, where Jim Getz, the Heidelberg Athletic Director, was principal. Charley was a great guy, funny and up for anything. I forget exactly how we met. He and I were both just around and we connected. He was from Marion, halfway between Tiffin and Columbus, and was a true anomaly. First, he was a good athlete despite his slight frame, and a lady's man, cocky, witty and sarcastic, just fun to be around. He could both take and give shit, which he would have to if he wanted to be part of the group. Pat immediately named him "Beach" for his "swimsuit model build," which stuck. His college girlfriend Carol Mosesohn, a Jewish princess from Syracuse, sarcastic and in for anything, soon joined him in Tiffin and worked in a dentist's office not far from Doc Ross, Becky and Kathie at the time. We all bonded soon and I would later be a stand-by best man in their wedding in Syracuse. The guy showed up.

Before all that, one night Pat, Russ, Larry Watson and I were lounging around in Charley's apartment before going out on the prowl ourselves, and Charley was nervous about something, unusual for him. Apparently a married lady in town, prominent, had taken a shine to him and had asked him over to her house in the country for a dalliance on a night her husband would be "late." Charley was pondering it. Naturally we would be his "counselors" with lines like "You don't have a hair on your ass" and "Never over, never in" until he started to puff up and finally left for the rendezvous, leaving us to sit. But not for long. By the time he turned the first corner we were in Larry's car. He knew the country roads, and we were in cautious pursuit for several reasons. First, we were perverts, but second, the husband was known for rambunctious tendencies and we weren't sure if he could take a joke if he came home early. For some reason, Charley thought pulling into the garage and closing the door would be the canny thing to do. Russ in the back seat, was getting that maniacal grin on his face, there might be some action here. By now it was 9:00 PM.

We drove by, saw Charley going in, and drove to the next farm, parked and ran through a field, corn naturally, coming up on the living room side of the house. Three of us looked through the window, Pat was too short and ran to get a bucket he had seen and she was modeling bathing suits, one after another, come on Charley for Christ's sake, pounce. We were getting bored. It was 10:00 PM. If they did it they would probably go upstairs to the bedroom since he had already parked in the garage and stupid seemed to be the theme of the evening, so we would miss out.

Russ's grin had turned to thoughtful. He had seen a huge rock beside the garage and since Charley drove a Volkswagen there would be room in the garage for us to wrestle the huge rock into the driver's seat of his car. On top of everything else Charley couldn't have been dumb enough to lock his car. He wasn't, but I've gotta say it took all of us for a proper placement of the rock. We then returned to the window. And they were gone, presumably upstairs.

We ran back through the field, sweating and filthy, got in Larry's car and drove back to the farm where we drove in, honked twice and took off back to Charley's. We weren't back in his place five minutes, had gotten beers and were still sweating when he came in panicked with no idea we had ever left.

We all had magazines in front of our faces, Pat's was a *Playboy*, upside down. Our heads were vibrating and we were choking and crying. How many Big Pet moments can you have? Charley never noticed. After about fifteen minutes of Charley's pacing and shaking, Russ dead panned, "How'd it go?" Pat and I ran for the door, Larry, the bathroom. The last words we heard were "you cocksuckers!"

Chapter 33

On My Own

Paul Tipps, the Chairman of the Ohio Democratic Party, was resigning to go into the lobbying business with uber-lobbyist Neal Clark. "Tipps and Clark" would vault to the top of the power chain, with Speaker Vern Riffe and "The Governor" himself and his to-be successor Dick Celeste alongside legislatively. Pat would succeed Paul as party head until they had their next vote. Initially he had everyone's support—in Columbus. Bear in mind I had never asked any of the above for anything.

Everything looked good for me initially. But no one knew Pat better than me. Given full control it would be a tenuous situation at best. In his way he would offend people every day without trying and he wasn't beneath trying. When I mentioned this to him as a friend, he turned on me letting me know I owed him everything, which was not the thing to say to me. I didn't owe anybody anything. He provided an opportunity; I did the job making him look good. We were even. He knew right away that he had said the wrong thing to me but he never took it back. That hung over him as our friendship dwindled. He knew I was right but went out and shot himself in both feet. At the next Democratic Party Caucus, he would be voted out by a wide margin and immediately become toxic. What a loss. He had held the party together for years. Both Paul and Vern had warned me this was coming, to stay away to save my future, for which I was grateful since it meant that they had my back, but where were they for him? A word from either of them would have saved him. It was Pat that severed our relationship, not me. I would always be available for him. We were friends.

Frank Clegg saw the potential my pairing with Randy Osborne offered but wanted me in the office more, on the phone. That was never my style, much later it would be forced to be. You needed to develop relationships which can't be properly done on the phone. Nowadays you can't get anybody on the phone so you are forced to email or text. Of course, nobody "reads" those, only scans them at best so I don't know what the trick is now. Both those methods exceed my skill sets so I just stuck with meetings, scheduled or otherwise, but I never met with anybody without an agenda in mind to benefit both of us. And I never asked anybody for anything, only offered opportunities. That is how I maintained my relationships. Those were the days. Nobody taught me that, it just seemed inherent. You can judge its merits for yourself as we move forward.

Pat and I still hung out and socialized and I prospected as it was to be a big year politically: 1980, with Republican Ronald Reagan running against Democrat incumbent Jimmy Carter. Plus, I needed a vacation. Tom Watters had gotten into real estate back in Pennsylvania, married and moved to Fort Lauderdale and bought some properties to rent. He also bought a plane and flew all over the state in search of more. Smart man. He invited Becky and me down to stay in one of his places any time. I had to finalize my own agenda first, but she was in so it was a tentative yes, I would let him know.

In every election both parties have challenges in districts where their "candidates" can't conceivably overtake the incumbent for a myriad of reasons, ranging from superior qualifications to sparse opposition to gerrymandered districts. In those instances, the respective parties still have to support somebody or nobody of substance will run in the future. With Paul and Pat on the outs for the Dems that problem was compounded. Paul and Vern asked me if I would be interested in providing guidance and direction in certain districts where the candidate had no chance to win, but place and show counted for a lot for the future. I would have their recommendation which would be big. But then I told them about mine and Pat's situation. This had to be made to look like his idea or it would only compound everyone's problem. If it could be done it would solve everybody's. They saw the problem and would get back to me.

I had one more opportunity to scope out before we would leave for Florida. Three guys I didn't know--Phil Craig, David Krakoff and John Bubanich--had broken off from a public relations firm with which I wasn't familiar, but upon inquiry, heard questionable things about. They wanted me to join them in their new political consulting firm, Craig, Krakoff and Bubanich. They felt they were amply connected with the Repubs and wanted me for my connections to the Dems, as an employee. As you have seen, I didn't employ well, but I didn't take on unnecessary debt well either. During our initial meeting several saliant thoughts ran through my mind as to directions I could take them, when Craig mentioned their connection with Gary Jones, the second (by far) most connected liquor attorney in the state, behind Connor. I would let him know when I returned. As you will find out later, trips to Florida didn't always promise a happy return for me, but this one would, for a while. They were surprised and delighted to learn that I was a Repub personally but lived up to my commitments professionally. That concept seemed foreign to them and I took note.

    I checked into the Michigan grapevine regularly to keep up, just as I did at Nemo's. One story jumped out at me. You already have heard of Ken Tureaud, the flamboyant running back/safety/Geography grader. He had spent a season with the Cowboys, then allegedly hit the jackpot by discovering and marketing 3D advertising around the country. I had seen it; it was amazing, and I had his 3D card for a while. Now the story was he was developing Jupiter Island in Florida, which I had heard was the hottest real estate in America and just up the coast from Fort Lauderdale, where I would be heading. I called Watters to arrange things and he was intrigued, too. Hell, we would fly up together and pop in.

    I drove down early so Tom and I could get Becky set up, then I called Ken who was glad to hear from me and told us to come right up. He would be hosting dignitaries if we didn't mind but we would be welcome. I told him we would be flying and he said he would have "Gordon" pick us up at the airport. Just call. Becky wasn't scheduled until the weekend, so the very next day up we went, a half hour flight, and Gordon met us. He was obviously a Tureaud acolyte, with some substance, I would find out, but with an agenda of his own. No toady. He met us in a Mercedes convertible and took us to Ken's home on the Island just across the Intercoastal Waterway. It was an elegant three story with a Banyan tree circling through its core, bottom to top. Naturally, The Man was in a meeting. Gordon gave us a tour—all top of the line. Then Ken came up, looking prosperous, gave us hugs and introduced us to the hierarchy of New Providence Island, Nassau, if you didn't know. Of course, I did, so did Tom. Then off to his flatboat, a floating night club, for a tour of the Island, on the Intercoastal. It had six stanchions, three per side, with huge bottles of champaign overflowing in each, a butler to serve. We were included in the conversation and when asked what I did I said "I run political campaigns." Tom said he was a "smuggler." We got some attention. Ken introduced us, we all chatted, we caught him up on our lives, he said little of his because of his guests and we were given the tour. Very impressive. He never stopped drinking. Back on his dock we returned to the house and minutes later a helicopter landed on his lawn and another executive type got off as Ken greeted him, the Prime Minister, we were told, their boss. They joined Ken and the P.M. on a lower lever and we went with Gordon. As we exited the room, I noticed that Ken pushed a button on a pool table and the table rolled over and a scale model of a huge island development fell into place.

We ate and chatted with Gordon for an hour and my day was made. It seems Gordon was in from Denver to convince Ken to get involved with his company, recently purchased, Trailerboards, which put advertising on the sides of trucks, much like you see on all highways on billboards. The appeal was that all the trucks traveled designated routes, either cross country or city wide, so you could target your message to your specific audience. I started to drool.

The day I left Columbus, Pat had told me that the Repubs had targeted Democrat Senators Church, Bayh, Leahy, McGovern, Culver and McClellan specifically as vulnerable in this fall's election. To pick off several of those would give them control of the Senate, and with a Reagan win against Carter, the whole Congress. Huge stakes.

I envisioned putting giant yard signs (Billboards) on the sides of selected trucks with the targeted senators' messages on them into problem areas. Contrary to what you may think today yard signs still win more elections than any other medium and this would be <u>now</u> and <u>MINE</u>. I asked Gordon what it might cost to do so and he had proposed $100.00 per truck per month for the standard advertiser and imagined the same for the pols. Dirt cheap. Plus, the targeted senators were Dems so the Teamsters shouldn't have a problem and I knew Hoffa, Jr., his father's successor. The catch escaped me: there wasn't one.

Gordon was as excited as I was and we had hoped to catch Ken after his meeting but when it ended all the Nassau crew left on the chopper and Ken disappeared. About a half hour later he came out all slicked up in a suit with a suit bag and bade us adieu with no time to chat. Gordon jumped in as Ken was headed for the airport for a flight to New York, and offered to drive him so they could chat. Not ideal but would have to do. We joined them as we were set to leave too. Ken's last words to his man were "Call New York, tell them to hold the Concord." Wisely, our topic never came up on the way. I gave Gordon my number and asked him to call me before he talked to Ken so as not to misspeak. I had some thinking to do too. Everything had to be in place before I made a move. And it had to be the right one.

It was good that I had a vacation ahead of me because I had a lot to consider with a lot at stake. I have always seen value in things other than what their original intent was for, but to me it was perfect. The average voter back then, not so much now with all the media attention every election gets, didn't even know there was one upcoming until they saw the yard signs pop up everywhere, and they always read them. Putting the same message on a billboard on a truck (all sizes) in motion in targeted areas day after day, first of all is unique, unusual and bold, but saves room for <u>content, no more than five words</u>. It was perfect for the stretch run of a political campaign. Nobody could credibly argue against it.

With that settled, of course I had to see the finished product and Gordon's organization in Denver. Would his people buy in, could they produce? It was all new to Gordon, he had only heard it once from me and would have to sell it to Ken and his partners in Denver. Ideally it would be me doing that but circumstances had dictated otherwise. I knew I could sell it to Ken, face to face. Everything in what little I knew about his career suggested he would see the value immediately. I would have to let that part play out unless called upon.

Finally, should everything fall in place, to whom should I introduce this in Ohio? What I had seen happen around me recently made it obvious, the Speaker. It might save Pat, but then it would be his, and Pat had already stepped into it with me. It would do Paul a world of good, especially in his new lobbying career, but he would likely look upon it as doing me a favor. As you can see, I was trying to rationalize the obvious move to myself. No sir, it would be Vern. But first I had to clear it with Hoffa, Jr. Hence Brennan and Holmes, at Nemo's. Most critically, nobody could present this at the top but me. I would be doing them a favor. Think about it. Look at what just happened to us in 2021.

Becky and I began a wonderful vacation. The last several days had energized me. For the first time I had the plan, not someone else, and the means to fine tune it. I had better access to Hoffa, Jr. than anyone and he had more at stake than anyone, plus we would be using trucks, hence truckers, hence Teamsters. He could be the star. These days away gave me more time to think, calm down and prepare. I only told Becky the rudiments so as to avoid the attendant pressure a vacation didn't need. Then I went for a swim.

One of the releases I deployed on vacations by the ocean that always relaxed me and brought me calm was a residual from my Marine days. Late at night, usually around midnight when the beaches would be clear, I would pick a spot with obvious land marks, strip down, hide my clothes and swim out through the surf for about a mile, then turn and swim back until the surf zone, then just lie back and let it take me home. So relaxing.

It just made everything else so clear, gave me perspective. This would be my path forward if I played my cards right.

We did our normal things, beaching, prowling, dining, seeing friends, running, etc. Becky had become a runner and was taking it seriously but my past was beginning to catch up with me leg-wise. I was near forty, hadn't played basketball in five years, but still played racquetball and lifted. We closed out our vacation by taking the Watters to dinner in Miami Beach. A fine time.

Chapter 34

Friendships

Gordon had gotten the "Go ahead" sign all the way around and the next step was my visit. He was a big Broncos fan and Bill Laskey had finished his career there several years previously. Bill was having problems at home and needed a break, so Gordon told me to bring him along. So, we flew out and spent the weekend, all on Ken's dime. Trailorboards was real and anxious to meet me. They were shocked to see what they potentially had and answered all my questions. I told them my plan. Go to Speaker Riffe, then to the upcoming Convention in New York and the targeted senators' campaign managers. Play our cards. Any overtures before then would only dull our message. Everybody would be doing that. Besides we only needed three months before the public and it would take one week to get the message on the trucks, upon a signed contract. Money would be no problem. They hadn't even thought of the Teamster connection. They promised we would be their sole focus in the interim.

Bill's presence helped and he too was impressed and told me Tureaud stories of his own. "Turtle," as Ken was known at Michigan, had broken the mold and truly was world-renowned. Of course, Bill's nickname was "Worm," hardly more glamorous, and he was only regionally renowned. Mine was "Clevy." I wondered what eventually that would gain me.

Janie Laskey and Caroline O'Donnell were two of my most favorite "friends' wives" of all time, not to slight any of the others. I had been to just about everybody's weddings but both would die tragically, far, far ahead of their times and it really impacted me. Both of the illnesses were usually controllable. I was with Bill later in Valdosta, Georgia when Janie died. Jack Admire, another friend and former Ram and I drove down through a snowstorm from Columbus and Cincinnati respectively at the end and Mack Shilling, up from Texas. Jane had come to Columbus when Logan was born to visit Becky and me. She was special. I hoped she and Bill could work things out and they would, but he wanted to get away and talk, so now we were left to make the best of the weekend in Denver.

Gordon had rented us a convertible for the weekend from the Airport and I had explained to him of my mission so he was cool with it. We thought of heading up to Vail and he called ahead for reservations at a lodge, plus meals. We were set. It was a beautiful day well after the season, an easy ride, with the mountains, the two of us—Bill and me—and a case of Coors. I let him talk and I just listened; we had done this before and it was just what he needed. Halfway up we stopped to rent a couple horses and went riding in the mountains, the Coors spilling all over the place, hoping the horses knew where they were going but Christ we were getting hungry. Bill knew the lodge we would be staying in and its manager, so if he would be working after season we would be set. He was and we were. He fed us samples of buffalo, bear and elk. Lots of Bourbon. Bill and very few others could ever drink with me and he was getting maudlin, missing Janie when we went to bed. Word to the wise here: when someone "needs to talk" let them, don't advise, they need to talk. The next day Bill drove down the mountain straight to the airport. Two missions accomplished.

Upon return, I called Nemo's for Brennan, Number One, and began to ask when I could—and he interjected "it's done." It was fucking done. He told me to come up to Detroit, not Washington, and talk to his aide with the details, deal only with him throughout. Straight from Junior himself. I asked him "what about my pitch?" He said "Fuck your pitch" and hung up. I could see Larry smiling over his Vodka and Soda. I had only sketched it out for him from Florida just before I left for Denver. Relationships. I had never asked anybody for favors, only brought them opportunities. Remember that.

I recounted my research and ultimate strategy to Vern the next week and he was impressed, especially with the Teamster stamp of approval. I went on to say that this all had to come from him, not me, if it was to proceed further. To the National Dems I was nothing, even on his say so. He was the Man, a Tip O'Neill favorite, the Speaker of the BIG House; it had to be his and he had to be fully prepared. I would be his aide. At the Convention in Madison Square Garden in two weeks. I was already planning to go as Pat had asked me as moral support in his bid to salvage his position. Pat was not to be told of the plan.

Vern got the exact summary I prepared for Hoffa, word for word. I could write the shit out of a summary. If both of them READ it, there would be no questions. If there were questions, I would be there to answer them, as Vern's aide. I specifically mentioned the targeted senators. It was my shot. I had drinks with Vern away from the pack to fine tune. He had read it.

At the Convention so had O'Neill and his aides and they presented it to the senators' campaign managers. From the top down it was the way to go. Five of the six took fourteen trucks apiece for three months, September, October and November, of various models and varying targets with varying messages. I gave them Gordon's card. Naturally, he had come to New York to sit in too. The connections were made, soup to nuts. All five senators on board were reelected in November; the sole holdout lost his race.

Of course, Reagan won, soundly defeating Carter, and the Repubs took control so I couldn't gloat but I was secretly glad. I had done my part, got nothing for it other than my commission from Gordon and owed nobody at all. I even had some favors coming but calling them in was not my style. People would know and Vern knew. It made Gordon. Incidentally, because of the Teamster involvement this would be strictly a Dem weapon.

Pat was let go later that year at the Dems' year-end caucus and was bitter at the world. He never knew of Trailorboards, was too distracted, even though we would room together at the Convention. There was nothing I could do for him and I might even have been a negative in some people's eyes for the way I appeared on the scene out of nowhere.

Chapter 35

Back to Reality

The only other thing of consequence I can recall about 1980 was coming home from something in Cincinnati one afternoon and seeing cars parked along the highway on both sides just sitting and apparently excited about something. I was thinking and not paying attention to what was on the radio but impulsively I pushed a button and "The Miracle on Ice" was counting down: The USA was defeating the Russians in Hockey in The Olympics, the biggest upset in Olympic history. As the countdown wound down everybody started honking and you could actually hear the people in the cars cheer. I am a big crier when things hit me just right and I could have floated home.

Craig, Krakoff and Bubanich weren't my type of guys, weaselly like a lot of the guys from P.R. firms they had left, but they needed me, they were two out of three smart, they had offices and were willing to pay. Frank didn't like it but Randy and I were making entrees into places he would never know without me and Randy was the perfect partner. I had more than held up my end. Nobody was aware of what happened in New York except Vern. Pat was the typical Irish Loose Cannon and I tried to be there for him, but he made it hard. Of all the enemies he had made, he had always been his own worst. Now people stayed with him but stayed away from him to do so, if that makes sense. He made it clear he didn't wany any help from me. "What could

I do?" Connor, Cardi and Schaf tried, with no better results, "What did I know?" We all just left him alone for a while. The only person he would talk to was Marlys.

We had put together a pretty good group of carousers over the past year when Pat was off the rag, Becky and me, Conner, Marlys, newbie Danielle Folquet, who would eventually marry New York Mets star Lee Mazilli, a wise cracking foil for Pat, plus Charley and Carole Wachtelhausen, transplanted from Tiffin. I had gone back there several times to facilitate the sale of our properties there with Mom in no condition to maintain them. All but the house were on Washington Street, the main drag, and occupied except for my old Downtown Athletic Club spot, prime but sloping with the town. Our CPA, Dominic Ranieri, went to our church, St. Joseph's, had an office across from it and had done our taxes for years, and he recommended Pat Dell, an attorney around the corner, to list our properties, also a parishioner. Two good Catholics serving a third, what could go wrong? Ultimately nothing did, with those transactions. Stay tuned.

Schaf had worked his ass off for the Republican ticket and State Senator Tom Van Meter advanced to Congress, but heard nothing of his own future. He felt abandoned but never complained. So, I called Woody Hayes, fresh off troubles of his own, having recently been fired. I had met him once before, long ago at an OSU basketball game and had liked him immediately. He was a big, active Republican and Reagan supporter. But I didn't know him and he wouldn't remember me. Anyway, I called him at home, he answered and I explained what was being done to one of his favorite players. He heard me out, had no questions (when I state my case few people do) and said "I'd like to have lunch with you sometime, give me a call." I said "I'm a Michigan Man." He said "I know."

Two weeks later, Dick Schafrath was appointed to Van Meter's vacated state Senate seat, where he would serve several terms before retiring. No way, without Woody's intervention. One of my biggest regrets: I never called. In later years I would get to know Bo Schembechler and I realized Woody was lonesome for people like him. A lot of people in Columbus had abandoned him. Maybe later we would talk. We never did, a big regret.

Then Phil Craig of CKB had a very good idea that got my attention. Truth be told, it was a good thing he did, because these three weren't my type. To put it bluntly, they were connivers. I usually use that term affectionately about my dogs, because dogs are the kings and queens of conniving, with those sad ass looks they give you until you cave to their evermore increasing demands, but not here. I mean it conventionally and negatively. Still.

At that time in Ohio, the Ohio Liquor Control Board regulated all of the licensed beverage (liquor, beer, wine) permit holders in the state, and they abused their power effusively. Years before, the bars had joined forces to create the Ohio Licensed Beverage Association to defend them and represent their rights to the OLCB, a good idea. But over the years, the two entities, OLCB and OLBA, had gotten too close to the point that now it became obvious that the bars were grossly underserved. The top two attorneys defending the permit holders, my friend John

Connor (the vast majority) and CKB's friend Gary Jones (the rest) could attest to this: the OLBA was seriously underserving its members and was ripe for some competition. Phil recommended the formation of "The Ohio Retail Permit Holders Association (ORPHA)." There were over 25,000 permit holders in the state with only a tiny percentage represented.

I was to be membership director; CKB would take care of the representation and conniving. I would bring Conner, they would bring Jones, both of whom would benefit hugely with an expanded client base. The OLCB would be intensely pressured and would be up against me, Connor and Jones but CKB would front me with some media and promotion. I wasn't going to be a pioneer anymore. I had graduated with honors. When I felt the prospected area was properly salted I would venture out to enlist membership of bar owners. That was the deal. I would even write the ads for the respective newspapers. CKB hadn't accounted for any of this but they couldn't deny its propriety. Additionally, I didn't think that any of the CKB trio could convince more than a handful of outstate permit holders that they were the answer and they knew it. I closed it off with "You guys feel free to make all the cold calls you want." Not for the first time nor for the last I had added one sentence too many. Their focus now turned to putting me in my place. Arrogance is a vice I have always allowed myself, regrettably.

On Monday morning all was agreed to and where to start. It was obvious to me; we should get all of Connor's and Jones' existing clients to sign up immediately and work outwards from there on their referrals. We asked them what to charge for membership. They already knew the value from their own experience with John and Gary. The prospective members wouldn't, so we let the first members set the value. Nobody at the table had even thought of that, not even the attorneys. Cost as a factor was eliminated. We came out <u>way</u> ahead.

Next, I wanted Jere on the Board of Directors, which set them back, but Connor agreed. He had been to an Open, became acquainted with Jere, and would be his attorney when and if needed. Jere had branched out from the Golf Courses and had some bars in Tiffin. He was grooming his nephews, who were replicas, to be as savvy as he was. Mary Whalen, his longtime girlfriend, was his perfect match and a friend of mine and Becky's.

All this was new to CKB but the attorneys loved it. The ball was in CKB's court but they were losing control. It made me wonder why they had left their old firm. I honestly think they thought they could control me, that I was just some journeyman jock looking for direction. Now John and Gary were with me.

Of the three, Craig was the point man, Krakoff the prototypical Jew and the brain man and Bubanich the slick empty vessel who hid his value somewhere in his slickness but God, could he come up with some funny lines on occasion. I could have liked all of them if I didn't have to have anything to do with them. Those were the parameters.

Things would have gone better if I had just done everything but I did everything I could, while CKB went around town taking credit for everything I did when I was traveling, which was often, to full houses. We far, far, far exceeded expectations as to membership, but the ads disappeared and I continued on pride alone, taking first year memberships to around one thousand, more than OLBA's multi-year total. CKB contributed nothing and when I was in the office they would leave. They had chosen a board in my absence. Jere was on it as were Dick Allen and Chris Miller, two local campus bar owners that were savvy and, I surmised, appreciative of my efforts. There were four other board members who I knew only slightly from my meetings. Connor and Jones seemed delighted. They weren't on the board.

Come Convention time, CKB came to me for advice on a speaker and I suggested State Senator Dick Schafrath whom I had just nominated for the NFL Hall of Fame in Canton, who obliged. We had a packed house and Schaf was in true form. In less than one year, we had become formally the number one voice for the permit holders of Ohio, a huge success.

The next day Becky and I returned to Florida for a much needed vacation. I had to admit I was proud of myself. I went for one of my swims. The next morning Jere was on the phone. I had been fired by a four to three vote of the board. All I had done fell apart by the next "Convention." Connor would have nothing to do with ORPHA, hence its collapse.

Lesson learned? Hell no, I expected it since my extra sentence.

Once again, to quote Super Chicken "You knew the job was dangerous when you took it, Fred." Onward.

Chapter 36

Recovery

I needed things to lighten up, a little humor in my life and there was always plenty of that plus Becky was my rock and her defense of me over what transpired with CKB was what got me redirected. Sure, I would be justified in whatever action I chose but one day Randy Osborn and I had an appointment with an estate planner at Porter, Wright, Morris and Arthur, directly across from the Capitol. We arrived slightly early, so we lounged in the waiting area which had, for my money, the best view in town. High up, panoramic, you could see the entire downtown.

Now, I mentioned before that Randy was a collegiate wrestler and built like it, even had some budding cauliflower ear, but was the mildest mannered, family oriented, religious friend I ever had. I had told him what happened. He just shook his head. As we stood gazing I noticed some movement across the Capitol, a full block away. Three people had emerged from a building and were obviously sneaking down the street like they had robbed a bank. I had never seen a skulk like this one. It was Craig, Krakoff and Jones, the lawyer. Obviously terrified. I pointed them out to Randy. Then they crossed the street to enter the underground garage beneath the Capitol where we had parked. Randy bumped me and said "Let's go!" I was shocked but Randy was at the front desk asking the receptionist to hold our brief cases, that we would be right back, and headed for the elevator. Being the follower I was, I followed.

Now there were three floors of underground parking under the Capitol but coming in we had parked on the main level where the attorneys parked and as we exited the elevator I saw Gary Jones' car pass by, headed for the exit gate, where he had to pay. We ran in pursuit and he saw us in his rearview mirror. He wouldn't make it. Being a lawyer, he jumped into the entrance lane and up the ramp and out the entrance. They said he was a good attorney. C & K were in the car. I couldn't have asked for a better episode. They knew I would be coming and I had hired a thug. I forget how the meeting went.

That sufficed for me and later Randy and I laughed about it. We eventually did get some business from Porter, Wright. I was satisfied and so was Frank, for now. That would be my main focus for a while.

Charley and Carole got divorced but were still friends and Charley started seeing Marlys. Pat was still waiting for something to come his way. I started my own company "Networth Corporation" to consolidate my licenses and added "Lobbyist" to the list and had a couple of targets in mind, the state pension systems for one. I advised Pat to do the same, which of course eliminated it from his tiny list of options. Connor remained a friend, and an enemy of CKB, which put them out of the liquor business for a while. ORPHA and OLBA would eventually merge and years later Craig would become its director. A survivor. I never saw K and B again. Schaf had settled in as a state senator and Danielle had moved to New York where she would meet Mazilli.

We sold our properties in Tiffin satisfactorily, all but the house, which was a load off and Mom was regressing but under control, thanks to Linda. Time to make some plans for Becky and me. Cuddles had passed and was succeeded by Ebony Snow, "Ebbie" a black and white cocker spaniel who immediately took control. Becky's Mom, Helen, always cared for our dogs when we traveled. We would always miss Cuddie but we would catch up later.

I would do two more campaigns for Vern that he routed to me the next congressional year, as a favor to both of us-- neither candidate with a prayer, but willing to represent the party against strong incumbent Repubs. This is supposed to be humorous and I include them because if you were curious in the first place you would never be able to dig stories like these out on your own. Vern just wanted to put earrings on these pigs but knew I would do my best.

The first was Mike Coffee, a county commissioner from suburban Cleveland. He had "everything" in place: always a bad sign, and just wanted me to "fine tune some strategy; get some perspective" (show me how it's done). I went up to meet with him and his campaign committee, which was essentially his office staff. How more objective could you get? We met outside in his campaign tent in a vacant lot decorated with yard signs with the catchy slogan "He's your cup of Coffee" (and he was the underdog?).

It was an ungodly hot and humid June day and they were waiting outside the tent, a good sign. I got out of my car and Mike, about my size, came to meet me, hand extended, and said,

"You must be good if the Speaker sent you" and shook my hand. He had handed me two coffee beans which instantly clung to my palm, melting, just what I craved after a long drive. I mean, where do you start? My first inclination was to wipe my hand on his shirt but, first inclinations never worked well for me historically. His "staff" all had Coffee buttons on, a bean over the slogan.

Now I sat down and talked to them, asking all the questions. The incumbent was imbedded, had ridden in with Reagan and gotten off to a good start, had all the money he would ever need. Up against this. I liked these people; they knew the odds and were doing their best. Nobody could salvage this. I just tried to make them feel good about themselves and to keep it about Mike, all the positives. Any negatives would only chase people away.

I reported to Vern and he agreed with my judgment but asked me to stick with it for his benefit. Just go along, see it through and also see what I could do for Bob Moon in rural Ohio a wealthy Sydney farmer, a challenge of another kind, again up against a sharp up and coming incumbent Republican. So long as I kept getting paid.

Basically all Bob Moon had done was announce his candidacy and submit to a few interviews in the local (Sydney) paper. Bob Eilert had remarried and moved there where he had purchased a prosperous diner/restaurant/catering business at the town's crossroads called The Spot. His wife Barb was from there and neither of them knew Farmer Moon, not a good sign. I would also find out that Mr. Moon was wealthy for a farmer by yesterday's standards. He was also stubborn, even for a farmer, didn't think he knew everything but damn close and had a married daughter living in Washington, D.C., so he felt he was "connected" at the highest levels. Where was Mike Coffee when I needed him?

On the plus side, he had no staff or strategy, just a connection to "all the farmers in his district," a sprawling mishmash of counties gerrymandered together to reflect demographics to influence elections by the party in power, the Republicans. I had to figure a way to get to scratch so I could start from there. His campaign didn't have any money, he was self-funding as we go. I hoped he meant that because Farmer Bob's hip was about to take a bruising.

I had a wild idea and it would take even wilder ones to make a dent in this campaign, so I put the question to Bob. "Exactly how many of your farmer friends can you count on to come through and pony up and organize events for you in their individual sections of the District?" When it dawned on him who was, I said "Get 'em on the phone, right now." He didn't have their numbers. I almost said "I'd thought you would have had them memorized by now" but choked it back, never too old to learn. I did say: "Bob, do you know that your Congressional District runs though Senator John Glenn's Senatorial District on the east and that he is not up for reelection this year and would willingly support your candidacy to unseat an up and coming Republican incumbent?" Bob hadn't thought of that. I then said "Did you know that I know both John Glenn and his top aide and that Vern Riffe, the Speaker of the Ohio House of Representatives, who sent me to you, also put John Glenn in his Senatorial seat?" More news for Bob.

I then leveled with Old Bob: "Bob, if we don't do two things right now you are going to embarrass yourself. We're going to have to go to Washington and get some funding, you can't self-fund your campaign. No one ever has and won. Then we are going to stop in at Senator John Glenn's office and see if he will attend a fundraiser for you in his District (and yours) this summer."

Bob's response was "We could stay with my daughter in Washington." Oh Jesus. But then he said, "Where I am going to get the money for my campaign in Washington? I don't know anybody in Washington except my daughter." I said, "Bob, we are going to get the money from lobbyists." He huffed, "I don't know any lobbyists." I said "Leave that to me."

The next day I called Vern to see if his staff could find me a list of lobbyists who opposed Bob's opponent's every move congressionally and if he would check with Glenn about a fundraiser. Of course. He liked my strategy. The lobbyists weren't going to give Bob Moon, the farmer, squat but they would allocate thousands to an opponent of a legislator that voted against their interests. Then I began to prepare a pamphlet of Bob's candidacy to show the lobbyists and for the campaign. I excel at that and this would be my best work. Hell, even I would have voted for him.

When I had what I needed I told Bob to set a date, no weekends, and told him not to make any plans with his daughter beyond the overnight. We could use one of their cars. I knew where to go. Bob thought the brochures were "ok" as he coughed up the cost. Glenn was open to the fundraiser. Bob had not called any of the farmers, but would. I made an appointment, tentative, with Glenn's office, to drop by when in town. "Was there anything else they could do?"

We set a date and Vern's staff made the appointments with the lobbyists, guaranteeing their full attention. A dozen the first day, six on the next, a Friday, Cocktail Hour. I requested twenty minute sessions with ten minute intervals for travel between. They at that time were all in a row on K Street, Lobbyist Row, in converted Brownstones, six to eight to a building, all competitively lavishly furnished. I had very carefully prepped Bob that we were here because they are against your opponent, not necessarily for you. Give them the brochure and let them guide the conversation. The brochure contains everything they will want to know about you and they will <u>have</u> to keep it for their files, they have bosses too. Most important, <u>we have to stick to a schedule</u>.

Now what follows is why I am pretty sure that when the time comes I am a bang-zoomer for Heaven. Everything was precisely arranged. We had a 5:00 AM flight out of Columbus to Washington, where Bob's daughter and her husband were supposed to meet us with <u>both</u> cars, one for us to take to our scheduled meetings, the other for them to take our luggage back with them until our arrival that evening. Of course, one car. Daughter had prepared a nice breakfast for us, a "Good Luck" breakfast, to "get us off on the right foot." We got to the house after I had explained en route the dilemma, a longer ride to the point I was no longer assured of "where the fuck I was," hence belabored directions from people who weren't familiar with that area to which I needed to be.

Bob was in a pout. Sissy had made a "special breakfast." We missed the first meeting (my call), we would be late all day otherwise because I "didn't know where I was going" (Give me strength Big Fella). Once parked, it was easy and we picked things up and at meeting number two, order had been restored.

We walked in, introduced ourselves, and sat down. This was where Bob was supposed to offer the brochure, but no, let's chat first, get to know one another, after all, I'm a candidate for Congress. Once again, these guys need our brochure as much as we need their money. They have records, too. Give them the brochure, let them scan it, answer a couple questions of interest to them. I was surprised they didn't ask Bob for ID, but his picture was in the brochure, then wait for them to write the check. They just have to rationalize it. The guy was looking at me as he wrote the check. I think his eyes said "Good Luck." His check was for $5,000. I reinterpreted it to mean "Good Brochure."

At meeting three, actually two, we shook hands and Bob handed off the brochure, then circled behind the lobbyist to look over his shoulder as he scanned it, what's in that thing anyway? The lobbyist looked at me. I just rolled my eyes, and on it went. We made ten of the twelve, missing the first and last, no time for lunch and after missing breakfast, an old farmer was a dangerous animal. But I got us to Sissy's. By God they had better be drinkers. All Bob could talk about was the $40 K he had raised, Vern and I had nothing to do with it. We had a nice dinner and I drank some bourbon and went to bed to let them catch up. I said any breakfasts had to be at 6:00 AM because I intended to at least try and make up the meetings we missed and still make our 4:15 PM flight back to Columbus.

We were set to go by 7:30 AM the next day, almost out the door, when Bob asked Sissy to join him for lunch "some place nice" downtown. He had just finished breakfast. She caught my eye roll and wisely declined, telling us to leave their car at the airport. She recognized the burden and gave me a hug when I thanked them for their hospitality. Her husband was laughing.

For reasons you can only imagine, by now we only made thirteen of our intended eighteen meetings and raised $90 K for the Bob Moon campaign. He was excited; I was both pissed and embarrassed. Had we followed the schedule and heeded my instructions we would have made at least $100K, nothing by today's standards, but enough back then to fully fund an unknown challenger--make them credible. We had stopped at Glenn's office in the Senate, and being Friday, neither he nor Dale were there, but we were given royal treatment and a commitment for the Fundraiser.

That was totally up to Bob to arrange. As I recall, Bob's district constituted about eight rural counties from Sydney, his home base, to New Concord on the east, Glenn's turf. He needed to contact the Democrat Chairman in each to arrange the one big fundraiser with John Glenn's attendance and support for not only Bob but every Democrat candidate for office, but primarily Bob, in the entire district. I gave Bob the names and numbers of each county chairman, step by step instructions and Glenn's "can make" dates. Bear in mind once again: I couldn't do this for him. These chairmen didn't know me from Adam and I wasn't the candidate. The Congressional candidate sets the tone for the District. The chairmen do his bidding, theoretically.

I needed a break and went up to check on the Coffee Campaign, near Cleveland. They were into it. Mike was all over the place, and since it was a suburban district, he had an easier access to his voters. He had an engaging personality. He stuck with the coffee beans. After what I had just been through it was a welcome refuge. I had come unannounced, so they didn't expect me; and the tent was full of volunteers hustling about constructively. It would be this campaign that convinced me of the value of yard signs and grass roots efforts, even now. While Bob had eight large rural counties to canvas, Mike had three suburban counties and was already an office holder in one of them. You couldn't dislike Mike Coffee; it took all I had to tolerate Bob Moon. I couldn't get over the fact that in Bob and Barb Eilert's Diner, The Spot, in downtown Sydney, his home base, nobody knew Bob Moon. Nobody didn't know Mike Coffee. I had been so wrong about his tactics at the outset. They were delighted to see me, Mike especially. What he did wouldn't work ultimately but nothing else would have either. I would get him $5,000 from Vern. What a lesson.

The next week I checked back with Moon. Had he contacted the county chairmen? Not yet, but he would call a couple of his farmers who were "connected" and said "they would take it from here, Bob should leave it up to them." Okay, by now you know me, how would I react to that? Tic, tic, tic! I said, after a pregnant pause, "Bob, if you don't call the county chairmen today the Glenn thing is off." He went into a pout and said after a while, "but I don't know any of them." I was back in control. I then said: "Bob, if you haven't 'gotten to know' all eight county chairman by next Monday, we're done, Vern and I are gone. You and your farmers can take it from here." I reminded him that I was the one who gave him the county chairmen's numbers in the first place and I would be checking. I finished up with: "Bob, you are running for Congress in a sprawling, rural district over eight counties and you don't even know your own county chairman? Hell, from what I can see nobody in your hometown knows you!" And hung up. Fuck Bob. I secretly thought that the main reason he ran for Congress in the first place was to be close to his daughter. Lots of great statesmen started out like that.

I told Vern and he understood and said he would call Bob. He couldn't afford to have no candidate opposing the Republican Incumbent, especially after raising the PAC money. I said Bob would have to call me. Vern said to keep using the Glenn leverage. Vern would also call the county chairmen. About a week later Bob called, said he had complied, the county chairmen were "informed." But were they aboard? I checked. They had heard from Vern, not Bob, and a couple had heard from a constituent representing Bob, something about a fundraiser with John Glenn. I decided to see things through. Bob thought he had won, brought me to my knees, his view of things confirmed, but this was for Vern.

Weeks later on the night of the Glenn Fundraiser, some sixty miles from his home, Bob picked me up in Columbus and we drove to a restaurant/bar in a town I forget, where Bob's

"King of the Farmers" had arranged everything with all the other farmers. I had warned Glenn's people not to expect much but they were aware of the risks and it was close to home. We arrived at 7:30 PM and no one was there but the staff but the place was reserved. Vern wasn't coming, which kind of surprised me. It was to start at 8:00 PM. Just before 8:00 the King called and <u>left a message</u>: he couldn't make it either, something came up. At 8:00 PM in came John and an aide, thankfully not Dale.

We sat and waited. John Glenn, U.S. Senator, world renowned astronaut, in the center of his district, his aide, the Guest of Honor, the to-be next Congressman of the District and me, his campaign manager, the guy to blame for any glitches. Waited until 9:30 PM. NOT A SOUL.

We had a good time. John never mentioned a thing about it, not a word, nor did I. Bob was chattering like a magpie to Glenn as the aide and I rolled eyes. At 9:30 PM I dismissed the staff, gave the bill to Bob to settle up, rental and all, and we parted company. I got paid. Bob was on his own. Other than tense chit chat on the way home, we never spoke again. There was nothing constructive to say. Later, both John and Vern commended me. Moon was overwhelmed in the election.

Coffee lost, but did his best.

Back then, these were unusual but not extreme cases, believe it or not. An incumbent has a three-to-one advantage going in, with a staff in place. Any challenger will just instinctively turn to his supporters who agree with him on principle for assistance and direction. To do the absolute opposite would be smarter, then do the absolute opposite of what they say. Hire a good independent pollster, then hire a professional campaign manager, hire a proven fund raiser and <u>then</u> deploy your supporters, under their supervision. Most importantly work your ass off. Family obligations are no excuse. These days, forget it. Buy a gun and lock up. Lots of ammo.

Chapter 37

On My Own

Those two campaigns were two generations ago, pretechnological. While prehistoric by today's standards, they weren't uncommon then at that level and that level was second only to the presidential. For all the wonders of technology it ultimately eliminates character from the equation by giving cover to the cretins of the world. You seldom hear the word "character" today in conversation, but I still use it and value it. Pretty much everyone I have featured in my tale <u>thus far</u> had character of a sort, even the bad guys, excepting CKB.

As I mentioned at the outset, I am eighty and for 15 years have had a serious neurological disease, Inherent Neuropathy, a <u>progressive, degenerative</u> disease with no cure. I can't really walk but do bounce around the house when alone at home without the cane or walker I require outside, depending upon the weather. I have virtually no balance and am in constant pain in my trunk, legs, hands and feet. The only time I have any comfort is when I am in my recliner in our living room, where I also sleep. I can drive but not to travel. To brush, shower and shave is as long as I can stand if I hustle; imagine me "hustling." The pain centers in the hands when I'm seated which I am now since I'm writing this. When weather permits I've got an electric scooter that I can handle to ride around the nearby elementary school, Greensview, where our son Logan attended, and a big park where I can play with the dogs and converse with their owners when I'm up to it. Becky accompanies me when she can. We miss Digger so much. Whenever they come over, we take Pauly and Tommy with us, so proud. I still wear my MAGA hat and nobody says a thing. My pain averages about an eight on a ten scale. There is no relief.

This section of the book is the busiest, when the opportunities appeared along with the bad guys. You often had to deal with the bad guys to advantage the opportunities, especially in politics. I was never far from politics, particularly in a capital city of a major state.

Either age or my condition has made it more difficult to recall with as much precision the minute details of my active participation in the prime years of my career in Columbus because the rosters continually changed with the elections. As I said, this book relies on recall, not research, and with that in mind, I won't assign names when in doubt, nor will I necessarily impute blame because when you're dealing with legislators you're never <u>really</u> sure who is behind what. Usually, you are though.

Retrospectively though, had I known I would be so afflicted later, I would have scheduled things differently and taken the low hanging fruit moneywise before attacking the accepted norms of the government bureaucracy, which astounded me. My limited experience and the pursuit of my licenses was still fresh and my Economics major at Michigan and time at Dun & Bradstreet prepared me for what I discovered. Ohio government was 100% corrupted financially, due mostly I hoped, to ignorance.

I am not going to go all "blow for blow" on you here but essentially to summarize: The Ohio State University's Foundation was teetering to stay above the $1 M amount and pulled out all the stops to hide it. OSU was, I believe, the largest college in America at the time. Michigan's Foundation was near $20 M and the Ivy's were over $50 M. Why? OSU was openly spending the principal, which was supposed to be the investment base. Think about it. Donors leave their hard earned fortune to the Ole Alma Mater to grow its stature through investments and it's used to pay bills? I knew the two guys in control. One had worked on the Brown Campaign, from the office.

The second even more egregious abuse was what was commonplace in the Public Pension Funds. There were five in all: Public Employees (PERS), State Teachers (STRS), School Employees (SERS), Police & Fire (PFRS) and State Highway Patrol (SHPRS). Collectively, they made up the largest state system in America, each independently and internally managed by senior members and those <u>they</u> hired. Jesus Christ. <u>Plus</u>, each member of each system had 12% of their earnings deducted from each check they received in compensation, usual and natural, to fund the investments made, except that 12% was <u>included</u> in the year end profits/earnings statement. So, if the investments themselves earned 3%, the employees' statement showed 15% (12% + 3% = 15%). Piss poor to the average worker, properly disclosed, which it never was. The Ohio Pensions were essentially doing the same thing the University was. What to do? Collectively, between OSU and the Ohio Public Pensions (OPP), the status of hundreds of millions of dollars of taxpayer money was both being mishandled and misrepresented by those responsible. Essentially you have "money managers" off the street and "in-house" managers at the helm of the largest public pensions accounts in America. Moreover, they were <u>never</u> audited. Who knew what the real figures were? I did some research and came upon <u>The Milliman Report</u>, an annual fiscal review of Public and Private Pension Performance, and found that all five of the state's Public Pensions were in the lowest 5% of the country.

I have a routine here, all prepped, of what I could have done with the material at hand if I was the sort to audition at a comedy club, but I'm too shy and humble, so I did what got me where I was and went to Vern again, fully prepped. I had never seen Vern sigh before. He told me to keep a lid on things while he did some checking around but before I left, I told him of an idea that came to me during my research. Another book I came across listed the nation's top independent money managers and five in Ohio were in the top fifty, really the top twenty-five, three in Cleveland, one each in Dayton and Cincinnati.

He saw where I was going with this. Those five weren't managing any of the Pension Funds and would have killed to do so. I had asked; so had they. The Pensions would stay "in-house," they were doing fine, thank you. In fact, they were hiding. This was way off Vern's beat--the Legislature--but he saw the dilemma. The pensions were failing. Nothing was more important. What didn't really dawn on me until I saw Vern's reaction was the fact that we couldn't let this become public knowledge. My limited research proved accurate upon Vern's staff's scrutiny. What to do? Well, this was state government, first and foremost, so covering it up was the first and foremost priority. The pensions had the jump on this; that had always been their plan. But shit, what about my plan? What would Vern's plan be and would it be inclusive of my interests? Becky was covered by the PERS Plan and it was the biggest offender.

I made sure Vern was aware of my concerns and that I was the guy with the solution; they didn't have to go looking. But first they had to be confronted and agree to change at the risk of exposure. In my mind at least. I wanted to go to the five Ohio based elite money managers I had discovered to judge their interest, but held off without an opportunity to advantage, which was wise because later that week Vern asked me to sit tight while he made some moves. Shortly thereafter the Ohio State Endowment Fund Manager retired. Had a message been sent?

I went on to other things to let things play out, which was against my nature. I should be prepping the Ohio Five and developing a plan. "Look out for myself" is what everybody else did in Columbus politics.

Of the five Ohio Pension Funds, two--Public Employees (PERS) and State Teachers (STRS)--were by far the largest, both at about $50 M. Police & Fire was next followed by the Ohio Highway Patrol and School Employees (SERS). All were foundering. Police & Fire was positively toxic because of its tenure regulations. Cops and firemen could retire after twenty years, the work was hazardous so insurance was through the roof, and it was not uncommon to see forty year old retirees, people in good health, long lives ahead, taking advantage. Shortly I would meet Dewey Stokes, a local cop who had risen to become a multiple term National President of the Fraternal Order of

Police, which didn't help me now, but would've then. We would later become great friends and business partners. Thirty years later as you will see from the attached clip (metro clip), the pensions' problems remain.

I don't know for sure but have to think that one of Vern's staff either let it slip or outright outed me to PERS, because the word got out somehow that I had gone to Vern and exposed their status so now, naturally, everything was my fault. I know it wasn't Vern, because nobody ever told him anything, he just knew it, being Vern and all. Anyway, no more waiting. I informed him of my status and he was as pissed as I was. He had only talked to Governor Celeste. I moved on to other things, let the Pensions sort things out without ever really leaving anything behind. I still officed at Clegg's and Randy was established at several law firms and brokerage houses through my connections. Frank's sons Cap and Skip had taken over and were more than up to it. I missed the occasional side show Frank would host, but I had a lot of buddies there that came out of their shells in his absence. Tingley was still pounding his OSU football beat.

One day at lunch up the street at one of Dick Allen's bars, I ran across Steve Daft, a bar buddy and mortgage broker, who was a great guy himself but a slimeball magnet. This time he had a matched set, Joe Marsalka and Don Cullen. Steve had taken the liberty to anoint me for them. I was the answer to their prayers. Joe was the point man, he put on the show, Don was the money guy, had all the answers and all the "promises" of money. I had just what they lacked, legitimacy.

What they needed was funding for two sports teams they wanted to bring to Columbus, an Arena Football Team and a Columbus franchise for a team in the fledgling American Basketball League. The franchises were already theirs. The new Fairgrounds Arena, just off campus, would be the site. A good idea, if legit. So far I hadn't believed a word they said. I kept thinking about Abbot and Costello. Joe told me he had a meeting with Steve Schott, Cincinnati Reds Owner Marge Schott's son, about funding the next week and wanted me to go with him, so out of courtesy and curiosity I accepted.

Joe picked me up at Clegg's and we drove to Cincinnati. Joe had on a nice sports coat and slacks with a blue sock and a black sock under slick loafers. I wore a suit, black shoes, socks and belt. Joe had a way of rambling as he spoke, like every word he said was gospel and accepted as such, kind of off-hand, like there could be no doubt of his veracity. He was a born liar.

Steve Schott, and this just came back to me as I was writing it down, was the biggest BAH I have ever encountered or ever will. Even his Mom avoided him. We met at the Reds' offices in the stadium. From the outset he interjected his views into everything Joe said, not even pretending to listen. Joe never missed a beat throughout even though Steve denigrated him at every turn. When Joe finished his presentation, totally unaffected by Steve's rudeness, he asked "So, what do you think, Steve?"

Schott said "I'll give you what you want if you do it here." To which Joe responded "Oh no Steve, this is a Columbus Franchise, we have signed a lease with the Fairgrounds. Weren't you listening?" As we left, Marge was storming down the hall. Oddly enough, on the way back I did have an idea for a funding source but not until I became convinced of their legitimacy, a ways off.

Several weeks later we met at the Fairgrounds. Their updated arena would be available on schedule next summer. They seemed anxious about Joe's tenacity, was there any word on an investor? Don said they were in talks with several. On the way out I mentioned Jerry Greer. Jerry was a major mobile home dealer and sports-nut known to be a shrewd businessman. I knew Jerry only slightly and he was the one I thought of on our trip to Cincy. They both knew of Jerry and made an appointment and I attended. Jerry asked a lot of tough questions, appeared to be satisfied and wanted to run it by some others too. Several weeks later a partnership was in play and initial funding was secured. I would get a cut of the profits, should any occur. I would need a contract. I didn't know who the investors were. I wasn't involved in those meetings.

Chapter 38

Our Wedding

I had occasion several years past to be in Phoenix on business and visit old friends who had moved there, principally Van, who would join Dick with the Suns for a last hurrah, hopefully a winning season. He had gotten remarried to Kathy, a far better fit, and after taking care of business I stayed with them for a few days in their Scottsdale home.

Petroff and Kroll had both moved there and remarried and Dick Kuhn an old friend from Tiffin and high school classmate Bob Altwies, our high school's "blind quarterback" (who was actually very good) and his wife Mercedes, a class younger from Calvert, were my targets. I really missed Big Pet who was now known as "VERY Big Pet" and "Seeds," Bob's wife. Kroll was now a bookie; Kuhny, a prosperous landlord after devising a method of trash collection for the city's schools, had married Barb, his perfect mate. Dick and Bob and I ran around together in high school; Kuhny played at Columbian. Kroll, of course, stood out.

He had always been a lifter but now, being a bookie, he took it to the max, looking EXACTLY like "Mr. Clean." He had also affected a shifty, thuglike look and smoked cigars. When Big Dave assumed one of his roles he took it to the extreme, was all in. In a class by himself, with a few others. If you haven't noticed yet I attract characters.

It was August and Tom and Dick were getting ready for the season and a bunch of pros got together in a downtown Phoenix gym most days to scrimmage. I would go down with Tom to shoot and fill in, as needed. It would be come and go for hours, with the pros in various degrees of readiness. One afternoon all of a sudden all activity came to a halt. There stood Connie Hawkins, Legend personified. For you youngsters (Pauly and Tommy), he <u>might</u> have been the greatest basketball player of all time. "Might" because he was deprived of that opportunity until the tail end of his career by "holier than God administrators" in the NCAA and then the NBA, that declared him to have had a role in a point shaving scandal when he was a freshman at Iowa. Just like with Tom, Dick and me and most others on the floor, freshmen couldn't <u>play</u> as freshmen. How in the hell could they shave points? There was the crime.

He joined in and so did I as things were winding down. I was on the court "competing" with Connie Hawkins when Bob Altwies walked in. He had told me that morning that he might stop by the gym since he knew where it was and we hadn't connected yet. Now, back at our Calvert Class Reunions I would be a legend, too. Connie's lore began on the playgrounds of New York and the famous Ruckers Court, where he, Wilt and countless others made this sport the one by which all other athletes in the world are measured.

The next day, my last in Phoenix in the 100 degree heat, we went up in the mountains, Tom, Dick and I, for the final day of the Dick Van Arsdale Basketball Camp. They taught the kids, schmoozed the parents, thanked all involved and closed it out with each of them, coming from opposite angles to the hoop simultaneously slamming down two vicious dunks in the same basket. Quite a show. Nothing but class. When we got in the car to come back it was 60 degrees.

It was the right time for Becky and me to tie the knot and make things official. I knew that because it just seemed so right, like it was meant to be. It was so good to see Becky fulfilling her potential and developing the confidence in herself that all people need to succeed, something I doubt she would have developed in Tiffin, although she had started out very successfully with administrative duties in the Ohio Attorney General's Office. Lots of politics there, office politics, the worst kind. Also, neither one of us took any shit. A German female and an Irish male, teamed up and in sync, are a great debate team.

I brought it up and she said "sure" and smiled. Cary Grant and Grace Kelly in real life. Cuddie woke up from a snooze and we gave her a celebratory "half a b" (half a biscuit). Really it was a tender, special moment and we went out to dinner to celebrate, laughing and kidding and planning, just like it's supposed to be. We wanted it to be special event, in Tiffin for the ceremony and reception and to Rome for the honeymoon.

After the Brown campaign I had maintained my Youngstown contacts, primarily Eddie Flask and Carmen Policy and upon hearing about our wedding from Bill Brown they called to congratulate me. These were connected guys, all around not just politically, if you get my drift, and close to the DeBartolos as well. They had a friend, Father Marocal, who had risen to the top in the Vatican and could arrange things for us there. I thanked them and said that would be great. I would let them know. WOW!

I was really happy. I had finally done the right thing at the right time for the right reason. Our Moms were happy, mine relatively, since she hadn't handpicked Becky and wouldn't remember if she had, and we had some planning to do.

For me, who to be in the wedding? I wasn't twenty-two, thirty, thirty-five or forty. There would have been a roster of candidates in those years, all of whom I would be proud to have now, but I would be forty-two at the time of my wedding. I wouldn't even invite most of those people now. It would be an imposition. Also, I had been in a lot of weddings in the interim and hadn't kept regular tabs on most of them either. Best man was easy: Jere Carrick and I connected and both of us were loyal to our friends and careful of our enemies, either keep them close or avoid them totally. We both had them and always would. Pat had scratched himself by his actions. Mills was always in for anything and he was an usher along with Jack Wickert, the most confident man I ever knew and probably as good a clutch shooter as I had ever played with, filled it out. Becky's maid of honor was Marlys Brown.

We got married on August 27, 1983 in St. Joseph Catholic Church in Tiffin at high noon, with a reception at John Egbert's Riverview Inn, the old home base for the New Riegel Open, that lasted from right after the ceremony until beyond midnight. My old classmate from Calvert, Father Dan Ring, was the officiant. My sister Shirley and her husband Joe kept Mom under control-

-my sole concern; they got her a little looped and took her home by 3:00 PM. I wouldn't see her until we got back from Rome.

It was really a gigantic open house for all our friends who wished to party. I had called a few of my Michigan and Detroit friends and left word at Nemo's. All of our friends who required invitations got them. Our Columbus friends were all there, even Pat. Connor, Charley and Cardi, of course: a couple hundred attendees in all.

Being Membership Director of ORPHA and politically connected, plus being tight with Connor and Cardi, got us most of the booze dirt cheap and John Egbert cut us a big break as we had filled his motel once again. We packed the pool and Jere had a beer truck with taps on its sides next to the diving board and catered all the food (including a pig roast); his nephews Tony and Tim Paradiso were the DJs. We lacked for nothing. Ann Arbor, Detroit and Nemo's were well represented as was, of course, Columbus. Lowell Kiefer, the deputy sheriff, was a guest, an old friend. Anything went and did.

Friday night there was a Bachelor Party at Jere's bar The Hardware Inn Saloon with open invitations extended to all.

Becky and I retired to our room at midnight at Riverview with the reception peeking out. We got up at 3:00 AM to head back to our apartment in Columbus to change and pick up our bags for our trip to Rome. Cardi took us to the airport for our 8:00 AM flight first to New York, then to Rome with a stop in London, where we viewed landmarks from the air. No sign of James Bond; he would be undercover.

When we landed in Rome, there were Carabinieri all around, the Italian police. It was a sobering moment as we realized this was no longer America (maybe shortly but not then), but the birthplace of Christianity, always under siege in some manner or other. You could wear sandals on airplanes back then and we were glad we had because the long flight, plus all the booze, had ballooned my ankles to where shoes (loafers) would have been impossible. We found our bus, as per Father Marocal's instructions, to take us to his choice for a hotel, The Forum. The drive in took us directly into Rome's heart and within awestruck minutes Becky, on my nudges, looked out the front window past the driver to see, 100 yards away and closing fast, the Coliseum. The driver stopped just in front, turned the corner and there was the Forum Hotel, an old style Roman relic, well preserved. We were the only ones debarking. As we did the driver smiled and said "Viva Father Marocal." As we entered, the Concierge greeted us and took us to registration. Our room was on the sixth floor of the nine-story hotel with a patio restaurant/bar on the roof. The Concierge took our bags, escorted us up and I told him I'd get him after I exchanged my currency at the desk. He smiled and waved me off, citing Father Marocal. We dumped our bags, used the restroom--bidet and all--and went to the rooftop bar. What the hell, it's our honeymoon, maybe <u>one</u> drink.

As we got off the elevator, to our immediate left was the Coliseum and we were high enough to see inside. It was literally just across the street. But then to our right, almost next to us, was the Forum, where Roman law was made under the Caesars, in ruins, but preserved for centuries. Motherfucker. We hadn't even noticed the bar which was of course perfect for its surroundings. We just sat there and sipped our drinks, awestruck.

Becky and me in Rome on our honeymoon, here at The Forum, just getting started. Access to the Vatican, a car in the underground garage and me, a Rome veteran, at the helm. It could only be perfect. And it was.

Father Maracol was back in the states on furlough, but had told me not to miss visiting Tiburzio on the Via dei Condotti, the Avenue of Fashion, and ask for Tito if I wanted to buy my bride a wedding gift from Rome, which of course I did.

But first I had to convert traveler's checks to lira, check out our wheels in the underground and tip the Concierge. The key was to keep them on your side but he declined, citing guess who. I told him I would get him when we left and he agreed to that. The car was a Fiat convertible. I started it up, let her breathe, turned it off and went for a walk, clear to the corner in front of the Coliseum where we grabbed a table at an outdoor Trattoria and for the first time realized how tired and hungry we were. We hadn't eaten since the reception except for some snacks on the plane. We had nine days in front of us. We had a Roman pizza and some Dutch beer and just sat there for hours, watching the natives ignore their surroundings and the visitors, like us, aghast. Hang on! Now this was thirty-seven years ago and I am eighty and have a Neurological disease, albeit one that does not usually attack one's memory, but to recall with precision and then amply describe the time we had is far beyond my capacity. Suffice it to say we didn't miss anything that could have topped what we saw and it was the time of our lives. The Vatican was supernatural. Everywhere you looked you had to look away, overcome by the splendor. Our audience with Pope John, II and his blessing to our small group, each personally, was almost overwhelming. His audience to the masses every Sunday to hundreds of thousands of pilgrims was humbling as they dropped to their knees screaming "Ile Papa," pleading for his grace, then cheering afterwards as he waved.

Of course, we hit Harry's Bar, off the Via Veneto. For those unfamiliar, there is a Harry's Bar (or was?) in every major tourist city in Europe and North Africa, where "Casablanca" was set, modeled after "Rick's Place" with Bogart and his crew. It was a must for me back then, but Louis Armstrong had died just before my first trip and you had to daydream again a little now.

All the churches, the catacombs, the monuments, the basilicas were thoroughly toured. The first thing our driver did out of the chute was get lost but since he was me all we did is laugh. We eventually got everywhere, then just drove around until we got back.

Mostly we walked everywhere at a casual pace. We went to the Spanish Steps with the huge Hassler Hotel looming above and the Via Condotti, the Avenue of Fashion, easily topping Detroit's, streaming below. Every fashion designer of world repute competed for the flashiest displays. Bring your allowance. We window shopped until Becky found something she would actually wear but mostly we sought out Tiburzio for her wedding gift. We made several passes, looking ahead at all the signs all flashing spasmodically when, on a pause, I looked straight at a plaque on a marble wall of a building next to me that spelled out "TIBVRZIO," nothing else, in the exact middle of "The Avenue of Fashion." Above a step up to my left was a door with the same message. The sleuth in me said "This must be it," so I opened it.

There was a small display on a glass table and a lady came out. I said "We're the Clevengers from Ohio," when she interjected, "Ah yes, Father Marocal" and turned away. In a couple seconds out came a little superbly tailored Italian with a big smile and hand extended to Becky first and then to me in congratulations. Tito Tiburzio, jeweler. He invited us in his elegant office. The lady brought champagne and we drank and talked for about fifteen minutes, him giving us tips on where to go for anything we sought. Then she brought out a tray of elegant bracelets. Tito asked Becky if there was one in particular she liked. After her assessment she chose one, a twenty-four-carat gold beauty. I took out my lira and asked the price. Both of us knew this was my gift to her but let's just say it was a bargain. It became one of her all-time favorites--until she lost it.

I'll skip ahead now to the adventurous part of our trip: driving down through the mountains of Italy to the boot then up to the Italian Riviera to the Isle of Capri and Pompei. While the old saying "All roads lead to Rome" might be true I can attest that it's also true that NO roads lead out of it. For all our driving from site to site on spec we never saw any "outskirts," so I just hired a cab to lead us out towards our destination and off we went, I would take it from here. As we headed south it got darker and darker as the Apennines enclosed us then at Naples we were back on the coast and sun again. At Salerno we hopped on the coastal "Highway" for the ride of our lives and headed back north, Amalfi, Sorrento, The Isle of Capri: the most beautiful places on earth. We made the stops, took our time and enjoyed, especially after we stopped at an overhanging bar on the coast to get Becky looped. You see, the "Highway" was high alright, right on top of the mountain range that led up the coast, a half mile above the water, the Mediterranean Sea. It is a two-lane (generously), that wound around every curve with a large mirror hanging down so you see the oncoming traffic. No guardrails at all and no curbs on the sea side a half a mile below opposite us. We passed several cars caught in trees below that hadn't made it, just like Laskey and I had experienced in Vail. My bride needed some martinis to settle her down. The place that first appeared was actually hanging over the water with a thatch roof that slid serving trays under the straw roof when it rained, which it didn't. The only two patrons were obviously spies, carving up the world: dirty white suits, straw hats, needing shaves. The bartender left them alone and I bought Becky a martini and me a beer, then Becky another martini. Soon we were back on the road. Bec leaning back, chattering like a magpie.

You had to take a cut-off down to get to the coastal sights and we did that, but for a change of pace, I took a dirt road up, just to see what was above. Less than a hundred yards up we found a small settlement from a hundred years ago at least, almost primitive, no wires of any kind, no cars--just carts and at least one mule. I called out to a kid but he just went inside so we left. A hundred yards down, back to paradise. We stayed in Amalfi, toured, ate a great meal, drank and slept soundly. The next day would bring Pompei and Mt. Vesuvius.

There is no Pompei on the maps because it's gone, beneath Mt. Vesuvius lava centuries before. But it had been excavated and left in its last state, total ruination. Miles away Vesuvius looms and still smokes. Absolutely chilling. The cobblestone streets restored, in each home you can enter and determine what each family's last act was. Not much to say after that, but to visit Pompei after what we had just seen in nature's splendor on the coast left an impression. Amidst all that beauty, the beast still puffed, waiting. Big Fella.

We got back to Rome in time for dinner, no problem. Bang, zoom right to The Forum and then some exploring, to Old Rome. See where the natives went. It was packed, mostly with young people on the chase. Hardly any tourists. Lots of artists. We bought a painting of the Spanish Steps and its surroundings, which still hangs now, had another great meal and retired to the roof of The Forum for a night cap and some reflection. Not a bad week: two days to go. Actually, it was the time of our lives. With nothing more on our agenda, I turned in the car and we just walked, window shopped and watched new arrivals scurry about. Then a papal blessing, Mass, and back home, exhausted.

We drove to Tiffin, picked up Cuddie at Helen's and gave our Moms their gifts we had bought on the Via Condotti--easily the most conservative tops obtainable--and recounted our tale (different version).

One of the kindest acts I have ever witnessed took place at about this time and it overwhelms me now at the joy it brought my Mom at just about the last time she would be able to appreciate the event. John Connor made it happen: shortly after our wedding, our Bishop and the Baltimore Bishop came to Columbus to present my mother, Mabel Clevenger, with a plaque recognizing her brother and my namesake, Dan Costello, as Mt. Saint Mary's Greatest Athlete.

Conner did it as he did everything, completely over the top, commandeering the bottom floor of one of Columbus's finest restaurants and Mom was just beaming, press coverage and all. To me, she looked as regal as any queen.

Chapter 39

Back in the Flow

I had a lot of balls in the air with a lot of people of questionable character. I didn't have any of my money at stake, only what would be due me if things panned out. That's the cost of doing business in a political environment, especially the Capital City of a major state. Contracts would be nice and I would have them when dealing with proven entities, but the speculative stuff had to progress beyond where it was to be structured appropriately, essential when dealing with the characters I had attracted. The best ideas in the world are valueless if the wrong people control them. Stay away. Over time I would realize that another option was to take control myself, to make any conniver the connivee. Much later I would deploy that strategy to launch a major company of my own with old friends, people I knew I could trust, but not without the assistance of some new friends, yet to be tested. Right now, I had to make sure whatever steps I took would be consistent with Vern's view of the Pension Fund problem where hundreds of millions of dollars were being mismanaged and apparently nothing would change. OSU took steps in the right direction but the pensions apparently thought they had dodged the bullet.

I met with Vern with a plan, as always. I had always tried to point out how my ideas would benefit him too. I had always liked the idea of an "Ohio Super Fund," which I had floated before, as you'll recall. I couldn't get it out of my mind but I didn't know where it was in his. I didn't figure Vern for aspirations beyond Speaker of the Ohio House of Representatives, to which he had risen when I came here and would remain for twenty years. He was a kingmaker in Ohio and failing pensions on his watch would not bode well. He heard me out, had no questions and said "Dan, go onto other things." One thing off the old agenda. Our relationship had ended, our friendship, no.

The reason I bring this up again now is because if I have a good idea I don't give up on it. My longtime friends know that, don't you? Ever. And this was one of my best. Our Public Pensions, now in the billions, have used Fund Accounting since before I was here, still do and probably will until they implode. They just keep extending qualifications and reducing benefits. So long as Becky's unaffected, I relent, and that is a qualification.

I'm going to change things up on her because for the next twenty years government and politics would play a huge role in my life and Becky's, who has served nine Attorneys General in her thirty-one year tenure. What I have already provided for you are the parameters of what one who makes such a choice has to function within, i.e., absolute ignorance to unbridled corruption. Look around and you know my point is made. Ask Dave Bing. I am not going to burden you with example after example when the current Administration is doing that for me and I would lose my audience if I tried.

I'm sure that the Founding Fathers set out to do what was <u>right</u> for the country and I am just as sure they soon settled for what was <u>best</u> for the country, as politics evolved. Ever since then the definition and interpretation of <u>best</u> for the country changes as <u>politics</u> evolves. The definition and interpretation of the <u>best</u> has devolved to what we have now, pre-revolution. <u>Best</u> for whom? The Deep State, whose plan for us is enslavement. Tune the fuck in. On our watch. It's up to the good old boys to step up when they go for our guns. Follow their lead. Enough of that, we're living the nightmare.

    Becky and I began looking for a home of our own. We preferred Upper Arlington, a close, affluent suburb landlocked by others, with the best school district in the state, as we planned a small family. The first place we saw was perfect, a three bedroom ground level condominium in a gated community with a great pool and party house combination with guest quarters. We paid cash: lots of uncertainties in the career I had chosen. It's worth four times the price now and with the death of our final dog, Digger, we are redecorating. We had no idea we would be here this long but my disease and setbacks reduced our options to where this is it for me at least.

    On June 4, 1986 our son Logan, which means Wolverine in Indian, was born, and life changed forever. We were different people forever. Most of you know the feeling. He had dislocatable hips and a torticollis which is a neck issue. The doctor assured us both were correctable. It was a cesarean birth and I held Becky's hand at the extraction. Thank you Lord. Now, at thirty-five, he's a six foot, 205 lb. stud CrossFit trainer with lots of work ahead and pleasure for us, as grandparents.

    My "changed forever" life apparently didn't kick in for twenty-four hours though because that afternoon with Becky and Log safely ensconced in the hospital with Helen, I bought a box of cigars, called Miller in Bucyrus on the way and went to Shorty's retirement party in Detroit. It was a city-wide event originating at Nemo's. Of course, Mills was in, so we celebrated on the way up. As we entered Nemo's the first person I saw was Shorty, with Norm, Dave and Dooling then everybody else. I had called ahead so everybody knew about Logan. I got rid of the cigars within five minutes, the first to Nemo, then Shorty. Then party. Everyone was there, packed in. Sam was with Phil, who actually smiled. All the Good Sports. Hang on.

As rush hour receded we headed out to the party site, a huge church hall venue where the Bishop presided alongside Mayor Cavanaugh and a bulging crowd with a long table for irreverent speakers. DeBusschere was the first introduced by the mayor and he set a high bar for those that followed. Sweet Lips was in the crowd, blending in. Later in the evening I saw a table full of the Old People from the union wars, drunk and recounting old tales. They recounted my "interlude" with Phil at Nemo's with Buttons, and what preceded it years before. It was a planned hit on Phil at Nemo's in a delayed revenge plot for Phil's mauling of the Longshoremen's strong man during the wars. Phil apparently saw him coming in out of the sun with a crew on a Teamster election day to start a brawl with the place packed and, with a running start, smashed him across the face with a champagne bottle, knocked him through both heavy doors, dragged him across 8th Avenue and bounced his head off the fire hydrant, which became famous--a landmark. I just stood and listened; they never noticed me. After all these years, I knew. Mills and I left at 11:00 PM and drove home. I went right to the hospital and told Becky everybody had sent their best. Another Wolverine was in the world, doing fine, thank you.

The next day we brought Logan home. Helen stayed to help. Of course, I began the neck exercises for the torticollis right off and determined that the pool would be required to get the hips strong, that afternoon. Me, jump the gun? I finally held off until Helen went home but I had heard at least five hundred "Bless his little hearts" in the interim. When we took him to my Mom's she just held him and cried, fading fast. I was grateful she had that time.

Becky could take all the time off she needed and I worked from home when I could. We had the neck and hips corrected by the next summer's end. First, a cast, then triple diaper, then double diaper, finally single, with pool time every day; tilt, twist, tilt, twist on the neck during his waking hours. Develop those habits early. He was in mint condition for his first football season. We would meet Admire at Helen's in Tiffin, drop Log and Cuddie off and head to Laskey's in Milan to take his motor home and guests (always Joe), to Ann Arbor and the game. In place by 10:00 AM. Games started at 1:00 PM then. We would head back to Columbus from Tiffin on Sunday. So, I remained connected to my true roots, Michigan.

My lobbyist arm of Net Worth Corporation focused on trying to place Ohio companies from outside of the capital with state agencies to do business, usually with time and money savings technology they had developed, saving the state millions of dollars. I would charge them $1,000 a month retainer plus 5% of what they would earn should things work out, for as long as they did. If I devoted twenty hours a month to each client that would be $50.00/hour. Neither side could complain.

I am not going to begin another saga but just give an example, summarized, so you will know that incredible corruption existed in the state agencies as well as the State Pensions and how blatant it was. This state agency collected taxes--you figure out which one--and was run by minorities who did business only with that minority whenever possible. My client's technology did automatically what the current (minority) collection management contractor did manually. Automatically versus manually. Hmmm, now there's a dilemma. Either pay a staff of hundreds to do daily collection attempts or pay one Ohio company to do so automatically with their technology, each month, no people involved on either end. <u>All</u> the Ohio taxes.

I knew the primary minority conniver in Columbus was a local attorney who had stocked this particular agency with their minority executives. He was also the national attorney for a major law enforcement agency and he had gotten that appointment through the efforts of its national president, a non-minority and my friend.

My client was a family business from southeastern Ohio. The mother was a nice lady, the face of the company, and a shrewd business woman. Her sons were the technocrats and classy young gentlemen. What a package. The father was uninvolved, but a professional himself. The sons made the presentation and it blew everybody away. To this day I have never heard a better one. The executives didn't know what to do. They hadn't understood the presentation but they knew an entire division of their agency was in peril; they had to get to the conniver. Prevent this at all costs.

So did we. My friend and I effusively congratulated the presenters and saw them off. They were very impressed with his status nationally. We then drove down the street to their conniver's office on the top floor of an office building in German Village. Because of my friend's status we got right to the conniver. My friend described what he had seen and did a great job, even wondering if there would be a fit for the technology in their National Agency. I hadn't said much, no need to at this point. Now the conniver thought he knew me, we had met, but he didn't know the real me because he asked me to step outside with him for a minute. My friend went with us but had to use the facilities, so the conniver suggested we go up to the roof, it being a nice day and all. Odd, but fine with me.

As I recall, the roof was one story up with a tile border about a yard high surrounding us in thirty yard squares. We had walked up and I walked to the edge overlooking where we had parked. Always take the initiative to gain an advantage. To hand it to the conniver, he followed me along. I just waited; it was his play. To his credit again, he asked what my cut would be. I told him that was to be determined. He said he could make it happen for half. I told him I would run that by my friend, his benefactor, who at that moment appeared at the roof door. Knowing me, under the guise of wanting to see the view (it had been his beat for years). In the car my friend asked what had transpired and I told him. He was aghast. The conniver had been as well.

I did nothing and heard nothing for three weeks, tough for me. Patience has never been even a semi-virtue of mine; lack thereof, has been a major weakness, and costly. But this time it paid off. The agency was exposed. The executives running it were fired and criminally charged, as would soon be the officeholder. After my report, my client called to fire me, not because she suspected me of wrongdoing, but because if this was an example of how the state did business, she wanted no part of it. Country living can make a person naïve. The conniver came out unscathed and prospered through the years to where now he is probably the real mayor behind the feckless figurehead in place now. Some of you would get to know my friend in our later venue. I had nothing to do with what happened above.

These examples I have cited weren't rare, they are only representative of what I encountered personally, back then. Representative, not rare, nowhere near all. Everybody has a book out about political corruption, all more credible to the general public than I am. But I am more credible to my audience so take the following from me and I will move on. There are no "good" laws. They all hurt us more than help us. We have just witnessed a Covid 19 Bill granting Two <u>Trillion</u> Dollars we had to print, of which 95% of goes to liberal causes other than Covid, a sham in itself. The real disease was our government, now apparently secure for years, on our backs and those of our children and theirs. Get you some guns, lock in. There will be many more of these to come unless it's stopped <u>this year</u>.

Chapter 40

More Skullduggery

I had maintained my Youngstown connections socially throughout the years and occasionally would run things down for them or test waters, solely on a friendship basis. Coincidentally, Carmen Policy and Eddie Debartolo were looking to purchase the San Francisco 49ers of the NFL so that gave me an out. Eddie Flask would hold down the fort.

Soon after, I got a call from a Youngstown Insurance Executive who had heard of me and inquired of my services in his behalf. He invited me up for a tour and an overnight visit to discuss potential endeavors. So I went. I am not going to go in to great detail about what he offered or about his overall legitimacy as his is still an open case with a lot of agencies and I know of nothing to help them, nor do I wish to be called on. But I will recount our relationship, such as it was.

"John" was a big man: my height, about 260, with a totally bald head--rare back then—and he lived in a mansion with all the trimmings. He looked precisely like a younger Sydney Greenstreet for my older audience. The only thing missing was Peter Lorre. In his place was Mike, his son-in-law, and Rod, his technocrat, an insurance expert by any measure. What they offered was cutting edge and totally legal but unheard of at that point. It was something I <u>had</u> to run past Randy.

John provided an extended catered evening with fine cocktails before, during and afterward on into the evening, then downstairs to his sauna to flush out. We all got along and the focus was on me. I was being tested. I always passed these tests by telling the truth. I had all my licenses but was no expert. I relied on the contacts I made with people I trusted that were. With me, as you have learned, it was all about relationships. That way I am off hooks and we share the spoils; they will know more prospective candidates then I will, so we all benefit if it passes the tests. I passed mine and we had a tentative deal. A night well spent.

Upon my return I ran it past Randy and he saw no flaws and was excited about the concept so I sent John a contract after I had talked to Eddie Flask, who knew of John but not professionally. He hadn't referred me and doubted Carmen had. Then they came down to Cleggs to share their concept with Randy and several other agents, who were intimidated by John's presence. We were in business.

On the day of their visit the Thunderbolts, Columbus' first of two Arena Football League teams, were holding open tryouts at the Fairgrounds, so after lunch I took John, Mike and Rod out to watch, something new to all of us. Their coach, whose name I forget, already had his basic roster intact but a local or two wouldn't hurt. But close to fifty came. The best way to describe it is to compare it to a state fair, so the site was appropriate. Creatures galore, from cave dwellers to rock stars. If Joe Marsalka had known, he would have charged admission, but he became more intrigued by John than the candidates. I had warned John about my evaluation of Joe and Don Cullen so I introduced them at a break. It wouldn't be John's first rodeo. He would be on his own.

Things progressed, overtures were made and the products withstood scrutiny. John invited me to an event in Phoenix at the Camelback Inn for a chance to become familiar with the others nationally advocating the product and asked me to describe the way I built my network, which would only work in a capital city. The Camelback Inn in Scottsdale was new then, with a great view of the mountains and all else required for a top flight resort. I called ahead to Tom Van Arsdale to warn him of my arrival, then Kroll, Kuhn and Altwies. I saw them all. On the night we had planned to meet at the Camelback, do the town, one of the most beautiful storms I have ever seen rocked us. Lightning flashed across the mountain range, the Mogollon Mountains, if I recall, over and over for more than an hour, then just stopped. We were in an open air rooftop bar with a roof but no walls. It must have dropped 20 degrees and we were invigorated. I introduced John, Mike and Rod and asked them to join us on our prowls but they had schmoozing of their own to do. As we left, Mike chose to join us.

I think Kuhny drove. On the way into the city all the canals dug to house these sudden storms were overflowing; on the way home they were empty. Kuhn knew his Phoenix. At the first stop, as we were just entering he went over to a friend of his, hard at work on a hustle, and chatted with the guy, who was obviously busy on a routine. It was crowded so we took a table and ordered and I went to tell Dick where we were. As I approached, something about the guy he was talking to looked familiar. On closer review, it came to me and I let out "Dooogy."

Without looking, he said "Clevvvy." It was Bill Dougall, a fraternity brother and former quarterback at Michigan, earlier mentioned as a player in the Detroit minor league. Small world. You just can't ditch some people. He was working for the Suns so he knew Van too. We had a great night and by the time we left the 20 degrees had returned. Doogs and I are close to this day. He has a family in his wake, spends winters in Phoenix, summer and fall in Detroit, where he still coaches—and hustles. Never misses a Michigan game. Those were the days. Van lives next to the Camelback now.

All the while between these episodes I was broadening my base to include people with more experience and expertise than I that I could trust to provide support when I advantaged the access I still enjoyed to certain of the Public Pensions. The biggies, PERS, STRS and Police & Fire were off limits for fear of exposure, but SERS (School Employees) and OHPRS (Highway Patrol) were tentatively open to outside Ohio based management, SERS particularly. I had a good relationship with their Executive Director and had placed a good chunk of their portfolio with our Ohio All-Star team of five firms, which was working well.

On Wall Street at that time, hedge funds were breaking out, essentially a grandiose version of what we had done, described above. The big negative about them that I could see was accountability. There was bound to be blending amongst what they managed collectively and individually and how to monitor your individual investment. Plus, these people were unscrupulous by nature, especially in the hedge fund format. But what did I know? I ran it past my team and they concurred but were curious too. Before I could inquire further, one of them called me, out of New York, inquiring about the Ohio Pensions' prospective interest. As was my habit in all such matters I told the guy the absolute truth of my status with the Pensions, which he probably already knew. They would have to have done their research to get to me. He wanted to meet.

We did so the next week in stockbroker Randy Rogers' office in the same skyrise I had spotted my betrayers several years before, an impressive venue. Randy was briefed and was a born skeptic, just what I needed. The hedge fund guy was typical Wall Street, talked down to me while laying everything out, soup to nuts. It all fit. He provided support documents on all his contentions, answered all our questions. As we left, when I looked at Randy, all he did was shrug his shoulders.

The hedge fund guy took me to lunch and inquired of prospective clients. I told him I had several in mind and would make inquiries and present my package to him late that week or by Monday for sure. This set him back but he covered well. He had been impressed by Randy's questions but still thought he would be the one providing me the "package." I talked to my SERS manager, their Executive Director, and he talked to Randy and agreed to meet the next week. I prepared my package and sent it overnight so he would have it in plenty of time. I had doubled the normal stockbroker's fee. Both Randy and my SERS friend knew it and did their due diligence. Nothing negative showed up but that would be hard to check in the early stage of hedge funds.

At our meeting the guy brought an "associate"--a slickster, the closer.

That's often done, especially on a $5 M deal, big back then, which this was. I didn't bring Randy, just the SERS Execs and me. No questions about my package. The presentation was perfect, all questions answered and they presented us with a SERS contract, already signed. No sign of my package, though, so I inquired. "Oh, we'll get to that later" responded Slick, with a big smile, as we left. In the elevator alone, just the three of us, I said "No, we're going to get to the motherfucker now" and pulled out a copy. After we exited the elevator, I took them, herd fashion, over to a corner away from check-in, reached into Slick's briefcase and grabbed the SERS contract. I was right, Slick was in charge. I offered him mine, holding SERS' away.

The original guy spoke up "Dan, we're going to pay you a stockbroker's fee for three years. That's a lot of money." I said "I'm not in this as a stockbroker, I'm in this as a finder and you have had my contract for a week and besides, being a stockbroker, I know the normal contract is for five years. Randy was the stockbroker in this and he has to get paid too."

Then Slick actually reached for the SERS contract. I had been right. I put my hand on his chest, pushed him away slowly and said, "Be back in a minute." I returned to the elevator, took it back up to the SERS floor, handed the now wrinkled contract to the Executive Director and said simply, "I wouldn't." He'd seen my contract the week before. I'll never forget his response: "I won't." Case closed. When I descended the elevator, the hedge fund boys were gone. They would have screwed him at some point and what would have been his recourse?

Just reflect for a moment on what must have gotten through the larger pensions manned by home grown novices over the years. The cases cited here are only indicative of most of myriad examples I could provide. Things have changed somewhat, so I hear, self-correction, finally. I honestly don't know their status now. Who really does? I would bet it's between piss-poor and terminal. The attached clip from today's <u>Columbus Dispatch</u> supports that. Bring in another dead horse, get more of the same.

Chapter 41

Wrote My Own Laws

The inaugural Arena Football League season began and John must have invested because he was there on opening night to a good crowd. I forget who won, but it was fun, lots of non-stop action, back and forth. The Thunderbolts had some talent and a good coach. Nobody from the Fairgrounds had stuck. Joe Marsalka thanked me for introducing him to John. I thought John knew that the reason I had was so he would be wary of investing. Plus, Don Cullen was the money man, Joe the face man. I had stuck around to learn what to watch out for, not to learn the how to's of the business or to recommend it to anyone.

The League failed after one year, as did the basketball league. If there's a defense of Joe's and Don's management efforts it's just that they got no help or direction from the League, but then they had no qualifications of their own to begin with. The attraction to them originally must have been that they had recognized that this was a pure money grab, top to bottom, and they were in it to get theirs and get out. I can identify off the top of my head about a dozen steps a troll would have taken before even considering such a venture.

I could be a billionaire--a term never heard in those days--and never for a second consider investing in a sports team. It's just not me. Too much greed, too many assholes. We assholes need our space. We pick our spots, no more than two to a venture. And we always have a way out. I had introduced Joe and Don to two people who could have invested in their venture but never for a second did I think either Jerry Greer or John would end up doing so. Neither of them ever said anything to me about it. I had done everything but advocate it. Besides being the truth, it's my way out.

One time I dropped in on them to see how they were weathering the storm. Now I had never seen Joe in the shower but had the occasion ever occurred, I wouldn't have been surprised to see him roll his balls in ahead of him. He was on the phone, chattering away, and gave me the palms up wave to enter and sit, big smile and all. I sat and looked around at all the trophies casually as the Master preached the gospel according to Joe. He was trying to get an investor in Arena land to get in on the Hoops venture and "get his money back and more" when things got loud, no LOUD. Joe gave me the palms down wave and I went down the hall to visit Don and another effusive welcoming, "How's Trudy? (Becky)." We could still hear Joe's caller accelerating by the second, and it was John. Don tried to engage me and I shushed him. We looked at each other for five minutes listening, until the call ended and Joe came down to Don's office all smiles, shook his head and said "How's Becky?" Don winced. I said "John sounds pissed," to which he replied "Oh yeah, you know John, all the losing and all." I think the Thunderbolts broke even, record wise, all tight entertaining games to the end. Like everything was ducky.

Who turns up dead months later under mysterious circumstances and has a closed coffin funeral with no revealed clues as to cause? You guessed it, John. I went to the funeral and wake and got nothing. Hundreds attended, none of my usual Youngstown friends, which I thought odd, but absolutely no conversation about circumstances. Either everybody but me knew or nobody knew. You know I had to ask John's man Rod. He just smiled and shrugged, Youngstownese for "no more questions." Joe and Don didn't attend. Years later there would be rumors of John sightings in South America. Solid ones.

While it probably sounds like wasted time to you, my time with Joe and Don was anything but. They were the very best con men, perfect partners, and they knew I was on to them. They liked me, but then they had no souls so that wouldn't count for much. Years later, with the able assistance of one "investment guru" and personal friends, we turned the tables on Don in a most rewarding way. Stay tuned.

While we are on sports, around that time the biggest focus in the sports business world was on unscrupulous sports agents taking advantage of athletes on contracts and investments. Lambs to slaughter. Earlier a friend of mine from Detroit, John Noonan, DeBusschere's agent and attorney, perhaps the first sports agent, and I had recognized the problems and thought maybe we should try our luck at legitimate sports agency. There was a second tier receiver from Michigan, John Kolesar, coming out so we targeted him for our first client. He would be just fifty miles from Noonan's offices and I wouldn't mind the drive for a stop at Nemo's after.

I called Kolesar and introduced myself and laid it out. He had heard of Dave but not John or me so I filled him in and he seemed excited to meet at John's office at 11:00 AM in a week.

He hadn't previously been contacted. We figured for lunch, then a Q and A and our presentation. I drove up and we sat for an hour, no prospective client. I called, no answer. We both went to Nemo's. Fuck any sports agency.

After a few pops at Nemo's we figured, "What the hell, let's just fix it, since we're here and all," so we set about to write the textbook legislation for the regulation of sports agents in America, which over the course of the next year we did. With a lot of help. Noonan was an exact physical replica of Dooling with a slight edge in height and sophistication, and a Nemo's veteran. The first obvious obstacle was that Mark McCormack's International Management Group (IMG from here on out), a legitimate group, was housed in Cleveland. Legitimate, but they would take their liberties, and would automatically object to regulation of any sort, while Michigan possessed no such obstacles. So "Bear," as Noonan was known, of course had just the guy, Michigan State Representative Mike Bennane, whom he knew well. My guy in Ohio would be Porter, Wright, Morris and Arthur attorney and State Representative Bill Schuck, a friend with an MBA and Law Degree from Cornell, perfectly qualified. I was friends with Ohio State Football Coach John Cooper and Michigan's Bo Schembechler, who would be strong advocates, and I was confident Joe Paterno at Penn State would come aboard, which he did. Another friend, OSU's Athletic Director Andy Geiger, who would later be Logan's Pee Wee Football Coach, was another advocate. We were in business. Nemo? Two more.

In Ohio the timing was perfect. OSU All American receiver Chris Carter just lost his last year of football on Cooper's first year as coach by signing with the prototypical bad agents, Norby Walters and Lloyd Bloom. The table was set. I had run across McCormack in the political wars and we got along, but he would have a lot at stake and knew Vern too, and had a <u>lot</u> of money to throw around. Write the bill first, everything included, adjust accordingly, lots of media throughout. Bear was just as connected and would have an easier time of it in Michigan. I was glad Schuck was the author; he would leave no stone unturned.

I'm not going to burden you with a legislative saga to decipher here because back in those days the media actually reported news instead of inventing it. So, the included series of articles summarizes things well. We did write the text book legislation for the regulation of sports agents in America. Schuck made it stiffer than it had to be because he knew Vern would grant IMG some concessions but he would grant me some too. In Michigan Rep. Bennane didn't face the opposition we did and had Bear in his corner so their bill was even stiffer,

What's funny as you read these articles is OSU Coach Cooper mentions the need to pay college athletes a monthly staple to deter them from falling prey to unscrupulous agents. That wouldn't get attended to for thirty years: now, in other words, and I have written that too. More on that later as we wait out the Pandemic and see what's left. Everything is on hold now.

One other thing of note: The Sports Agent Legislation would be the second time the <u>Today Show</u> would call me to inquire of my availability to appear. The first time was the Trailerboard Election eight years previous. On both occasions, national disasters pre-empted my appearance. I would later have an even bigger reason to be invited, thirty years later, but our current disaster, unnatural, preempted that. C'mon, Big Fella!

The notoriety I did get, however, put me in touch with Major League Umpire Larry Barnett, a Marion native, who I helped structure the Umpires Agreement with Major League Baseball shortly thereafter, landmark at the time. Larry was a great guy, as was fellow umpire Rocky Rhodes, from Ypsilanti, and we hit a Michigan football game that Fall Season, three GAHs in one car. They wanted to tailgate at Dick Honig's house in Ann Arbor, even though Dick would be off refereeing another Big Ten Game, for some of his Dad's famous chili. Let's just say that my formula proved out. No more than two GAHs to a venture. The chili was great but as the day progressed I became more of chauffer than a host. After we dropped Rocky off, by the time we hit Toledo my considerable self-esteem was restored. Umpires and officials are usually always AHs of a sort. Comes with the territory.

Chapter 42

Mom's Passing

It was 1989. On the home front, Log was growing up and my Mom was fading fast, approaching 90. I am not going to dwell on the latter because it had reached the inevitable crossroads we all do. She was mildly suffering but only from frustration and loneliness, no pain. Christ, I'm crying now, remembering; for me that would be the worst way and I was her son. After a last stay at a Sandusky hospital and Upper Sandusky nursing home, she passed. I got word at my office at Clegg's. She made it to 90. What I felt was that I was so proud to be her son. I had hoped I would make her proud of me but she never knew what the hell I did except marry Becky and sire Logan. Maybe that was enough. It would have to be. Her funeral was as nice as funerals can be. God bless her. It was now MY family. She and Dad await us in heaven.

To brighten things a bit, the old Tiffin group was branching out. Bob Eilert had prospered in Sydney and moved to Florida with Barb. Log's Godfather Jim Huss, another old TU basketball player and part of the Michigan football caravan for years, did as well, to Palm Harbor, where he met Michelle, straightened around an established family restaurant and married her. Hussy was a problem solver with a saint's patience and rarely gave up on a person. Log's a lot like his Godfather. Hussy has a son a lot like Huss, last time I saw him, too long ago. I owed Bob and his was the first debt I would repay when my life's final project, yet to be detailed, would be rolled out, years ahead. Both lived in the Tampa, Sarasota, Clearwater, Palm Harbor area and were super friends. Becky, Log and I would vacation there often.

Fritz Smith's family had grown and they had moved to Tiffin from Upper Sandusky where he would later get out on his own with Sue to open a meat market and motel/restaurant, top shelf only, down the highway from the Riverview. His kids were good athletes and went to Calvert and I notice when we get our Alumni News he is one of our school's largest benefactors. My donations wouldn't be hard to top, as all that place ever did for me was its best to obstruct my attending Michigan. Love the classmates though, and never miss a reunion, mine or Becky's.

Jack and Sue Wickert got divorced and he hooked up with his soulmate, Ann, and moved to the Carolinas. Jere was disengaging his area interest gradually; his nephews, Tim, Duni and Tony, were mini-hims and he was a born mentor. They were into things up towards Lake Erie, last I heard. Jere would end up in southwest Florida near Fort Myers, where he runs a golf course with Mary and her son Joe, now married. Mary finally got her horses. Tom Bogner, now divorced from Terri (I was his best man, a high honor as Tom was a great friend since before his Eastern Michigan days), joined them and soon remarried. Now that I think of it, Tom and Jere (think "Tom and Jerry") would be a perfect tandem to run a golf course; Tom, "Mr. Hard Ass" and Jerry (Jere) "Mr. Smooth." Meant to be. Sadly, I've lost track of the others and too many have passed. I talk to Jere often.

I talk often to Paul Winterhalter, my old teammate and best friend in high school, still in Dayton and "Of Counsel" to his law firm his entire career. His wife, Ruth, has come through some heart problems and Paul's dealing with some eye issues, but they raised three daughters and grandchildren abound. What's funny is when we talk we will each recall different moments in our pasts. I'm trying to get him to write a book of his own. As Van says and I've told Paul, it's cathartic. He probably won't because he didn't think of it first.

My other "bestie" at Calvert, Dr. Bill Leahy, moved to Savannah and we've lost touch with Bill and Dawn but they've got lots of grandchildren so I'm sure they're busy. Becky and I loved Savannah. Once, on trip to Florida we stayed for few days with a very best friend from Michigan, Skip Hildebrand and his wife Ann. They lived on posh Skidaway Island, where golf carts were the recommended mode of transport. I miss Savannah and Skip was always a mentor to me at Michigan, a tough football player, a great student and one of those hell raisers who could get away with anything. We were roommates for several years. After he got his MBA he seemed to advance to CEO of some major corporate entities like that was what he had interviewed for in Ann Arbor. His younger brother Rick, also close, would become an airline pilot.

The rest of my high school crew, Ed Warnament, Jake Sauber, Tom "Jolly" Rodgers, Dan McGowen, Frank Mangiola, Ron Rochester, Jim Omler, Father Dan Ring and Larry Barrick were all great guys that carved out niches of their own but we could pick up without missing a beat. Several passed away before their time but I'll never forget them. Another, Phil Schenk, moved away in high school to Florida and after our 60th reunion several years ago, on a whim, I called him at the same number he had in Sarasota back then. He answered and after his initial shock, we had a conversation just like we used to. Up until 2000, I used to be able to remember every phone number I wanted to forever. No more. I forget basic recalls every day now, as you have and will see in this as we proceed. I still function well in the present but the past failures and accomplishments occasionally elude me.

One example: shortly after Noonan's and my involvement in the Sports Agent legislation I became, as a result of that, involved in another minor crisis involving the law firm of former Michigan football captain Tom Maentz, Scott's cousin, with one of his top partners, whose name I forget. This was not a crisis for the firm, but for a cause, not a client. I have good feelings about the experience, but can't recall what it was. What I do remember was that on my several trips to northwestern Detroit involving it, I was astonished at the absolute ruination of this once great city, top to bottom. Mile after mile of disaster. Too many years of Democrat rule, now beyond recovery. Dave Bing would later be the right guy to right the ship but could only come so close. When I moved to Columbus forty-five years ago, Detroit was seven times our size; now we're nearly twice as large as Detroit and thriving.

Of all my Tiffin friends, the only one that could have thrived in the political environment that existed was Jere and it would have been right up his alley. He could have been a strategist, an officeholder, a candidate or a lobbyist, all with the requisite seasoning, of course. He had been performing those tasks on his own behalf for years in overcoming the area's private sector challenges. Tiffin was his district's county seat and the incumbent, Republican State Rep Gene Damschroeder, lived elsewhere, but incumbency is nearly impossible to overcome if the challenger isn't totally committed and Jere was always juggling more balls than he should. Pat and I had been talking about our experiences for years and he was curious, but curious had to translate to commitment or everybody's time was wasted. Plus, Damschroeder knew all this and had been through it before.

Vern would love to get Damschroeder's seat though, so I asked Jere if he wanted a taste, to meet Vern, get a feel, and he did. He asked if he should bring anything and I said "just a check." I arranged a meeting with the Speaker's office in the Capitol for 3:00 PM the next Friday, hoping to extend it into cocktail hour across the street at the Galleria, Vern's sub-office. I met Jere outside, took him in and introduced him to Vern, who I could tell was pleased. Jere's about my size and nearly as good looking with one quality I lacked: patience. They shook hands and as he sat Jere slid a check across the table. At the same time Vern slid open his drawer and slid it in. It wouldn't be lonely to the point of overflow. These two would get along.

We talked and went across the street to follow up and several others stopped to pay homage and leave an envelope with Vern. Vern also focused on Jere the majority of the time, but never introduced him, which meant for the others to move along. At about 6:00 PM the body language, mine, suggested it was time to begin the weekend. Both Jere and I knew and I think Vern sensed that it was too late in the game to start over. It would have taken a lot of work, total devotion to unseat Damschroeder, but it could have been done. Anyway, Vern got his check and Jere knew. Best of all, nobody's time was wasted.

Now Vern's methods may sound like a temperate version of what goes on today on a grand scale but there was a huge difference. I never knew Vern to champion a piece of legislation that in his evaluation wasn't in the state's best interest. That's the reason he served as Speaker under both party regimes for a record twenty years.

A few years later Helen, Becky's beloved mother passed after a long bout with pancreatic cancer, our family nemesis. She had become devoted to Logan as well as hers and our dogs. Tom, Bob and Mike, Becky's brothers, were there to assist her and she had a lot of family with which to share our grief, which in Becky's case helped. With me, in my Mom's death, it wouldn't have. Everyone held up well. With pancreatic cancer, grief takes a backseat to relief. Bless her BIG heart. She was so proud of her daughter and adored her grandson. I think she loved me too.

Chapter 43

Raising Logan

My body had been breaking down for years from overwork, certainly not neglect. My Columbus "Y" team racquetball teammate John Norton was a Podiatrist and had been telling me that I had the worst feet he had ever seen, extra high arch, toes curled under that never touched the ground. I was never a big sleeper so I would get up early and either run, lift or play racquetball, sometimes all three, every day. My vanity forged my confidence and I was always prepared. Plus, I had my cadre of specialists for support, all with big egos of their own, which I loved. Between us we'd cover all the bases. But I had to be out and amongst 'em.

I had a lot of surgeries--knees, shoulders, neck--to repair damages and my doctor, John Lombardo, was a friend and fellow parishioner as well as the team physician for both Ohio State and the NFL. He warned me that replacements were inevitable, so why stop. John had a son about Logan's age and we would often discuss strategies on how to bring them along, diametrically opposed, as you might imagine. Log was a small boy but was swimming at two, in gymnastics by three and soccer at five when we started racquetball. Once, at about four, when I dropped him off at gymnastics and walked up to the balcony to observe, I couldn't find him until he called out "Dad" and I looked in front of me to find him at the top of the rope climb, forty feet in the air, hanging on with one hand and waving at me with the other. Another time the instructor printed the evening's lesson plan on a chalk board and when his fellow students, all several years older, dispersed to their assignments, Log just sat there looking at me. The instructor noticed and looked up at me too. I mimed "He's four, he can't read." The instructor slapped his head. Log was developing the basics to prepare him for whatever sports he would choose to specialize in.

About that time, I had an idea that I wanted to run past John since both our boys were approaching school age. I had met a producer of television specials who had impressed me, Dale White. He had a studio close by, Brainstorm Media, was always looking for projects and had a son of his own. My thought was since all of us had sons on the way up, why not have a weekly series starting with school in the fall (back then you could count on school in the fall) called "America's Student Athlete?" My thought was to feature up and coming high school athletes and programs from the area with both the athletes and their coaches, complete with film of training and live action and interviews. While John and I could moderate, there were three former Buckeyes whom John would know--Kirk Herbstreit, Clark Kellogg and Jim Lachey-- who were seeking to establish themselves in that field, a far better option.

Both John and Dale liked it and the timing was perfect. We interviewed all three and they were interested. Nowadays it would have to be Clark and either Kirk or Jim but back then the method we utilized was to work with the first two to commit, Kirk and Jim. Clark had prior commitments to check and was a day late. John really got into it and he had all the connections and status. I had the ideas, John the access and Dale was a master of production. Naturally, we won an Emmy. Dale was established.

Incidentally, all three of our host candidates hooked up elsewhere, thanks, in part, to John, Dale and me. That was "America's Student Athletes'" only season. The hosts have stuck. We really did win an Emmy.

That Friday as I celebrated the award with my guys, Ed Miller suggested I get an agent to take advantage of the window it opened. I thought he was kidding but he suggested I try his—Cam Talent Agency in Grandview. He'd gotten a few commercials and had nothing but good things to say, but hadn't told a soul, waiting to be recognized. What the hell. Ed had pushed my ego button, which went off easily, as you have seen. Ed introduced me and we hit it off.

Within a week I had my first "gig," a monumental challenge. I had been cast as a priest charged with marrying a couple at a new church in southern Ohio. There was a plot beyond that but it no longer involved me so I never knew what transpired. The bride would become a good friend to Becky and me over the years. Robin Gordon was a fine lady in every way and a super talent and soon became a part of our Michigan caravan and a valuable part of the Columbus Arts Community. Meeting Robin was the best thing the Emmy ever brought me although it did afford me "status" in the Arts Community. I did several "acting" roles for the BBC but my second biggest highlight was being considered for a role in an Al Pacino movie to be shot in Kentucky. My size squelched that, as per Pacino himself. I'd have stuck around longer but then Roger Moore got the one role I was made for. Seriously, there's too much standing around and waiting in make-up for me and I was never comfortable doing it so I probably sucked at it. My first Emmy was my last. The Agents were great. My friend, Dale Butland, was also a client and he was always working. Dale was good at most things.

About a year later Becky and I started to get Log into sports he might actually play. The first transition was from Soccer to Lacrosse, one of the happiest days of my life. Being the upscale neighborhood it was, Upper Arlington just had to play, at that time, a "Continental Sport" even to the extent of importing foreign coaches who couldn't speak English, so soccer was a rite of passage for your preschooler, at an age where sharing a ball is as foreign as the gibberish coming out of your coaches' mouths--always as least two coaches.

Lacrosse was big in Upper Arlington and was an American Sport. Simon Kenton used to play it back in the day when he and the Indians were on better terms. They were perennial state championship contenders in high school and had a legendary coach and great programs all the way up. Log would see it through and win two State Championships, much later.

He did gymnastics for four years, at a good school, but by that time as in most schools, the focus went to the girls, most of whom aspired to be cheerleaders and we had accomplished our objectives--strength, agility and balance--so racquetball, baseball and basketball loomed ahead. We had been practicing all three at home and at my gym, which had everything. So did Log, except for one thing—he just wouldn't grow. We had held him back a year to start kindergarten on the advice of his pediatrician, who had put two college stars through UAHS, one a Mr. Football on a state championship team, so we thought he would know what was best. Of course, he had missed the fact that Log was lactose intolerant earlier. Even with the additional year in preschool Log was still close to the littlest kid in his class but by far the best athlete. No football for a while.

His first baseball season was a disaster. He didn't know any of the kids and it rained every single day a game was scheduled. Typical Columbus spring. And it was miserably cold. Thank God for the batting cage. On the first game they actually played, still raining, he was in centerfield and a big kid got one and put it over Log's head. Log raced back, eye on the ball, stuck his glove up and somehow caught it as he tumbled over one of those flimsy picket fences straight into a huge mud puddle. He held on but actually had to be rung out and leave the game, with no at bats. He did want to talk about the catch though. The season's last game was our first sunny day. So much for spring baseball.

In the UA summer league John Lombardo coached a team and took Log in the draft. His first choice had been his own son Brian, a long, gangly kid. John had never seen Log do anything other than fart around in church, but he must have been prescient because if Log's bat touched the ball he was on base and if he got on first he was on third two pitches later. The problem was on the next pitch he was headed home, no matter what. He had my lack of patience and I found out what had happened to my speed. But it was fun—and funny.

I would take Log to practice and usually stay to watch. Brian was a couple years older than Log and would mature into a fine receiver on the football team but now he was all gangly and clumsy, trying to be a pitcher, John doting over him and misdirecting him all the way. Even my patience was being tested. I finally succumbed and said "John, I used to pitch, can I give him a tip?" Now if I'd pitched anywhere along the line I can't recall it, but Jesus. He said "sure, have at it." Brian had been taking a huge windup, arms back, left leg up, left leg down straight in front of the body, toward the plate, right leg down, release ball, go find ball. I cut the fat and suggested "Brian, stand sideways, facing third base, raise left leg slightly, towards third base, bring the ball back behind you and turn towards the plate, releasing the ball as your eyes see the target. Follow through. "Pop, Pop, Pop" you're out, batter. No wind up, just a stretch.

It was a fun season. Log did his thing and Brian developed nicely and we usually won. The league had a rule that after four consecutive walks in an inning no more walks were permitted, the batter had to swing, and one game with the score in the 40s John asked Log if he would like to pitch. Log was in, in relief, in the middle of an inning so with a new pitcher the four consecutive walk rule began again, to the consternation of the throngs in the stands. John got it waived, so Log got to work. Pitch after pitch right down the middle, head high with the umpire calling them balls and the crowd booing every call. He was a high school kid and getting nervous. Finally, he began calling every pitch a strike and the opposition began booing. Soon they began swinging and striking out. Every pitch, head high, right down the middle. Log's expression never changed.

Log was up first on the last half of the last inning, walked, stole second, third and home as the catcher panicked and dropped the ball on the final pitch. Log was the winning pitcher, 1-0 baby. John Glenn's aide, Dale Butland, would later also be one of his coaches.

John Lombardo would be my friend and doctor up until joint replacement time for me, then he turned me over to OSU surgeons, but I started out with Adolph Lombardi, a partner of then fading Tom Mallory, brother of Michigan coach Bill Mallory, together the godfathers and pioneers of replacement surgery, when the time came. OSU would get its shot later. Both served extraordinarily well. John's son Brian and Log would later be teammates on the Upper Arlington football team. John has since retired and moved to the Carolinas.

A scandal of great consequence began on John's watch as OSU's team doctor about that time and would balloon in magnitude and spread like a plague within the Big Ten Conference. I would end up in the middle of it without ever being officially involved years later. I will also state right out that in the thirty years since, and it is still an active issue today, the name Dr. John Lombardo had never publicly come up, for which I am glad. But how is it possible that THE Ohio State Team Doctor escapes public scrutiny, to the best of my knowledge, in the biggest scandal in Big Ten history when it started under his watch in his office: the abuse of young athletes by a team doctor. Now let me say right off, John can't be guilty of the alleged offenses. The guy who was, Dr. Strauss, later committed suicide after having "allegedly" abused thousands of athletes over decades, but John was in charge of the team doctors throughout. So far the University has foolishly doled out $50,000,000 to hundreds of former athletes who twenty and thirty years <u>after</u> the alleged abuses came forward to suck at the teat of a PUBLIC INSTITUTION. To cap it off, the school officials say no public dollars were used in the payoffs. So private donors' contributions were used? I don't think so. That well would go dry in a week. Do you sense a vent here? It was and remains Deep State money!

Some of the same charges would surface through the years at Penn State, Michigan State and Michigan and I have to say, through intermediaries, I was at least partially responsible for plugging the well at Michigan, at least for now, but with the leadership in place there now that cork could pop at any minute. The same minds that seek to run the country already run our universities. Christ, wake up! They are recruiting weak life failures and paying them to discredit our legends.

When I was at Michigan, team "physicals" consisted of Doc Burke sticking a popsicle stick in your mouth and saying "Ah," good to go. So, when similar charges surfaced there during my time in Detroit I was shocked. I figured some guy got cut and was seeking retribution, especially since I knew Dr. Burke and Dr. Jerry O'Conner, the only two in my time. Of course, there were others over time that I didn't know.

It haunted me and I thought "what would I have done if it did happen to me? I was a marginal player and if I were the only complainant, I would have likely got cut. I would probably ("choke it down" would be a bad fit) have tried to put it out of my mind and soldier on. The one thing I would never have thought of was "I'll wait for thirty years and assemble a team of fellow 'abusees' and sue my university at a time when they will be sympathetic to my plight." Nope, that wouldn't have occurred to me. Neither would I then assemble over the internet a team of bottom-dwellers that had played a sport but failed in life to climb aboard while the tap is still open. How in Christ had this plague taken root? They were being recruited. "Get your free money at the Old Alma Mater."

Now as I said, Ohio State is at $50 M in settlements at the moment and inviting more. Is there guilt at OSU, at MSU, at PSU, at UM? Of course there is. The offenders are long dead or already in jail. The problem is the scavengers, who have hired "lawyers" and the Administrations who encourage it and ostensibly piss their tax dollars and endowment funds down the drain in the name of "justice." No sir! Worst of all is the public who tolerate it. These people, the Deep State, are running our fucking country!

Ask yourself: How many complainants would it take to equitably settle $50 M? Just at one university. Would you want to at least hear from the victims? That's today's media. "Give poor little abused sonny his due." Don't make him testify, he's too fragile.

Chapter 44

Father and Motherhood

Becky and I were in a period of our lives where we could devote our attention to our only son, just as planned. Aside from his lactose intolerance, he was perfectly healthy; but he just wasn't growing. After checking with Dr. Carl Backus, his pediatrician, and John, we saw a doctor they recommended, who would provide steroids, carefully monitored, in certain such cases. After much research and deliberation, we began a series of injections over two-year periods that did help, in that he finally started growing, but he had a lot of catching up to do. By that time his skills were fine-tuned, his speed exceptional and we just had to wait for his body to catch up. He had become a racquetball youth player champion of our club, Sawmill Athletic, had selected basketball and lacrosse as his sports, and was going to try football when his size allowed. I worked with him <u>every day</u>. Later I would include his friends; he would be playing on a team and they would be on it and Upper Arlington has a rich tradition, so one needed to prepare accordingly. UA was a landlocked suburb with no room for expansion and no desire for another high school. We had 35,000 residents; Columbus and its suburbs were booming—and expanding.

Skip Bozarth was a fellow Tiffinite and Seneca Hills veteran as well as one of our traveling basketball troops, having played at OSU and then at Tiffin University after his first wedding. He divorced and remarried Kathleen and returned to the Columbus area to a nearby suburb, Hilliard, where he worked for a horse transportation business, transporting race horses from venue to venue. He was my best friend in Columbus, along with another Hilliardite, Bryan Hansen, a Green Bay native and salesman extraordinaire. Both had sons older than Log, athletes too, going through the Hilliard system, and Log got to know both fathers and sons. It helped him, gave him someone to look up to. Log would also go drinking (pop) with me and the fathers on Friday happy hours and became comfortable in saloon life.

Charlie and Marlys had married and also lived in Hilliard, just across the river. They had a son Grant, slightly younger but not yet bar broken, and no athlete. On Fridays from then on we had to play dodge bar, but it was fun and Grant finally caught on that the olives and cherries on the bar weren't for beaning customers and the bars took our pictures off their walls. Life was good.

As I said, UA had the top rated school system in the state and when Logan did start he did fine and adjusted well. His Elementary School was a quarter mile away, with a radio station and a park between so ready access was an advantage. Our Friday evening cocktail hours also included two "contractors," Ed Miller and Joe Triplett. Both originals. Ed was a procurement specialist with "rack" being his specialty, i.e., scaffolding. "You need it, I've got it." On a moment's notice and in a growing big city, it was always in demand. Joe did anything, always had work for his crew, who were vagabonds who seemed to float from job to job, always busy, drunk and high. Joe never brought his crew, thinking they might be bad influences on Log. Better to learn bad habits from the pros. Both liked Log and were very respectful of his youth. I didn't want Log to be uncomfortable around adults but to be respectful and this was my way of exposing him. The only time I have ever seen him intimidated by an adult would be years later, while in his teens, when he would meet Ron Kramer. He got over that fast and was made to feel special, slightly different from my own first meeting, at least at the outset. Ron would shower him with memorabilia, friends for life.

As you have probably deduced by now I was never meant for the corporate world. I could only be effective when I did things my way but I was always prepared for all contingencies and by and large was an original thinker. I never did business through intermediaries. No one else ever delivered my messages, leaving them open for interpretation, and I always had ample references. Take me or leave me and more people chose the latter than the former, principally because far fewer established companies did business that way. They would be comfortable throwing money at a problem and having someone to blame as opposed to investing in a solution and cutting someone in forever, once the problem was solved. That was fine with me and would save me problems down the road. In my world the next slot over was dominated by greed and power and higher levels of success and failure, some of which I'll provide evidence of and had ready access to, should I desire. But this is about <u>my</u> life, what <u>I</u> did, for better or worse, not what I chose not to.

My experiences chronicled thus far in my chosen profession are by and large extremes to establish basic parameters of what <u>can</u> happen. Coincidentally, in just the last few weeks, here in 2021, former friends and prospective associates of mine made headline news on just how out of control their lives can get and have gotten. I have had dealings with both in my past, before they got so caught up in power and greed and I will touch on them later, but for now read the attached articles for an overview of where their methods have gotten them. I am still standing.

Now I knew Paul Tipps, Vern Riffe and Senate President Stan Aronoff very well and Neil Clark socially, but we were never destined to be close. We wouldn't have blended. I'd get to know Larry Householder very well and we shared some adventures. Wait until I tell you about the Ukrainians.

When Log reached fourth grade our parish, St. Andrews, offered a Diocese-wide basketball league so naturally I coached and Log played. Another parent, Bill Khoury, assisted. His son Billy had to be the shiftiest looking kid I had ever seen and was even smaller than Log; they were my two guards. We had eight players and all played equally time-wise and we won the League. We did have some size and enough doppyness to confuse most opponents. Naturally, Billy led the League in steals. He should be up for parole soon. My statue still stands in the vestibule. Bring on the next level.

I also entered a team "The Bogey Inners," in a county league. The Bogey Inn, then a favorite watering hole, sponsored us for two years, grades five and six in the Central Ohio Basketball Association (COBA). That proved to be the polar opposite from the church league, experience wise. I asked Skip to assist me. Most of our players were from UA and neighboring Dublin and the parents were wonderful, just so long as their little sonny was the captain and featured player. We would soon find out that a former Michigan and a former Ohio State player didn't know their respective asses from a hole in the ground when it came to judging talent and that our team, collectively, didn't possess it. Our opposition would all be starting their third years. Also, soccer practices came first. How would I adjust to those parameters? Among all those veterans?

We were 0-30 our first season and 1-32 our second, along with a long one-game run in the tournament. Our sponsor loved us, even providing a pizza bloat after our tournament run. We were so proud of the kids for never getting big-headed. The parents just adored us; we were in their wills. Skip spoke to me again just last year. I was able to retire on top with that tournament win.

In grade six we let Logan play football, but I had been throwing routes to him since second grade so he started out as the Upper Arlington League's best receiver despite being two and three years behind most others in experience. Andy Geiger was his coach. His own son Greg was even smaller than Log and just starting out. This was the point at which the parents suddenly found time to pay attention to their sons' status as an athlete you know, whether or not to let them come out early or wait for their class to graduate. To their credit, the coaches didn't let parents influence their sons' status and were unified in this as a condition of continuing to provide their services. When they began playing for their respective middle schools though, all bets were off.

In the final playoff game we came from behind to tie in the last minute on Log's touchdown catch. Then, on the kickoff, the opposition fumbled after a long return and we recovered, forty yards away with time for one play. They swarmed our quarterback who was looking for Log, who was double-teamed, but he was a big kid with a strong arm and he scrambled to the right sideline and saw Greg Geiger, meekly waving at the goal line. Just before going out of bounds on the right side of the field our quarterback, a lefty, spun and hurled a perfect spiral right down the sideline towards Greg, who was lasered in and caught the ball in this chest, clamped down and fell backwards into the end zone. Mehraban to Geiger for the win. Andy was ecstatic. Poor Greg was mobbed. Perfect ending.

Ever since he was able to, around six, I had always had Logan do two things to subtly prepare himself for later: jump rope, 500 reps in ten minutes or less at wake up five days a week; and, whenever possible, dribble two basketballs around our complex, a half a mile, aiming for ten minutes or less. He was pretty good about it, especially when he got good at it. I wanted to teach him to juggle, a hobby I got from Kuhny back in high school, but wisely settled for two out of three since I couldn't do it anymore. These were little things, to stimulate the nerves and make up for his slow growth. That, and the racquetball and gymnastics, served him well and the swimming complemented everything. Too much swimming can ruin an athlete, unless of course he is a swimmer, as I learned in the Marines. But enough or less is great. This reminiscence brings to mind that since Log was born I never went on one of my midnight swims or pursued my other unsatisfied urge--to parachute out of a plane (although Logan did later experience that with his fraternity brother Justin

Krok). I had jumped out of helicopters into the ocean and always wanted to sky dive.

Before Logan was born, Becky and I went down south of Dayton to do so, me only, and ran into a neighbor as we were leaving and asked him to join us, just in conversation. We never figured him for a candidate but he said, "Heck yes" and jumped in. We had our usual cooler of cocktails. It turned out that not enough people showed up for the first jump at noon, after training for an hour in preparation, so they were only going to go up once that day, at 3:00 PM. I was pissed and walked to the car to grab a beer. A fellow trainee observed it and turned me in. I was barred from the day's only jump. By now our neighbor was pumped and we had to stay for his jump. It was successful and he was all excited and we had to reload the cooler for the ride home. After Log was born, the urge was purged.

When Log got to middle school it was football, basketball and Lacrosse for the duration, size be damned, he was a "mature small" by our rationalization. There were two middle schools in Upper Arlington, Jones in Old Arlington and Hastings in New Arlington, where we lived. The Old Arlington parents felt it was their birthright to run the schools, as both Jones and Upper Arlington High School were there first, old school logic. Hastings was looked upon as a "prep school." During Log's class tenure at Hastings the Jonesy's came close but no cigar and there was plenty of talent to choose from at both schools. Both were well coached in all three sports and state championships were expected, as usual. Log's quarterback from his first season, Bobby Mehraban, had a cannon arm, nobody could cover Log and the cast was formidable, lots of great kids and plenty of characters that remain close today. The same could be said for Jones. They all became close in high school but they would be tested.

Chapter 45

The New Regime

Vern retired in 1995 after twenty years in control of the legislature, the last of it in tandem with Republican Senate President Stan Aronoff, another friend. He was succeeded by JoAnn Davidson, another Republican, but things were in place and running smoothly. I liked JoAnn and we made tentative plans to move some things along but I got sabotaged right out of the chute by a Davidson disciple who felt I had dissed her at a meeting where she had sat in for the state office holder with whom the meeting was scheduled. Truth be told, I probably did. I had made it a point to always deliver my own messages. Here's a rule: If you don't they'll be garbled by prejudice. Every time. And this woman didn't like me going in. Imagine that. JoAnn knew enough about my proposal to know it was potentially the best thing on her agenda but she let it stand, even though she stood to benefit more than my clients and me, ultimately. Fuck it. I had enough to do.

Paul Tipps had been running his Cincinnati businesses and getting involved with financier Marvin Warner on some ventures requiring connectivity, which Paul could provide. Paul's daughter Penny, as mentioned, had established herself as a lobbyist as well. Then, from out of Cleveland came Neil Clark, a rogue dynamo and boat rocker in the lobbying world. He bragged about how connected he was in Cleveland, but things had changed in both places and Neil knew it and figured he would establish himself in Columbus where it counted with the power brokers. His target was Paul and then Marvin, wrap things up. I knew him but there was no connectivity there, no synergy. Usually with me, after a period of time, it's one way or another. With Neil it was just a feeling that I didn't need him in my world; I could never have trusted him. If he ever gave me that much thought he would have come to the same conclusion, but could have. I can't ever recall us having a real conversation.

Paul joined Neil to form State Street Consultants, destined to be most powerful lobbying firm in Ohio. Soon Penny Tipps came aboard. Their clients were the polar opposite of mine: major companies with control as their objective and the money to purchase it. Other lobbyists flocked to be in their employ. That's when things began to change in Ohio. Stan Aronoff made the transition to lobbyist and attracted others and soon they would need their own speaker. When Larry Householder of Perry County succeeded Davidson, another Republican, they probably thought they had their man, but Larry's own ambition made Neil's look like a whim. I had yet to meet Larry.

Out of the blue one afternoon in a bar I again ran into Steve Daft, my drinking buddy and mortgage broker who ran with Cullen. Don and Marsalka had parted after the sports fiasco and I hadn't seen either of them in years. Apparently Don had found value in coal slurry ponds, old coal mines that struck wells underground while mining and had to be abandoned. The water rose to the surface and ponded, then hardened over time as the coal rose to the surface and apparently had value as an energy force once again. The largest mass of coal slurry ponds in Ohio were in Perry County, just east of Columbus, Householder's base. Cullen's partner in this was Steve Lambert, whom I had met previously. He had a lot of snake in his lineage, another pro. There was almost a scent about them. Daft asked me if I knew Householder. I figured this could be the excuse I needed to get to, so I said yes. I fully intended to inquire of the new Speaker the true value of coal slurry ponds in his district and to warn him to watch out for these guys. The perfect entre.

The next week after a morning session of the Legislature, I walked into Householder's office unannounced and introduced myself; I was invited to have a seat. He had heard of me so I laid it out: what was the potential value of the coal slurry ponds in his district? He had no idea, but his interest was piqued. He wanted me to introduce him to Cullen and Lambert. I had a Hoagie moment from back at Michigan: "No you don't, no, you don't <u>want</u> to meet them," but he did, even after my generous warning. That Friday, with the legislature not in session, Cullen, Lambert, Daft and I found ourselves walking on a coal slurry pond in Perry County with the Speaker of the Ohio House of Representatives and the Perry County Commissioners. Can I lobby or what?

I had warned Householder about Cullen and Lambert but he just shook it off, seeing opportunity. He included me in everything and always drove when in his district, having to pause at every corner to greet constituents. He'd done his research and knew that these ponds were all over southeastern Ohio and if they could be reclaimed, he would be a hero. He always asked about Vern and his management style. I was curious as to why, until I realized he was testing me, since his was the polar opposite. I finally just told him, "Everybody's got their own style, Larry, whatever works for them."

I had been around labor leaders from the get-go--the best, in Detroit: the originals. They all knew that the stronger their union got, the more power they had, and they would use it to make their Union even stronger. There were primarily the Transportation Unions: Teamsters, Longshoremen, Stevedores, Airlines, Railroads, etc. A lot of the others were constricted by supply--coal, oil gas, etc.--and laws. A tougher challenge. I pointed out to Larry that the first thing he should do was find out what Ohio laws permitted so he could proceed from a position of strength and never have to back water, then get the unqualified support of the Coalminers Union. What everybody has to remember about the Teamsters is that they got too strong under elite leadership and ultimately couldn't handle it, exposing themselves to government control and Mafia corruption. Hoffa, Jr. has them stabilized now, albeit weakened. Greed kills.

After a final cautionary alert about Lambert and Cullen, we went our separate ways on this issue. But again, we too were just getting started. When we would get involved again later, Larry had picked up some tricks from the guys and our clients had far more of their own.

Chapter 46

The Important Years

As Log's class completed middle school, the high school won the State Championship in football on a team of future college stars that their first year coach inherited from his predecessor, who had been fired for "usurping his authority." He would find work elsewhere within a week. They had won "in spite of" rather than "because of" Darrell Mayne, the new guy, but it went to his head and he became intolerable right off the bat.

The incoming classes from Jones and Hastings were the next best chance Mayne had to advance that far, so he promoted both middle school coaches to the high school, ostensibly to bring them along to compete right away. Hastings had defeated Jones in their annual finale on Log's last minute catches bolstering a final drive--and Mayne and the varsity welcomed them in grand style to the varsity. A great start.

The best thing the high school had to offer was an elaborate (for that time) weight room and a former OSU linebacker Will Connery as Strength and Conditioning Coach. Will was a combination monster and teddy bear who ran a tight ship and always made time for everyone, especially those who wanted to work. He is a close friend to me and Log to this day. He made the team.

The middle school coaches brought along completely folded to the whims of Head Coach Mayne who tried, apparently, to redo everything they had done very well in their original roles: fit the kids to their positions talent-wise. He immediately put the classes' top talent, Hastings' QB Bobby Mehraban, to center and defensive end. Bobby had been Log's QB for three years, was about 6' 2", 175 lbs. as a sophomore, and could put a perfect spiral on a dime (or a Geiger) at sixty yards. But he was left handed and "would disrupt the flow of the running game." Couldn't have that. The second Hastings' QB, Andy Means, was a year away maturity-wise, giving Darryl time to fuck him up too. THE QB was going to be the son of a former OSU QB, regardless, but he was qualified and went on to play at Minnesota. Nearly every pass he would throw in his two year tenure would be to his buddy, a qualified receiver, who would go to Navy, but <u>every</u> <u>pass</u>? Once, in Log's two years as a starter, Becky and I were in the stands next to a parent who was listening on the radio. John Cooper had retired by then and was the color man. On one particular play Log was wide open for a winning touchdown and ignored again, prompting John to comment, on the radio: "Clevenger's wide open every play." We just rolled our eyes.

<u>West</u> <u>Point</u>—Immediately after Log's junior year and a State Championship Lacrosse season, Becky and I took Logan for a visit to West Point, something I would recommend to all parents of intelligent, athletic sons or daughters with the ability to do so, if only for perspective. Because of my uncle, I could have gone there and my parents took me way before it was consideration time and I still tingle at the thought. There they were: all my boyhood heroes, especially MacArthur and Patton,

in statue form, along with all the others stationed around the Soldiers' Field, all but Patton facing inward, George the ultimate soldier, facing outward, the rebel.

We left Columbus on the Thursday after school ended, early, and the weather was perfect, everything in full bloom, especially as we hit the mountains, the Adirondacks in Pennsylvania and northern New York. Thursday was our travel day with reservations at a motel just outside The Point, with a recruiting tour scheduled for Friday, then down to New York City, where Becky and Logan and never been (and I had never driven in) and on to the Prep School for West Point, then in northern New Jersey, for a Saturday inspection. Because of both his grades and his size, if he (or they) showed interest, this would be his first step.

On Friday morning, precisely at 8:00 AM, we were greeted by a Colonel in charge of recruiting for an impressive welcoming, then turned over to a very impressive lacrosse-playing cadet for our tour. At the time, Log *might* have weighed 150 lbs. and stood 5' 8" and the cadet was my size, but Upper Arlington was renowned in both football and Lacrosse recruiting circles for its quality student athletes and we were shown the greatest respect.

The facilities were the absolute latest and pristine, perhaps best represented for our purposes by the weight room, yet to be visited by the cadets on this day, but we checked in later to see precision perfected. Everything in use, nothing out of place, all put away in the hour allowed. Nothing on the floor, just as before, ready for the next group. Same with them. Every cadet lifted to some degree.

In our classroom visit, the cadet laid it out. Basically, classes were not for teaching but rather for asking questions, reviewing, clarifying and confirming what the cadet had learned himself by reading what was assigned in the text books the night before. Tests could pop up anytime, unannounced--I am sure to eliminate any chance of cheating (I'd made the right decision), like what had occurred in their past.

We hit all the historical sites as well on the rest of the campus like we were honored guests. The most impressive site overlooks the Hudson River at the spot where the British were ambushed with a giant chain blocking their planned attack on the patriot stronghold of New Amsterdam, now known as New York City, the ultimate victory of the Revolutionary War. The entire chain used in the ambush is preserved on the grounds. Just like Pompei, for the briefest moments there's a chill in the air.

By mid-afternoon, fully impressed, we followed the Hudson river south for the Big Apple, slightly over an hour away on another gorgeous day looking forward to doing the City, only recently recovering from 9-11, the Ultimate Ambush. All along the way on the radio there were mentions of another threat pending and a possible shutdown of the city even possibly today. Undeterred, we got off at the Midtown exit and I tried to get my bearings to begin our tour but even after a few minutes it seemed like _every_ car was heading for the tunnels. Now it was a rush hour Friday but _every_ car? The radio reporters formally acknowledged the threat so I got in line for the Holland Tunnel to New Jersey, playing it safe. The city would be no place to hole up in a crisis with your family. By the time we exited into Jersey, the incoming tunnel was closed down. We drove the short distance to the Prep School and got a motel, hopefully far enough away. There was a threat but it was thwarted. Better safe than sorry, but that's another trip I owe Becky. Log will get there on his own.

The West Point Prep School was a retired Army Base, the complete antithesis of up north, as its successor was being designed, years away. It looked more like a prison for deranged pissants so our stay was brief but we were shown every courtesy. The Colonel had phoned down with instructions to show us the plans and I hear it's the model now up north, but all in all, a great trip. We went home via Philly and the Poconos on another beautiful day, getting details of the vanquished threat along the way. We made the best of it.

In Log's senior year, with the "Combo" of QB-WR gone and Means primed for a breakout season, two other receivers previously relegated to defensive back status, but top shelf talents, Will Morgan and Corey Bentine, were slotted with Log to finally utilize everyone's specialties, scoring touchdowns in bunches. Plus, we offered a strong running attack and a huge line. Mehraban had become a tight end and had the best hands of all. What could go wrong? Mayne put a huge sophomore at a new position, center, where he had never made a snap and put Means in the shotgun. We were picked to win the league and have a deep playoff run.

Game one, we received, Bentine almost broke one. Our ball, thirty yards away. The first three snaps Means had to run down and dive on. Nice way to get comfortable for your first start. A couple series later, Andy Means went down for the count with a broken collarbone, having yet to complete an unharassed pass. Now get this: In comes a sophomore nobody's ever seen before to quarterback and Mayne puts him under center. We would later find out his throwing range didn't extend to flankers. Means out for the year, a sophomore with no experience and girl scout range in his stead, and there stood Mehraban. What would you do? We ended up the season 4–6. Mayne got fired. Duh! The sophomore quarterback never even went out for the team his last two years.

The last game of Log's freshman year, he broke his big toe after having his breakout JV season and had to miss basketball. A lot of talented kids passed on it to prepare for lacrosse so that's what Log decided to do after he recovered. The basketball coach, Tim Casey, was top flight but lost a lot of talent to lacrosse, whose coach, Ted Wolford, was legendary. To his credit, the basketball coach turned out winners every year and to play all three, consecutively, was just not done. The Jones kids hadn't played basketball in middle school, while the Hastings kids did and they were good but all passed up basketball for lacrosse in high school, having fallen behind. We were loaded as usual, and won State Championships Log's junior and senior years. Every year at spring break time there was a preseason schedule around Annapolis where we would stop over for a three-day round-robin tournament with the nation's best teams before picking up the kids and heading for Florida, usually in groups. Fine times.

When Log graduated from high school he was about 5' 10", 165 lbs., quick, fast, strong and talented and a B student. Michigan was off the table and hadn't begun their lacrosse program yet. No Michigan, but at least he made it to the border, enrolling at Toledo University, which offered club lacrosse. Toledo turned out to be a perfect fit. He played lacrosse, graduated in four years with a business degree, met his wife to be, a perfect daughter-in-law, made a bunch of great friends, had a ball and was right on the way to be picked up for our trips to Michigan games on Saturdays. When he returned to Columbus, he was just under six feet tall and weighed 190 lbs., strong as an ox. Like me, he hadn't interviewed for jobs his senior year. We both wanted to control our environment. I wanted to live in Detroit; he wanted to live in Columbus. We both wanted to choose what we did, not be chosen. We were both "people" people, our futures were going to be determined by relationships and the opportunities they brought. He asked my advice and I suggested he bartend for a while to see what developed. My workout buddy, Dirk Bengal, managed a big hotel, Embassy Suites, out by the airport and was looking for a bartender. Log was a perfect fit, as would be the clientele--traveling businessmen. In short, Log managed the bar and the behavior within and Dirk counted on him to control things. Naturally, a prominent rookie bartender needed a new Cadillac, a big black sedan. He didn't <u>always</u> ask my advice but his college car was one of my old ones, so, live and learn. That <u>was</u> scary. He lived at home at first and moving out would mean sacrificing the car. We didn't mind; live and learn. It had always been just the three of us and whichever era's dog, everything always on the table.

    Becky was the stabilizer of the house, as well as its backbone. By now she had managed multiple sections with the Ohio Attorney General's Office under nine AGs for nearly thirty years and was respected and revered by her fellow employees and it carried over at home. She was uncannily perceptive as a judge of character, much more so than me and I was good. So would be Log.

My own career was more of the same, different casts and characters. When Log was born I trended away from Clegg's and largely operated from home. Stockbroker Pete Fuhlbrigge and Insurance guru Dale Carpenter came aboard as specialists and great friends and the originals remained. New characters, situations and opportunities kept presenting themselves, but you have the gist. Occasionally the outrageous arose, this time from Householder. Over the years, we had become "buddies," not friends, because everything we involved ourselves in was worlds apart. So naturally, bring on the Ukrainians.

There had been another coup in the country and somehow Larry had gotten wind that the new Ukraine Prime Minister had emptied the treasury and was looking to reinvest (launder) it in America, maybe over a billion dollars (how times have changed). "Would my Ohio Money Managers be interested?" They were also interested in purchasing tractors, which is where Larry came in. He had been over as their guest to evaluate the situation, perhaps to construct a coup of his own with my guys as legitimizers. Now he didn't say that, that was my interpretation of what he did say. I ran it past Dale and Pete. The Ukrainians were coming to Columbus to close Larry's deal and he could arrange a meeting with my managers if they were interested. They didn't see a downside in meeting at least, here in Columbus, and Householder <u>was</u> Speaker. How Larry himself had gotten wind of the whole thing was an unknown. He and Lambert had attended an Ohio State-Michigan game as my guests the previous years, so that scent lingered. Fuck, my managers could always say no, leave it to them.

Four of the five said yes out of curiosity and, of course, hope. The Speaker's involvement swayed them. The fifth wanted no part of it, or anything Householder. I just presented the opportunity for their consideration, as always. Their choice. The first thing we needed to do was determine how to cut up the pie, if one appeared, between them, me and of course Larry, but we had to know the amount to be invested. Using $50 M as a base, we determined that 1½% per manager (6%) and for Larry and me, as finders (3%, 9% total) would be the minimum, with 12% the maximum. After all, this was found money for all of us, but it was my find through Larry.

So, it was arranged for a week later in an office building between Columbus and Delaware in what would now be the Powell area, certainly off the beaten path. Householder's meeting with them, ostensibly about tractors and agriculture, preceded ours and as it broke up I took note. I was looking for two things, the expression on Larry's face as he came out and whether or not Lambert was in the meeting. The Speakers' face was noncommittal and no Lambert but what a sight emerged. These buys were barbarians. A peace treaty negotiation with Geronimo came to mind. They looked like they had cut each other's hair simultaneously the night before and two wore work boots with their ill-fitting suits. It soon became clear that all they cared about was laundering the money and getting their own 5% (each) and moving on to wash some more elsewhere. No questions on investment strategies at all. The $50 M figure didn't faze them.

Naturally, my managers' reputations could not afford involvement with such creatures and they seemed to blame me. They couldn't get on the highway fast enough. I had gotten them access to our state's public pensions and they had prospered but a nation's treasury was verboten because of work boots and bad haircuts? C'mon. How's that for rationalization? It has carried me through lots of times. As I left, Larry pulled his car from behind the building and asked how it went. I told him and he apologized, apparently sincere. He had told those same hoodlums that the money for the tractors had to be paid up front before shipment, which he felt queered the deal. What the hell, just another experience. Just as an aside, the Ukrainians weren't intimidated at all. Imagine yourselves in the identical situation over there, then.

Point of order: Always be aware of greed, but nothing ventured, nothing gained.

Canoe Trip to Schafrath's Livery (Mike Ambrose, Dick Schafrath, Dave Krakoff, Linda Admire, Jack Wickert, Judy Schafrath, Jack Admire, Dan Clevenger, Becky Clevenger, Ann Wickert)

Helen Schultz (Becky's Mom)

Our Wedding pic w/Pope John Paul II at the Vatican

Mom with Cuddles (Dad's Picture on the Wall)

Dan Costello Plaque

Costello Honored

Dan Costello, the late brother of Mrs. Floyd Clevenger, 75 Orchard Park, Tiffin, has been inducted into the Mount Saint Mary's Hall of Fame in Emmetsburg, Md.

The son of Mr. and Mrs. Edward Costello, Dan was a member of the prep class of 1910 and graduated from the college in 1914 and currently ranks fifth on the list of all-time basketball standouts.

Costello, who died in 1936, led the Mountaineer team in points scored during his sophomore and junior years. As captain during his senior year, he set season records in scoring (267 points), and points per game (17.8). These records lasted 25 and 35 years respectively.

A native of St. Mary's, Pa., Costello was also an excellent shortstop and second baseman on the Mount baseball team. A four-year-starter, he hit for a career average of .375, including an incredible .418 during his junior year.

Major League scouts were so impressed with his speed and versatility, he was signed by the New York Yankees after graduation and became a close friend of Babe Ruth.

Later, he played for the Pittsburgh Pirates and for Vancouver of the Northwest League.

Dan Costello Article

Cuddles Ann (Cuddie)

Ebony Snow (Ebbie)

Laskey Family (Becky, Janie, Beau, Margaux, Lance)

Clevenger Family (Oct.1986)

OCT. 1986

Logan (July 1990)

FATE STACKED THE DECK | 319

Logan & Arnold (Arnold Classic, 1992)

Logan & Coach Bo (1993)

Logan's & Laura's Wedding (09-18-2015)

Logan & Randall McDaniel NFL Hall of Famer (1997)

Becky on a Cruise

Logan's Graduation from the Univ of Toledo (2009)

Digger Jewel (Diggie)

Emmy for America's Student Athlete

Striking back

Ohio State head football coach John Cooper (C) addresses reporters Tuesday after Rep. Bill Schuck (R) introduced a bill to regulate sports agents' contacts with college athletes. At left is Dan Clevenger, a financial consultant who helped Schuck write the proposed legislation.

Schuck's Sports Agent Regulation Legislation

Cooper backs bill to protect athletes

COLUMBUS, Ohio (AP) — Ohio State University football coach John Cooper says he favors cracking down on unscrupulous sports agents, but also believes student athletes should be paid.

"It's time we gave these kids some money," Cooper said Tuesday, when asked about football and other stars who fall prey to agents offering them lucrative professional contracts at the expense of their college eligibility.

Cooper, at a news conference to endorse a bill to protect student athletes, said most coaches agree that college players should get at least a modest amount.

He suggested that $50 a month would help poor students avoid the temptation to sign contracts that would end their eligibility.

"Some schools might oppose it, because they couldn't afford it," Cooper said, commenting on collegiate rules that ban payments other than scholarships.

Cooper, beginning his first year at Ohio State, said in endorsing the new sports agent regulation bill that he backs it "100 percent ... this is something we have needed for a long time."

Rep. William Schuck, R-Colum-

bus, said his proposal is almost identical to a measure that also was announced Tuesday in Detroit.

Schuck's bill expands an recent Ohio law that resulted from former Ohio state All-America wide receiver Cris Carter's loss of eligibility last season after he signed a contract with professional sports agents Norby Walters and Lloyd Bloom.

Carter's action violated a National Collegiate Athletic Association rule.

Sen. Eugene Watts, R-Columbus, who sponsored the existing law, said he had not seen Schuck's proposal and wanted time to study it.

Although Watts' bill was tougher when he introduced it, it emerged June 14 as what he called "essentially a disclosure law," requiring student athletes to advise their coaches and schools when they have signed such a contract.

Schuck's measure goes further by establishing protections for student athletes that he said correspond to those given all consumers. "For instance, under the legislation, only written contracts would be considered valid. Athletes would have two weeks to study a proposed contract and a three-day, cooling-off period to rescind a contract ..." he said.

Ohio State University head coach John Cooper, right, and Dan Clevenger, a financial consultant who helped write legislation that would regulate sports agent's contacts with college athletes.

Cooper Backs Bill to Protect Athletes

Cooper backs agents legislation

OSU coach proposes aid to shield athletes

By Mary Yost

If all universities could afford it, coaches would like to pay student athletes $50 a month in addition to full scholarships, Ohio State football coach John Cooper said yesterday.

He said the compensation might help keep students out of the clutches of unscrupulous sports agents who give them cars and clothes to persuade them to sign professional sports contracts.

"Absolutely, it's time to get those kids some money," Cooper said.

HIS REMARKS came in a news conference at which he endorsed proposed legislation announced by state Rep. William Schuck, R-Columbus, to regulate activities of sports agents.

Cooper said he is "100 percent behind" Schuck's proposal but thinks paying students also would help keep unscrupulous agents at bay.

The only reason the National Collegiate Athletic Association has not changed its rules to permit such compensation for football players is that not all schools could afford it, Cooper said.

Schuck said his proposal does not give athletes special treatment. "It provides equal protection," he said, by applying provisions of consumer protection laws specifically to dealings between sports agents and athletes.

Schuck's bill expands on a law enacted this spring under sponsorship of Sen. Eugene Watts, R-Galloway, that requires agents to give universities at least two weeks' notice of contracts proposed for student athletes.

Schuck's bill would:
* Require a three-day cooling-off period in which athletes could cancel contracts they had signed.
* Prohibit agents from bribing athletes or giving them anything more than "ordinary and reasonable" meal, travel and lodging expenses in connection with contract negotiations.
* Prohibit agents from having more than 5 percent ownership in investments he makes for an athlete.
* Give an athlete access to an agent's books for all dealings with that athlete.
* Allow athletes to seek triple damages in suits for violations of their contracts.

Schuck announced his proposed legis-

lation in tandem with a news conference by a Michigan legislator for a similar bill. Schuck said he and Michigan state Rep. Michael Bennane, D-Detroit, have been working with sports agents for several months to try to clean up their business.

Schuck said his bill is unlikely to make it through the Ohio General Assembly in the few weeks it will be in session the rest of this year.

But he plans to reintroduce the bill in January. Schuck said he announced his proposal yesterday hoping other states will look to it as a model.

THE ANNOUNCEMENT comes after the indictment of former OSU All-American wide receiver Cris Carter by a federal grand jury Aug. 24 in Chicago on charges of obstructing justice and mail fraud.

Carter is accused of lying to the grand jury about taking money from a sports agent while playing collegiate football.

Two New York sports agents also were indicted.

Cleveland-based sports agents, International Management Group, were major opponents of Watts' bill as it moved through the House of Representatives in the spring. William Carpenter, IMG senior vice president, said he wants to study Schuck's proposal before commenting.

Ohio State football coach John Cooper, right, talks to reporters at news conference yesterday.

Cooper Backs Agent Legislation

SPORT TALK

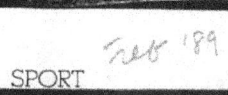

WILL THE U.S. BE READY FOR ITS OWN WORLD CUP?

Soccer's World Cup is coming to the United States in 1994, which brings up a significant question: Does a country that views soccer on a par with archery deserve to host the most-watched sporting event on the planet?

One of American soccer's leading lights says yes. "FIFA (soccer's ruling body) would love to have the American market," says Anson Dorrance, the University of North Carolina's soccer coach, who also points out soccer was the most heavily attended sport at the 1984 Olympics in Los Angeles. "They say, 'Here's a sleeping giant; let's wake it up.' They need us if they're gonna grow."

Even so, can the U.S. drum up enthusiasm for soccer between now and 1994? "It's a participatory sport," Dorrance observes. "People play it, but they don't watch it. It has to become part of our culture. When soccer games start to be something we talk about on Monday morning, it will be part of our fabric." Dorrance points out that "Brazil has all these problems with the World Bank, but their international reputation is good because of their great soccer team. The U.S. helps out with famine relief and our international reputation is miserable because we don't have a good team. I've got a patriotic incentive. Part of the American image is tied up in the sport."

Dorrance is doing his part, and maybe too well. The 37-year-old's men's soccer team reached the NCAA round of 16 in 1987 and was to play South Carolina in Columbia, S.C. That same weekend, his women's team was in the NCAA championship game against Massachusetts in Amherst. A coaching wizard he might be, but not even Dorrance could be in two places at once. What to do? "You always go to the national championship," said the double-duty coach, who journeyed to New England to direct his female charges to the NCAA title. The men, meanwhile, led by Dorrance's assistant, beat South Carolina and made it to the NCAA semis before losing to eventual champion Clemson.

North Carolina, along with Duke, Clemson and North Carolina State have become dominant forces in the U.S. As with previous soccer powers, Clemson established itself with foreign athletes, but Dorrance says that success drew better U.S. players. "In the old days," he says, "it was felt that if you sent a player to the U.S., he wasn't going to develop. It's changing." —*Peter Gambaccini*

A BILL OF WRONGS

Legislative attempts to regulate sports agents are admirable and probably overdue. If substantive laws existed, for instance, we wouldn't be subjected to the Chicago trial of indicted sports agents Norby Walters and Lloyd Bloom, which is scheduled to begin in February. However, getting strong regulation passed will be difficult, and probably not all that altruistic, if a proposed bill in Ohio is any barometer.

Representative William B. Schuck (R-Columbus) will introduce a bill that would place the strongest state restrictions yet on agents who misrepresent themselves to athletes.

Provisions in the bill mandate written contracts contain descriptions of agent services and compensation, as well as detailed disclosure of the agents' background and the opportunity for an athlete to consider the contract for 14 days (with a three-day cancellation period after agreement). Admirable. Also self-serving, because the legislation conveniently creates more demand for companies such as the Net Worth Corporation,

a financial services group that helped Schuck write the bill.

"Yes, it is very self-serving," says Dan Clevenger, a vice-president for Net Worth. "I'll admit that. I don't care about the athletes. People like you and I are getting screwed everyday by people who don't know what they're talking about and purport that they do."

Ohio combatants took shots at each other after the legislation was announced last summer. International Management Group, a Cleveland-based sports representation agency, claims that people like Clevenger who only advise athletes about the handling of their money aren't subject to the proposed bill. "If that investment house thinks it's good for athlete agents," says IMG vice-president Bill Carpenter, "we think it's good for the investment house itself."

Carpenter also points out that Ohio passed a 1987 agent-athlete statute that forbids players from taking money from agents. Clevenger laughs at that legislation, perhaps angered that IMG assisted in writing the bill. "The dumb legislator took it to them and asked, 'What do you think of it?'" Clevenger says. "They said, 'We don't need this, we don't need that, we don't need the other thing.' So, it comes out as a joke, just stupid."

The new legislation figures to be in trouble if only because Ohio legislators spent much of 1987 debating a bill on the same subject. "If something like this doesn't happen now," Clevenger says, "it surely will in the next few years."
—*Steve Rosenbloom*

Ohio, Michigan Lawmakers Toughen Sports Agents Laws

Toughest Agent Bills Pending

2 State Reps Propose Major Restrictions to Protect Clients

BY RICH ROSENBLATT

State representatives from Michigan and Ohio on Aug. 30 will introduce legislation that, if enacted, will place the strongest state restrictions yet on agents who misrepresent themselves to amateur and professional athletes.

The legislative move comes on the heels of indictments in Chicago last week against three sports agents and Eagles wide receiver Cris Carter, a former Ohio State University player.

Currently, 12 states—including Ohio—have statutes regulating agents' dealings with amateur athletes.

"This new proposal not only regulates the process of contracting [before an athlete becomes a professional], but it regulates the relationship between the athlete and agent after the contract is in place," said Ohio state representative Bill Schuck, author of the Ohio proposal.

According to Schuck, the bills will be introduced by the end of the year and could become law by mid-1989.

"The intent of the bill is to punish and eliminate the bad apples," said Schuck, "those people who intimidate and take advantage of athletes and just siphon off their earnings without providing bona fide services."

Michigan state representative Mike Bennane is the author of the bill for his state. Support is expected to come from athletic directors and coaches from the major universities in both states.

Schuck said, "We are not saying that all agents are bad. It's just that the potential for abuse is extreme where you have large amounts of money coming quickly into the hands of relatively young people who do not necessarily have a great deal of business experience."

Schuck's proposal would require agents to provide athletes with contracts two days before signing, while giving the athlete three days after signing to back out of the deal. The agent would also have to disclose his total compensation, while providing prospective clients with information on his background, current clients and other affiliations. All contracts would have to be in writing.

Penalties being considered range from a fine of up to $50,000 (part of the Michigan proposal) to imprisonment for a year, forfeiture of right to compensation under the contract and restitution of possible lost wages. □

Bennane's Michigan bill allows a $50,000 fine.

Schuck's Ohio bill would weed out "bad apples."

MANUFACTURING
Racket Makers May Unite
Tennis racket manufacturers, desperate to revive participation and sales, may collaborate on an inexpensive racket for beginners. 2

TELEVISION
Cable's Role In Barcelona
Olympic officials are studying how to add cable TV to U.S. coverage of the 1992 Barcelona Games. 3

BASEBALL
Little League Under Scrutiny
The Pennsylvania attorney general's office is looking into alleged discrepancies in Little League's financial records. 3

FOOTBALL AGENTS
The Top 25 Of 1988
Contracts secured by Marvin Demoff rank first among agents handling NFL rookies. 47

CABLE
USA Hikes U.S. Open Fee
USA Network has renewed with the USTA for the Open and the Women's Hardcourt event, at a 50% increase. 48

Toughest Sport Agent Bill Pending (*Sports inc.*)

Strauss abuse survivors plead with OSU to 'do the right thing'

COLUMBUS DISPATCH 11/20/2021

Leadership attempting to ignore athletes, they say

Sheridan Hendrix
Columbus Dispatch
USA TODAY NETWORK

Three former Ohio State students who said they were sexually abused by university physician Richard Strauss decades ago addressed Ohio State's Board of Trustees Thursday afternoon, calling on the university to "tell the truth" and "do the right thing."

A dozen Strauss survivors and their loved ones sat inside the Longaberger Alumni House at the trustees' full board meeting Thursday to hear the three men – former Ohio State athletes Steve Snyder-Hill, Gary Avis and a person who simply asked to be referred to as a John Doe – call out Ohio State's leadership for what they say is an attempt to ignore survivors and move on.

"We don't want to be dismissed, we want to be heard," Snyder-Hill said.

"The OSU that I believe in is better than this," he continued. "I want you to listen to us ... I'm really concerned that if you have another Richard Strauss, that based on the actions I've seen from 2018 on, nothing is going to change ... Nothing."

Strauss survivors have come to speak at November's board meeting for the last three years, but they were not originally scheduled to speak this time around.

Snyder-Hill, who has been one of the most vocal of the survivors, told The

See **STRAUSS**, Page 16A

> "None of us got into this for the money. We got into this because we know what is right and what is wrong. We've heard your words. We haven't seen your action."
>
> **Gary Avis**
> A former Ohio State student and a manager for the university's men's gymnastics team

Gary Avis and two other former Ohio State athletes, who said they were sexually abused by university physician Richard Strauss decades ago, addressed Ohio State's Board of Trustees, calling on the university to "tell the truth" and "do the right thing" at the Longaberger Alumni House during the board of trustees' meeting on Thursday. COURTNEY HERGESHEIMER/COLUMBUS DISPATCH

Strauss survivors plead with OSU

METRO +LIFE

More sue over Strauss abuse

3 lawsuits against OSU added on 2-year anniversary of report

Sheridan Hendrix Columbus Dispatch
USA TODAY NETWORK

Dozens more men are suing Ohio State University over the school's knowledge of decades of sexual abuse by former university doctor Richard Strauss and its failure to stop him.

Three lawsuits filed in U.S. District Court for the Southern District of Ohio, two on Friday and the other on Monday, come on the two-year anniversary of a report commissioned by the university that concluded Ohio State employees were aware of complaints against Strauss and did nothing to stop him.

"With this suit, Plaintiffs seek to hold OSU accountable for its failures, and to ensure that something like this can never happen again," a lawyer wrote in one of the new suits.

At least 41 plaintiffs are included in the two new lawsuits, most of whom filed anonymously. Some of the plaintiffs include former Ohio State athletes on the wrestling, track and field, swimming and diving, volleyball, ice hockey, lacrosse, baseball and gymnastics teams.

One anonymous plaintiff is an Ohio man who said he was repeatedly fondled by Strauss during examinations when he was a high schooler between 1978 and 1981. The plaintiff's coach brought him to Ohio State to practice as a prospective student athlete. This abuse took place in some of Strauss' earliest years at Ohio State, according to

Ohio State has publicly apologized and promised "monetary resolution" for survivors of Strauss' abuse. They've already settled with 185 plaintiffs, totaling about $47 million in settlements.

the suit.

"The men herein, like all members of the class, came to OSU as starry-eyed teens to get an education, have a college experience, or to be Division 1 athletes, and were – as part of the OSU experience – subjected to the worst serial sexual predator in American college sports

history," a lawyer in one lawsuit wrote.

In 2019, investigators hired by Ohio State concluded that Strauss sexually abused at least 177 students between 1979 and his retirement in 1998, and that university personnel repeatedly failed to act.

Lawsuits filed against the university indicate that the number of victims was much higher. At least 360 plaintiffs have filed 23 lawsuits against the university over Strauss' abuse and Ohio State's lack of action.

Until the 2019 report was released, many men believed their experiences with Strauss were isolated, didn't recognize their experiences as sexual abuse or didn't know that university officials had been aware of complaints against Strauss for years, the new lawsuits said.

See STRAUSS, Page 4B

Strauss
Continued from Page 1B

Strauss died by suicide in 2005. No one has publicly defended him since alumni began coming forward with allegations in 2018.

Ohio State has publicly apologized and promised "monetary resolution" for survivors of Strauss' abuse. They've already settled with 185 previous plaintiffs, totaling about $47 million in settlements.

Earlier this month, Ohio State announced it would offer an individual settlement program to some plaintiffs in five outstanding lawsuits against the university. However, individual settlements are currently available only to plaintiffs in the five specific lawsuits. It is not available to plaintiffs who have filed against Ohio State more recently, including 23 other new plaintiffs who filed suit in April.

shendrix@dispatch.com
@sheridan120

More sue over Strauss abuse

OVERTIME

FROM A VAGABOND TO A VISIONARY

Chapter 47

Pick Your Battles

Whoever first coined the phrase "Ultimately all politics are local" was spot on. To be a well-rounded lobbyist in a capital city, you must also master the local politics as well as the state and national to thrive; especially in a boomtown as Columbus was becoming. We were no longer a "Cowtown" as we were known in my youth and we had managed our growth well under good leadership. I knew all the mayors slightly but would never have occasion to engage with them business-wise until Major League Soccer came to town in 1993 in the form of Lamar Hunt. He was one of the world's richest men and the founder of the American Football League (AFL), by then constituting half of the NFL. So many of my old friends had found fame largely because Lamar was a visionary. Our then Mayor Greg Lashutka, a former Buckeye who played with Joe O'Donnell at Buffalo, was a friend. He was a dominant presence, a born politician who managed the power brokers well.

Lamar was in search of investors for teams in Major League Soccer and I offered some prospects based purely on his track record and their level of interest, sans my recommendation. I was still a soccer skeptic. Lamar and I hit it off. My old roommate at Michigan, Tom Keating, had played for him with the Kansas City Chiefs and had been one of his favorites. It became pretty clear to me that my prospective investors were not what city officials were seeking and Lamar saw it too. I bowed out, all bridges intact, living to fight another day. If Major League Soccer was going to work in Columbus it was going to be with those investors supported by the power brokers influencing the mayor, back then the Wolfes who owned the newspapers, Industrialist John McConnell who would bring the National Hockey League Columbus Blue Jackets, the Galbreaths and Banker John McCoy.

In my last years as a lobbyist the power brokers evolved to be The Limited founder Les Wexner and his coterie of minions. The soccer team, The Columbus Crew, survived all these years and, as of this writing, is the current MLS defending champion. They were recently purchased by Jimmy and Dee Haslem, the owners of the NFL's Cleveland Browns and Dr. Pete Edwards, a longtime Crew Team Doctor, all who will reappear later. They have got a brand new stadium, their third. The Team never made any money, living off the city and its taxpayers all these years. But it helped make Columbus a Major League City.

We also offered the longtime AAA Baseball Columbus Clippers, then the top New York Yankees' affiliate farm team, now a Cleveland Indians affiliate. Of course the Indians just changed their name to the Cleveland "Guardians," disgracing themselves and the state in the new "Woke" subculture and the American Indians in the process. Dear God.

I could go on about experiences I've had but by now you get the picture, via extreme parameters. A lot of normal lobbying went on with a lot of normal people with legal and constructive objectives that I would direct to the appropriate targets. I would get paid and satisfied. But just like now on a mini scale for all the good we would do, others would bribe their way to inflict irrecoverable harm on the public and with the opening, compound it for years to come. It is far worse now and the stakes are off the charts. We can't recover from where we are now. Read that last sentence again. The people to fear now are our own, and in charge.

As you read of my Ukraine experience you might have thought me naïve to deal then with a regime as patently corrupt as it appears now, but that was twenty years ago, in Householder's first term as Speaker. The Ukrainian schism from Russian control was a major opportunity and Larry had the balls to seize upon it. They were the naïve ones then; the opportunity was never better. Maybe we were visionaries but it didn't hurt to find out and we did; no gain, no harm and we knew. I am proud of the way we handled it. How did the Bidens handle their shot? How did Trump? Night and day.

Back to the past, things were about to change in a very big way for our family. One Sunday in November 2006, one of Jack and Linda Admire's sons in Cincinnati, got tickets for a Bengals game so Becky and I went. It was a rainy fall day and we hadn't been to a pro game for years. Just a getaway day, no pace, just relax and enjoy. Until that is, about five minutes remained and we didn't want to get stuck in the mass exodus so we got up to leave, except I could hardly walk. As our section emptied out I was able to drag my feet up the few steps to the aisle and finally Becky found an usher who helped to get me to our car. What the hell?

When Becky got us home she grabbed a pair of crutches from my previous surgeries to get me in the house. I was no stranger to injuries or even joints wearing out. I had both knees, hips and shoulders replaced and my entire spine fused with no problems. (An aside here: If you are an active athlete and need a replacement joint, <u>don't</u> stop working out <u>prior</u> to the surgery. <u>Prehab</u> is far better than rehab. You will come back much faster. The joint is <u>already shot</u>; you are getting <u>a new one</u>). Dr. Lombardo sent me to the OSU Neurological Hospital for a complete workup since every other option had previously been attended to. They deduced inherent neuropathy, just one of myriad of neurological diseases doctors know very little about except that there are no cures. There will be much, much more about that later. The doctors didn't even have any recommendations and rotated me back and forth, which I truly enjoyed in that it helped me with my self-control until it didn't anymore and I started ticking. At just about that time Tim Stapleton called. Tim was a pal of Daft's from Syracuse whom I have never met to this day but I consider a good friend just from our telephone conversations. I dislike talking on the phone beyond receiving and providing information as a rule but Tim was always an exception. He almost always had some and when he didn't I did. This time at just the right one, he did. Without knowing of my problem, he had called to tell about a nutraceutical he had discovered that was the best curative energizer he had ever seen and was going to send me a sample. He was in discussion with an agent about repping it himself and Tim was no fool. The nutraceutical, which means all natural, was called Stemulite. It arrived two days later and by that time I could painfully shuffle around the house holding onto furniture with almost no balance. I ripped it open and immediately took a double dose, then another before bed. When I got up I could walk to the john with no help and little pain. Two days later, after two double doses a day, I drove to and walked into my next scheduled doctor's appointment with no cane or limp, minimal discomfort. They were astounded. My doctor, a surgeon who was retiring to the cowboy life in a few days, was the only one of the four that showed any interest in the Stemulite; the others just humored me when I lauded its benefits. I never took well to being humored; it always made me feel a little enraged and disrespected. Let me summarize here; I had come to them the week before, in pain and unable to walk. They diagnosed me with having an incurable neurological disease that they could neither cure nor offer relief for. Yet here I stood, pain-free and mobile and they laugh at the reasons why. I was in the middle of my stare when my doctor broke the silence with "Maybe we should test some of your product Dan." I got up, walked to the door and said "Maybe you should."

I talked to Tim about Stemulite's effect on him. He didn't have my problem but loved what it did for him, so much so that he applied for a distributorship. He had gotten to its founder, a

David Summers, PhD., out of Texas. I began to think this was a nutraceutical, all natural, with no banned substances. I had a neurological disease that affected the nerves, which ultimately affect everything, for which there is no cure. Apparently there were no cures for any of the neurological diseases. The only ones I knew of were Alzheimer's, Dementia and ALS, now Neuropathy. I had heard that an old roommate of mine at Michigan, Stan Kemp, had developed ALS (Amyotrophic Lateral Sclerosis), known as Lou Gehrig's Disease. I couldn't think of a worse fate or a finer guy than Stan, a punter/receiver at Michigan, then the Packers and until recently, an NFL Referee. I had seen him earlier at a tailgate in Ann Arbor. What do you say? I usually always have something, but nothing fit. I just gave him a hug, which I never do, which was probably worse for both of us. As far as anyone knew you didn't die of what I had, just progressively degenerated and painfully rotted away until something else took you. I learned that there are several hundred other neurological diseases: AIDS, Amnesia, Asperger Syndrome, Bell's Palsy, Cerebral Palsy, Cervical Spine Stenosis, Diabetic Neuropathy, Duchene Muscular Dystrophy, Encephalitis, Epilepsy, Fibromyalgia, Functional Neurological Symptom Disorder, Guillain-Barre Syndrome, Huntington's Disease, Joubert Syndrome, Lumbar Spinal Stenosis, Lyme Disease, Head Injuries, Meningitis, Muscular Dystrophy, Myasthenia Gravis, Myopathy, Narcolepsy, Parkinson's Disease, etc., on and on. No cures.

By then I was in my mid-60s and my body was worn out. Everything's been replaced or repaired to the extent that it could be, yet I continue to push myself, making concessions every year;

now, at 80, I still do. Inherent Neuropathy is being put to its ultimate test and my recollection is not what it was, yet the more of this book I write, the more I recall. I am used to the pain and the Stemulite still helps. My hands and feet are the worst and my balance is next to nil. I get a steroid shot in each sacroiliac joint every three months, which is a Godsend.

Naturally, I called Dr. Summers in Texas to tell of my experience with his product and a little about me, and also to recommend Tim as a serious weapon in his arsenal. He was a folksy old Texan and a serious researcher, tough not to like. I filled him in on some of my recent experiences and informed him that I worked out every day with the Head of Research for OSU Hospitals, Steve Devor, and that the OSU Team Physician and NFL Doctor, John Lombardo was my doctor and friend. I also mentioned that I had dozens of famous friends that I felt could benefit from his product and refer it as a favor to me should it have a positive effect on them. He jumped at the chance and sent me a case.

The first person I gave a bottle to was Steve, the second to Will Connery at the high school. Both were in excellent shape with no problems. The next two were Ron Kramer and Joe O'Donnell, both with tons of problems from the football wars. By the next week all four had responded favorably. Ron and Joe effusively. The best thing for Steve and Will was that it worked and brought them relief too. They had only tried it as a favor to me because they just accepted some pain by now, as no other pain killer had any measurable effect any longer. I then took it to John Lombardo for the NFL and he wanted nothing to do with it, even with Steve's approval, "all natural" be damned. He didn't care what good could result just so nothing bad happened on his watch, just like with the abuse scandal at OSU. Geldings. At that time, the NFL banned everything.

Soon Ron wanted some for Hornung and it worked for Paul too, then Tom Keating, three former All-Pros. Usually there is a process and a fee for product testing at OSU but Steve waived it and did it on his own time, no negatives at all. Like always, when I consider involving myself in ventures beyond my experience and expertise I consult trusted friends that do possess what is needed. Dick Honig and Don Eaton came to mind on a grand scale. Dick had become a Big Ten Official and was now the Dean of Big Ten Officials (football). He had also formed Honig's Whistlestop, a worldwide supplier of officials and other sports equipment based in Ann Arbor. Don had been a football player about ten years after Dick, Joe, Tom and me and now co-managed Don Canham's sports and safety equipment conglomerate of companies in Ann Arbor with his son, Don Canham, Jr., the public face of his Canham's museum of successes and Michigan lore. No better venue exists for a football weekend blowout or to distribute a product worldwide. Eaton was married to Canham, Sr.'s daughter, Clair.

I also had a friend locally who was CEO of a major distribution company as well. I contacted them all and sent them samples to try in order to see if they saw a fit. All did, both liking the product and the idea. I contacted Van for the NBA connection; he liked the product and saw a fit as well. If I was going to start a company I may as well learn how to from the best and widely renown financier Mark Kwame, who had done some work for Governor John Kasich the year before, met a local lady and decided to marry her and set down roots, just across from the Capitol. I had done some things for Kasich earlier, when he was in Congress and still stable, introducing him and things at events, so Mark advised me, gratis. He had liked the product but advised me to have more than one product to offer, at least three. Dick and Don agreed. I needed two new products.

Out of the night when the full moon is bright came a shyster known as Cullen. Cullen? Yes, Cullen, with as neat a product as I had ever seen. It was the standard green, yellow and orange safety vest seen at virtually every construction site or night time public function but Cullen's vest had LED lighting attached, either flashing or constant, controlled by a button next to the front zipper. You would see the standard plain, non-lit version as often as you would see orange barrels, but never the lit version because Cullen "had the patent." Uh huh. Right off, a "Trailor Board" moment hit me. The safety value was obvious, but the underlying value lay in the promotional value. WHAT construction company was repairing the intersection? WHAT police force was clearing the disaster area? WHAT school crossing is this? WHOSE ambulance is that? Just off the top of my head. There was also a bikers/runners version. Of course, Daft was with him, no Marsalka.

I brought in my friend and associate Dale Carpenter. He had heard the Cullen tales and had to see for himself. He saw the value of the product immediately but needed a push from me to see the potential, then agreed. He looked forward to dealing with

Cullen. Product one. Product two turned out to be the Bio-Back from Medolutions, LLC, a local company of two good guys, Rick Gerace and Fred Graff, who had a well-designed, light-weight back brace: simple, effective and inexpensive, the perfect complement. As I saw it the only way to market a back brace in a catalogue was via athletes on a website, also ideal for the safety vest and nutraceutical. We already had two established websites, Honig's and Eaton's, plus our own to be developed should things go forward. My local potential distributor would be ideal for us later and did turn out to be, much later. Even then, his was a Fortune 500 company.

We needed to get together as a group to brainstorm--make it real--so to speak, so we arranged to meet at Canham's compound in Ann Arbor. I brought both of the vests and the back braces (two), as well as a case of Stemulite. Will came with me from Columbus and Honig, Kramer, Joe and Pat O'Donnell (Joe's brother a former gridder) and, of course Eaton, our host, met for the better part of an afternoon. I didn't try to sell them anything, just show them things, let them try some Stemulite, plant a seed because insofar as I saw, all three products would fit nicely on their existing websites, especially with some Hall of Fame advocacy, readily at our disposal. Should they concur, we could start our own company, an LLC, to feature ours alone. I had talked to Van in Phoenix previously and he thought Bob Knight, Sal Bando and Oscar Robertson might also be interested, not as investors but as product advocates, for a percentage. Kramer could get Horning; all of us could get others as/if needed.

On the way up with Will, I was deep in thought when two other avenues had invaded my mind: the police and military. Another of my good friends in Columbus was Dewey Stokes. He was the unnamed innocent friend in my "conniver" segment. Dewey was a lifetime cop, became the President of the National Fraternal Order of Police, then County Commissioner in Columbus. He had been involved in city politics forever. Dewey knew at least everybody and would do just about anything for them so long as it was legal. If you haven't yet guessed the "Conniver" got his position as National FOP Counsel through Dewey. Our products were perfect for the police.

The other was the military. The only way to get to the military was through the General Services Agency of the Federal Government (GSA), where ultimately we really needed to be, but it was a process, well down the road. The annual GSA budget was then one hundred billion dollars a year and the money had to be spent. All of the services, Army, Navy, Marines, Air Force, Coast Guard, plus FEMA and the other agencies, too many to list, had to buy everything through the GSA. Every government agency. The reason I thought of it now was that down the road from Columbus in Roseville, lived a retired Medal of Honor winner, Ron Rosser, who kept busy in his later years by attending prominent military events. He should be made aware of us and what we had to offer. His advocacy would be a huge plus. Dewey and I would be the perfect tandem to pay him and his wife a visit.

There weren't any flaws in the strategy; down the road implementation would be harder than it had to be, largely due to me having to do most of it, as it also had to be. It was my project;

I had to learn how to get things done, things far away from my skills and experience. I couldn't have done it without Becky. In fact, she ended up doing it all. I couldn't even operate a computer. My hands were too bad, shot really, and I couldn't move my head far enough up or down to read one. She would have to print everything out for me and send all the emails. That was then. Now, fifteen years later, I write this out on a lined tablet, every other line, and it takes me a half hour per page, in print only she can decipher, then type. I knew what to do and could write it out but all the messages were typed by Becky for all those years, from beginning until now. To everybody. She is my everything and I have failed her so. Ultimately, people would fail me, too, all of us.

But we did it. Everybody was in favor of proceeding to set up an LLC. We would call it Pure-Pro Products, LLC, with a presence in Ann Arbor, at Canham's and in Columbus, at my address. Everyone came aboard. Dewey and I went to Roseville and spent a wonderful afternoon with the Rosser's. Ron loved his back brace, which we renamed the ProBack and he chilled us with his tales.

I selected Porter, Wright, Morris & Arthur across from the Capitol to be our attorneys and everyone came down and it was real. We were in business. Medolutions agreed to our terms immediately but two challenges loomed ahead: an agreement with Doc Summers and his Stemulite people from Texas and, of course, Cullen and his people for what we were going to call Night Safety vests. Nothing was going to be easy. But parts of it were going to be funny.

Chapter 48

Getting Started

When I was stricken at the Bengals game I was in the early stages of my Inherent Neuropathy, with balance problems and relatively moderate discomfort constituting my symptoms. It had not yet been diagnosed. I just figured it for overtraining or as part of the aging process. I thought at first Stemulite might be a cure, so dramatic was my recovery, but after about a month my balance was still affected and my back always ached, but <u>no pain</u>. It had a dramatically positive affect on everybody I had sampled. In Syracuse, Tim Stapleton got the same reports. We had something.

Now we had to get something, a deal with Doc Summers and his Las Vegas "backers," who he said had done nothing for him yet but talked of taking it public, which concerned me. Taking what public? According to Doc, other than through several small time distributors like Tim which <u>he had</u> found, he hadn't benefitted a dime from his "backers," certainly not from us since all our samples had been gratis. Tim as always had done his research and smelled the same rat I did. He had even heard that the main honcho of the "backers" group was a hermaphrodite who presented himself as a male or female, depending on what the occasion called for and almost never met in person, working through intermediaries or over the phone. Kramer, Hornung and O'Donnell had just returned from the annual NFL golf outing in New York where they took several sample cases to distribute to the attendees and were already reporting considerable demand for more. I had even gotten some calls. Our position would never be stronger. We had to present ourselves from a position of strength. As elegant as the Canham facility was, it wouldn't register with a Vegas hermaphrodite and his legions, but my local distributor friend's facility would. He loved the product and had a "Campus."

I called him to fill him in and inquire and he offered his main meeting room in his executive headquarters for a meet. He was as curious as we were and wanted to meet the guys. His company specialized in healthcare products. After our founding at Porter-Wright, I had called Bill Hooth at Noonan's. Bill was now retired, but his former firm in Detroit might be able to provide legal services for the upcoming negotiations and potentially future ones on a partnership basis. Porter, Wright was good for a cover, but their fees would soak us and Noonan would have been perfect for what lay ahead. He saw the value and said yes. Bear was retired, but Hooth thought John Papazian would be perfect and he loved it. The guys were all in and those that couldn't make it would be virtualized in.

I called Doc Summers and extended the invitation. He was well aware of the "Campus," was excited about the potential and was sure his "backers" would be as well. I wasn't so sure. Kramer was excited, for different reasons.

A date was set and I picked Doc and Van up at the airport, separate flights. Oscar drove up from Cincinnati; Dick, Don, Joe, Pat and Ron from Ann Arbor; Hooth and Papazian from

Detroit. Hornung, Bando and Keating videoed in, as did Knight. Full house on our end. We sent a van for our guests at the airport.

It worked. They were intimidated by the status of their surroundings and by those in attendance, especially when the host CEO welcomed them and turned things over to me, seated next to him. Doc was seated next to me, <u>not</u> with them. Kramer was trying to pick out the one he was looking for. All of our guys were prepared and <u>if</u> what Doc had told us was accurate we held all the cards, a big if. I laid it out, who we were, what we offered, what we needed, our plans forward; it took five minutes. Hornung, Bando, Keating and Knight loomed overhead. Kramer just loomed, looking disappointed: their leader wasn't there. Will Connery, looking a like a young Dick the Bruiser, was on the other side of Doc. Remember, he had never seen any of us before, nor a facility like this, I would bet. Van and I had taken him to lunch at the OSU Golf Course before the meeting and made him feel comfortable and then he would meet his heroes. The table was set.

Across the table, nobody wanted to go first; they were fully intimidated so they asked for a conference break fifteen minutes in. They recessed to a conference room and got on the phone, ostensibly to Vegas. Afterwards they seemed to be newly energized and the first guy, of the five, to get up began to present their positions. Hopefully some of you can remember the old Art Fern character from Johnny Carson's repertoire on TV long ago because this guy <u>was</u> Art Fern, shyster extraordinaire. Everybody just stared except Oscar, who just rolled his eyes. They were just trying to save face, get out of there alive, especially when

Papazian started grilling them as to whether they even had a position, which was overkill in my mind. We didn't need any animus and now, there it was. Being an attorney, he had to interject himself. My bad.

    Things broke up, we thanked our guests, saw them off, then thanked our host, who had given us all the credibility we would ever need. We chatted for an hour. Hooth knew Papazian had fucked things up, made our prospective partners adversaries. Doc was over the moon. I just hoped he hadn't signed his life away. Van and I took him to the airport. I didn't say anything to burst his bubble. Overall, everybody was impressed with Pure-Pro Products, LLC's potential, at this point, rightfully so.

Chapter 49

Locking In

The Medolutions negotiation for the back braces was a mere formality. They were up and running on their own. Both Rick Gerace and Fred Graff were great guys. All our guys loved the braces. We met at the Canham Complex, which I will refer to as Eaton's from hereon, since Don was a Pure-Pro member and ran the place anyway, and both sides were impressed. The only problems I saw was while tons of people have bad backs and <u>need</u> a brace it would be tough to pick one out of a catalogue. One would need to try it on. We would be relying on our Hall of Famers' endorsements to hold up. In my case, all of my neuropathy problems emanated from my spine, which as I have said was fused top to bottom with multiple surgeries. The brace provided stability but did nothing to improve my balance or relieve the pain. Only the steroids did that. But at least with Stemulite I was "walking" again and the pain had lessened.

Cullen would also make the trip to our headquarters at Eaton's to discuss terms for our deal. He was impressed but unfazed by his surroundings. He and I and Dewey Stokes along with Dale Carpenter, my secret weapon, made the trip; everyone on both ends had been fully prepped. Earlier we had all the guys, our athletes, in for a weekend photo shoot at Log's workplace, The Embassy Suites at the Airport, and over two days on a weekend we did photo shoots and commercials in Dirk Bengal's lobby, delighting his occupants who mingled between shoots. Log stayed busy throughout and later he and his future wife Laura would do some great commercials on the vest at a nearby park along with some other friends down by the Scioto River and downtown Columbus. Hugh Rich, an independent expert, had come aboard as our commercial artist and a member of our LLC. Everyone but Knight had made the weekend shoot and we caught up with him at an Indianapolis hotel the next weekend. He charmed Cullen's wife and he and I caught up, despite an NCAA conflict he had just attended to. Jack Admire arranged a follow up shoot with Oscar and Paul and his Golf Club in Cincinnati to wrap things up.

By the time we got to Eaton's, Cullen was in his comfort zone. Dewey had told war stories all the way up. Dale had a plan he would save for later, just sizing Cullen up. Honig had told us earlier that most of the products on his website were made in China and he went over annually to secure his Chinese network and confer with his Chinese manufacturer and had for years. Duplicating or improving the vests ourselves would be no problem. Cullen hadn't shown us a patent, which, in China, would be meaningless anyway. Eaton's products were largely Chinese sourced, too.

Cullen wasn't testicularly challenged either, by anyone's definition. In their primes he and Joe must have made a pair. He laid out his offer, very humbly, with virtually no details as to sourcing or capacity or strategy or funding--those were confidential--but he finished with a flourish: our cut would be 15%, just for doing everything. At first nobody said anything because nobody could, even Kramer. Then Dale popped up with an enthusiastic "I'll draw it up!" Everybody was looking at me and I just put my finger on my lips. Dale followed up with "Meet me in my office at 11:00 tomorrow morning and we will sign the papers." Then, to me "That okay for you Dan?" I said "You're the dealmaker Dale." Then he said "Let's get back, I gotta get on this." As we left, he looked back at the conference table and smiled.

At 11:00 the next morning, a Friday, we met in Dale's office. He came in with two copies of the Cullen contract. Cullen was beaming. By now I knew what was coming. Dale said to me "Dan, do you want to review this?" I paged through it to the "No recourse" clause toward the end and, with my best reluctantly act, signed "Dan Clevenger, Chairman" and passed it to Cullen. Cullen signed his and reached for our copy, signed that. We smiled and shook hands and Cullen thanked us and left. What we had signed gave us 85% of the vests, him 15%. As I saw Cullen out, Dale went to notarize and fax our copy to Honig and Eaton. Frontier justice. We changed the name of the vests from Cullen's "Night Armor" to our own "Night Safety" vests in the contract.

Honig had sent a vest to his Chinese sources and had gotten an acceptable price and the samples he received were a better quality, so we ordered fifty. If Cullen ever noticed our skullduggery he never let on. Daft later told me Cullen was proceeding without us, "couldn't afford to wait." It was all just part of the game for him. Move on. I would later see him in bars and he was folksy as ever. The man could take a joke. We had our three products. Now we had to target our market.

Our website was www.pureproproductsllc.com and its content was mine alone and I am proud of it. No fluff, only essential information, excellent presentation, superb video thanks to Hugh. We called our menu our "Hall of Fame Line of Products" and featured the Night Safety LED Safety Vest with Bob Knight regaling its merits. All our athletes were great about everything with only their percent on sales as compensation. Try that now. I have attached some of our fliers for review.

However that "best laid plans of mice and men" saying goes, it would apply now. Doc called and after hemming and hawing around it for a while revealed that apparently he had signed an agreement with the Hermaphrodite previously that gave away control and approval of any and all deals regarding Stemulite and that he (Herm) no longer saw any need for us. I told Doc that that was something he might have mentioned prior to our presentation and asked him to send the contract to me so our attorneys could review it. I bet that's not the reaction you expected. Doc said he wasn't allowed to share it with anybody. OK, BOOM! Then HE got mad at ME. I told Doc what Ole Herm had in mind was taking it public far before its time and throwing him to the curb; that he wasn't mad at me, he was just embarrassed so send me the fucking contract. I never heard from him again. Review in your mind what we had put on his table. He's dead now and I still take Stemulite daily and it still helps. We were going to call it Proformax. Go figure. I eventually did get the contract and Porter, Wright said "stay away."

We had come too far to turn back and we had committed to several Expos. We had two solid products, with complete control of one of them. I had been exploring the General

Services Agency potential and considered it a process worthy of consideration. What I hadn't figured on and should have right off was that none of us had any commercial retail experience to speak of. I was born into it and grew up in it until I hit double figures but a disinterested ten year old wouldn't be decently prepped for what we would need down the road. All I knew about today's retailing was that it was dog-eat-dog played by sharks and expensive to sit in on. Dick and Don would know more than me, but I had heard from a friend, Danny Tarpy, a beverage distributor, that large companies like Proctor & Gamble, located in Cincinnati, paid millions of dollars a year to large companies like Kroger's just for favorable shelf space in their stores. How did the little guy even begin? Sam Salvaggio, an exec with a company that had a magazine that featured up and coming breakout products in the fitness and sports world AND also rated the country's top retail sporting goods chains, actually came to visit me, inquiring of our vests. I had seen his magazine and sent him a video. He thought our concept was the best he had seen. I asked him if his world was anything like Kroger's and he said "Oh, yeah, only worse. Try to get paid!" His magazine rated the Top 20 Retailers in all categories and they all paid at their leisure, if then.

I had an old fraternity brother, Dick Adams, who was making a career at P & G and after talking to Tarpy I called him for confirmation, which he provided. We wouldn't be using grocery chains but sporting goods chains would be essential. Dick was coming up on retirement himself and recommended I talk to two retired P & G CEOs for counsel on entering the retail world. Good idea. I wasn't keen on paying to get in or not getting paid, once in. I knew I was naïve about this market but, man, one or the other. Our product had value, too.

I called both retired P & G CEOs, one after the other and Will Connery and I invited them to meet if they were interested and sent them our video. Both were West Point graduates and interested so we met, separately over a two-week period. Will attests to this day that they were the two most deluded out of touch with reality individuals anyone could possibly meet, the other end of the world we would be entering in the retail market. Startups were totally foreign to them. P & G was no start-up.

The largest outdoor equipment supplier in Ohio was just miles away from my home, on a major crossroad over Interstate 71 going through the heart of Columbus. I paid him a visit, announced, and he was prompt and eager to meet, having viewed our video. His "store" was about the size of a small college basketball arena with available foot space for maybe fifty people at a time, spread out. He had no idea of the extent of his inventory, it just kept flying off the shelf. He loved our products, both vests and back braces. We had our first expo coming up in a week at the Columbus Convention Center so I could only afford to leave two vests, one of each and the same of back braces to test market for a week, <u>not</u> to sell.

A couple nights later I happened to be going north on I 71 and saw our flashing lights from the highway. He had put our larger vest in his storefront window, flashing all night to everyone driving by. The next day his store was packed. The smaller vest (bikers/runners) was inside, flashing on products recently added to his inventory. I went in and his first words were (kiddingly)

"Hell, I don't <u>want</u> to sell them, I can't keep people <u>out</u>!" I felt better for a while.

Our first expo at the Columbus Expo Center went well and was well attended. We did a great job: Kramer, Connery and O'Donnell walking around wearing the vests and braces, the rest of us manning our well positioned booth, wearing either a vest/and or a brace, handing out cards, chatting people up, then we would alternate. Mike Ambrose, an "interested party," had a huge sign made with our website on it. Everybody knew who we were. A couple more of these and we could open up. And they were scheduled. We also were a hit at the "Arnold Classic" Columbus's largest annual Expo Body Building Event, featuring Arnold Schwarzenegger, who loved our presentation.

We had to come up with a supply strategy. Honig's China supplier could do it; he had provided the fifty samples that Dick had arranged, but expected amounts far in excess of that once we were up and running and my recent retail findings were concerning. Also, upon inquiry, not <u>all</u> of the GSA market looked unfavorably on Chinese made products but when it came to LED there were very few other sources and none of them were anywhere near the quality or cost. The main GSA attraction was the potential volume and the certainty of payment. Five, ten, twenty thousand units were routine orders and they paid COD, no rush on delivery. I had also found a factorer, Capital-Plus, Inc., through Daft, who would be willing and eager to reasonably factor our GSA orders. Bob Setzer and his daughter Renee ran the business and had heard what we had done to Cullen and thought it well deserved. We would have to give up some to pay a factorer but the GSA always paid and if they didn't, he was insured, the cost of which of course we would pay for. Far better than us ponying up.

Our next expo was the National FOP Convention, in Cincinnati, and Dewey arranged things: a great booth, center stage, full access to the Brass. We had added a video of our guys showcasing our products flowing constantly. Oscar stopped by for a couple hours and he and Kramer vested up and mingled. Perfect setting. I wore my Marine Corps t-shirt and got a lot of "Semper Fi's." We put on a fine show and they loved our products. Two things paled it for me though, more than others. First, among the FOP Brass, the Convention had become a dick measuring contest. This was what the new President-Elect viewed as his show and he felt that Dewey, with Pure-Pro, had deliberately upstaged him on his big event after backing his opponent in the election. Then he and his cohorts began to denigrate our products in spite, even though the rank and file had loved them. He said that the flashing lights would make them targets, to which I replied they were outerwear, not underwear and designed for special assignments, not everyday use. He thought I was being a smart ass (people often misinterpret me so). Anyway, nobody would talk to Dewey anymore and he is one who would talk to anybody. Upstaging a successor would never have entered his mind. The rank and file were embarrassed. We cut it short.

I began the long process of gaining GSA approved status and got some advice from vendors already approved. This would take a while and would be totally up to me working with the selected consultant. Without a consultant it could take years and there were a lot of pretenders, but once approved, the entire Federal Government was at our disposal and currently there were no LED safety vests on the menu. Some but not all permitted Chinese-sourced products. I was told our vests would be well positioned since China was far ahead of the rest of the world in LED technology. It had to be pursued and I had to endure the process and explore the market. It would be up to my partners to take care of everything else, businesswise, because they had the experience and expertise. I had to learn my part.

Chapter 50

A New Life

By now Becky had retired after thirty-one years at the Attorney General's Office, going out on top to rave reviews. It was a propitious time to go, before retirement benefits were cut further, which was on the horizon. Naturally, as she was freed up I was increasingly restricted. I could no longer hit the streets, and my network constricted accordingly, as did my client base. I couldn't trust my balance even to walk Digger, our young Beagle, whom I had typically walked three miles a day. Walking on grass was out and my pain was constant and increasing. Stemulite helped and was now an essential. You can imagine how this was going to work out.

Dirk Bengel had gotten transferred within The Embassy Suites Chain to Greenville, South Carolina and Logan hit the sales world, sans Cadillac, moving to an apartment with buddies downtown: another sheik on the loose. He eventually settled in with Pella Windows and Doors as a trade representative, working with contractors. He has worked his way up to an established status. He also married Laura Gall, an acquaintance while they were at the University of Toledo. She too was from the Columbus area (Westerville) and they met up in Columbus at a bar. As she tells it, she pursued him. She graduated Summa Cum Laude with a major in Finance and minor in Sales and Marketing and knows her stuff. Laura is a Financial Analyst for a worldwide data company. Believe me! She is a wonderful mother to their two boys, Pauly and Tommy, to whom as you know this book is dedicated. They recently purchased a new home in a booming outer suburb, Powell. It is beautiful and they continue to make it a better home every day.

I have always believed that people are cut out to be certain things and that finding your niche in time is essential to being successful. For example, two close friends from Michigan, Skip Hildebrand and Ted Forbes, were in my mind destined to be CEOs of major companies despite having two polarized styles. Skip, a former football lineman, would be very imposing and well prepared, almost decreeing his strategy to his board. Forbes, a non-athlete but with uncanny wisdom, possessed a perfect executive's personality and style. He would have his board thinking the decisions he made were their ideas. When I was recovering from my early surgeries, I stayed at the Phi Delt House for closer access to classes and I felt I had to ask Forbes, a non-Phi, but frequent visitor, if it was okay to use *my* car. Smoooth, he was. Two of my all-time favorites.

Two others, Bob Brown and Scott Maentz, were types in my mind too. Both played basketball and football, with Brown becoming the first father/son football captain in Michigan history. He had gone to prep school ("Finishing School," as he referred to the memory), then Harvard, after graduation, for his MBA. Brownie would own his own companies very successfully. Maentz, a natural athlete and cousin to aforementioned former captain Tom, I had pictured as highly paid board member of someone else's company. Both were great guys and good friends too. Very successful. Great reputations.

I had found my niche in Columbus, but my presence was required and there was a changing of the guard. I was no longer an imposing figure and the political climate was devolving, due largely to Neil Clark. Tipps would get out just in time and joined him in State Street Consultants.

We did two more Expos, one at Lucas Oil Stadium in Indianapolis, just me and Dewey, for all the Safety Equipment Suppliers in North America. This was the Big Time. Dewey walked and I staggered through every aisle of the entire place wearing our flashing Night Safety Vests. We were mobbed. We answered questions and handed out our cards and flyers. We also wore our ProBack Braces (thankfully). We didn't get a booth because there were over 1,000 distributors registered for $500.00 slots and it was a last minute opportunity. It worked out for the best but we were exhausted. The single other LED vest present paled in comparison.

The next week I got dozens of calls, many from Canada, all very interested, loving our website, wanting a sample for the Brass. Of course we had to order them so I would tell them to make sure of the desired design now and the majority said to "just send one of each." Dumbass me, I had planted the thought of design options where I meant Safety or Sports Model but it didn't matter as we had only several of either in stock. Don had sold the others on his site. Then I heard that Dick Honig was retiring and was selling his business, lock, stock and barrel. Unexpectedly, he had received an offer "too good to pass up." What about our source? Our samples? Our orders?

We had to regroup and figure this out because the next week I was to go alone to a big Expo at Wright-Patterson Air

Force Base in Dayton, Ohio. Thank God it was a single seat format at a series of tables. I was a <u>guest</u> of the host General, whom I had been cultivating for months on the phone. I hadn't told him of my disability, let him think what he wanted, but when I arrived, he got me a wheelchair and assigned a sergeant as a wheelman. <u>All</u> the leading airplane manufacturers and airports were in attendance. I wore my vest but had it on slow flash, and my brace. "We" stood out. Other than to stand up to greet and model I never had to move except to give out all my cards and flyers I had brought. I picked up fifty-six business cards from interested parties and received many phone calls the next day. I had our video running all day. A good hit.

I called Bob Setzer and asked if he would factor such orders: got a yes. Would he factor an order from us based on an order from them, just to see? Not from China, as I figured, saying I was just curious, knowing China's reputation. So it was up to Dick to work something out with his now ex-source once he closed his deal to sell. We couldn't do anything with no access to product. Sourcing, once secure, was now our biggest question.

I also thought we had a great website with all our testimonials by our Hall of Famers and superbly designed by Hugh Rich. Plenty of video and intra-actional content and live action footage. No frills, just all the information anyone would need. Classy.

Chapter 51

A Blip Left Unattended

When I first came aboard at Clegg's it was because at that time they offered the best life insurance products available through Phoenix Mutual, their sponsor firm. As most of you know, a mutual company's earnings are shared with its policy holders while a stock company shares with its shareholders. For cash value purposes for its policy holders it's an investment in a mutual company, an expense. At that time the leading insurance company's money manager was also Phoenix Mutual's. That is what made all our unique strategies work: utilizing insurance products as both protection and investment. After a few years, Phoenix got greedy and became a stock company and the money manager left for greener pastures. After that, other than free office space and good friends, Phoenix had no value to me.

At first, Becky's retirement package with the Ohio Public Employees Retirement System included health insurance coverage for the spouse, but no life insurance. I had an old policy that I had maintained and at that time I was young and healthy enough to get some inexpensive term life insurance so I did. Five hundred thousand dollars, fifteen-year term, guaranteed renewable at the same rate at $250,000 upon expiration. Done and forgotten.

Years later on a weekend, I had a bad case of acid reflux and a long expired prescription and I had to get a refill for that prescription on a Sunday.

My go-to hospital was and is Ohio State University Wexner Medical Center, fifteen minutes away, but likely to be busier than Riverside Methodist Hospital, five minutes away. Becky took me there for what we thought would be a quick in and out with a new prescription. This is all my bad but I didn't deserve what I ultimately got. Emergency rooms are always manned by the rawest rookies on weekends and an underlying reason I settled for Riverside was that, unlike OSU a teaching hospital, I expected the rookies would actually <u>be</u> doctors, more experienced and inclined to sign off on my script request. Leave it to me to encounter a zealot.

Let's just jump to the next morning in my hospital room, when my assigned doctor, an arrogant--and believe me I know arrogant--Chinese doctor comes in with my test results from the myriad of them run the day before by the ER Sunday staff. I have about twenty minutes to live, he told me. They found that when I slept my heart only beat every six-to-eight seconds. I had known that for years; it's called "Athlete's Heart"; checking, he <u>knew</u>. So I got dressed and left. My acid reflux had passed.

About a month later my fifteen year, $500,000 term insurance policy expired and my automatic renewal at $250,000 was denied due to pre-existing conditions undisclosed at the time of origin: complete and total bullshit. Riverside seemed prepared for this and disallowed my efforts to contact "China." I called my attorney Bill Lampkin and laid it out and he warned of a protracted stand off by Riverside to protect their Chinese doctor, more of whom they were trying to attract. God, even then.

So now at 80, I'm a cripple with no backup except Pure-Pro's success, my Social Security and Becky's pension from the state. I haven't been able to work at what I excelled in for almost twenty years. I am forced to do now the very tasks I always avoided in my prime and have forced myself to excel at them, all except for computer technology, which of course is critical to one's success. My hands won't permit it. Becky does all of that for us and by us I mean all the Pure-Pro work. Ten years ago she applied for a parttime position at a Marc's Discount & Grocery Store five minutes away. She does merchandizing in the closeouts section and truly enjoys her work. It's very physical, she gets her steps in and as she says it helps her keep her girlish figure. Her nephew, Tom Schultz, is an executive for the Marc's chain of discount stores, predominately in the Cleveland, Ohio area and travels all over the world as a closeouts buyer. Becky was a runner for years and did a half-marathon in the worst weather I have ever seen. She came in second in her age group, age forty-two at that time. Since then she has had her share of joint replacements, right hip and knee, left shoulder. I owe her my life and if what's left doesn't work I will be ashamed of myself instead of proud. But I am saving the best for last so hang on.

Chapter 52

Getting Started Challenges

While we waited for Dick to find a reliable Chinese vest source, I began the process of getting us GSA approval, a process totally unfamiliar to me. I had screened about a dozen consultants. I had been advised by experienced GSA companies to involve myself in the process, as it was not uncommon for predator consulting firms to stretch the process out and bleed you dry, but I would have anyway. If I apply for something, I sure as hell want to know what I have got, how it works and what it entitles me to, especially since it is being paid for by Pure-Pro money. It took six months with me up their asses, in a curious way, every step of the way. We got our GSA license.

Dick's original Chinese supplier could be counted upon when he was responsible for a menu of products on a regular basis when Dick was in business. He did do us another 50 sample vests but we would need regular bulk orders to sustain him and our Expo candidates had moved on. Eaton could always be counted on for distribution. That was no problem, but our members had nothing to sell for long enough to quit looking. Our GSA consultants raved about our vests and knew FEMA, the biggest agency, would love them. To retain my sanity, I began the pursuit of AAA, locally at first, then nationally. No GSA approval required.

I can't bring myself to recount that experience. It has to be the poorest run company in America because apparently no one is in charge and the higher up you get the dumber the contact. These were safety vests with LED lighting and room for a big AAA flashing on the back of each one. How better to announce your company's presence at every emergency venue? To protect your driver and your client! The passing drivers. Get the name out! Apparently no one was authorized to make a decision. Just short of my "BOOM" stage I said "Can you at least give me an endorsement?" The guy said "Be glad to, that's a helluva product." We never sold them a single vest but their endorsement was huge. The process took three months. They allowed our claim of being the "best outdoor nighttime safety product in the world."

After securing a supplier, our biggest problem would be getting the partners reinvolved. Then Kramer died of a heart attack. At the Detroit funeral his son, Kurt, told me I was the last person he ever talked to via phone records. I had just called to chat and vent, bring him up to date. Everybody was at the funeral, all our guys, all the Old Packers and Lions, lots of friends from the old days. Bart and Cherry Starr had flown up from Alabama and picked up Paul and Angela Hornung in Louisville. I brought everybody up to date. I was going to proceed with the GSA pursuit. I was not going to fail in what might be the last thing I ever did, nor let them down. I asked for their continued support.

What I needed was a cause and in the drive home with Becky and Logan, just maybe one came to me. Back in Columbus Pelotonia was coming up.

Several years before here in Columbus about one hundred cancer survivors, led by one of them, all from the OSU Cancer Hospital, decided to develop a fundraising event to fund further cancer research at the Hospital with OSU's blessing and little else. Now there is no evidence that any of the survivors, other than the leader, had any experience or expertise in launching such an endeavor, ambitious to the max. They were planning a state-wide bicycling event over a three day period to attract donors to the cause. They called it Pelotonia. It would be held over a long weekend.

They started out door-to-door, neighborhood-to-neighborhood, then approached businesses downtown, soliciting pledges: grass roots to the core. Every survivor had a minimum that they <u>had</u> to achieve, preferably surpass, to ride over various routes to saturate Ohio, hundreds of miles. They divided into teams and <u>each</u> <u>team</u> had SPECIALLY DESIGNED T-SHIRTS IDENTIFYING THE CAUSE. Naturally, the media kept the public up to date, anything Ohio State, although OSU had nothing to do with it.

The Inaugural Event was a pronounced success, raising millions, and becoming nationally newsworthy largely due to the leadership of the Pelotonia CEO, their original leader. I called his office, got his aide and laid out my plan. She reviewed our website as we talked and got excited about its potential. Sponsor logos on our vests including Pelotonia's own, for every rider over three days, saturating the state while promoting safety as well as cancer research. The Corporate Sponsors would pay for the vests. Cause, Sponsor, Event over flashing LED Night Safety Vests. What's missing?

The aide was sold but the CEO was "in conference" and not to be disturbed. I left my number and was about to ring off when he came on the line saying "Who the hell is this?" Apparently she had pushed his button when finishing with me and he started in on her with me on the line. Even if I were the type to look past that enroute to a pitch I doubted he would be in the mood to hear one so I just hung up. A couple days later I tried again and a different girl answered and I was told he wouldn't take my call. Aha! A BAH! Still, I couldn't free myself of the concept.

To date over fifteen years, Pelotonia has raised over $250,000,000 for cancer research at the OSU Cancer Hospital and is nationally renowned. During the Pandemic they kept going, modified of course, much of it virtual, and they are back at it this summer. Look them up. What I had planned would dwarf that in year one. The BAH is gone but he set the tone and his successor, a good guy, is the perfect successor. I stored my idea for the future.

Chapter 53

Frustrations – Opportunity

The China situation was devolving faster than we were progressing. The GSA people would know far better than the average civilian and I would run across it every week, usually through the military, a prime target for our products. They would be the ones confronting the enemy should China become one. My political experience and Marine service put me in a good position to navigate those waters (sorry). I would make fifty calls a day to prospective GSA clients for our products. I forced myself to get good at it. If I put my mind to it, I can acclimate myself to anything but I had to purge the memory of the potential we lost at Lucas Oil and Wright-Pat because of lack of access to the product. Time and the political scenario became adversaries as well.

I would run across a Prime Vendor, Randy Webb, the crème de la crème of GSA membership, who loved our vests. He also liked our back braces and inquired about adding them to his menu. Prime Vendors had ready access to all GSA targets and he had dozens of products to offer, most procured from companies like ours. It seemed the answer until I told him they were made in China, then he laid it out. If a Prime Vendor had even a single Chinese made product on his menu he ran the risk of being wholly banned from doing GSA business, but he might have a solution. He would be willing to meet with us in Ann Arbor to discuss it as we were <u>close</u> to the solution. We set it up at Don's Ann Arbor Headquarters on a date our critical people could make. Randy was impressed by the venue but only Don, Pat, Will and I were there from Pure-Pro, less than I had prepared him for, fewer than we had expected. We had a good meeting and developed a trust but our experienced partner was missing. Nonetheless, his "solution" was sixty miles up the road in Lansing, where a GSA Approved School for the Blind, a National Institute for the Blind (NIB), was turning out dozens of products for the GSA market year after year. Substituting the "Made in China" label for a "Made by Disabled Veterans" label would be the answer, cost be damned. But could a blind person duplicate our vests? Randy said "Let's go see. I'll spend the night and we'll go up and see in the morning."

I had a procedure scheduled the next morning in Columbus, but Randy had dinner with Don, the perfect host, and stayed over, then drove to Lansing in the morning spending most of the day. Don was blown away. He had brought the vests and they saw no problems. They showed him some samples of previous similar products and it looked like this could be the answer pending costs and of course orders. I wondered if Randy wanted to market our vest why he didn't place the order himself. On the spot. The answer turned out to be he was in negotiations to sell his business, a Prime Vendorship, for multiple millions and couldn't afford the untimely interjection of an unproven product with no record currently made in China. His back was obviously killing him so he had gone the distance for us and opened the door. I couldn't help thinking "what if we all had been there?" Now it was up to me again and I set my sights on

FEMA. We needed a huge order and now we had an option aside from China insofar as suppliers went. He also loved our ProBacks.

My efforts to become informed on all GSA procedures over the past year had taught me a great deal. I had developed relationships with other vendors, consultants and literally hundreds of genuinely interested targets for our products. Sometimes they would even call me. Other prime vendors confirmed what Randy said. I never liked phone business, but when that's your only option, you had best develop a tolerance for it. I perfected it. I was <u>good</u>. Of my fifty calls per day (on for an hour, off for a half hour) at least five would recommend an Expo I should attend. Accepting my inability to do so they offered to recommend our website to the attendees in our behalf. They wouldn't be allowed to hand out our business cards.

When we received a bid request it would pop up unannounced on the computer and be there for forty-eight hours, no contacting the sender so no questions or the bid disappeared. Get it in or not. The Government's fiscal year ended September 30th, so most of the bids appeared from May to the end. The budget <u>had</u> to be spent or face reduction the next year, something nobody wanted to face. Since ours was the <u>only</u> LED safety vest and there were dozens of back braces, the consultants told me our bids would likely appear in August and September. Our bids were usually for between 2,500 to 5,000 units so I would use the Chinese pricing without identifying the source and I couldn't get any of my questions answered. I didn't know if I could even get the order filled at either source if our bid was selected. What I <u>did</u> know was the China situation was accelerating monthly into a total ban if the consultants could be believed, but it wasn't likely to affect FEMA since they operated worldwide. My FEMA contact told me they definitely had interest as I told him of my source dilemma. He had samples of both vests and both back braces. He advised me to use that as a selling point: either Chinese or the School for the Blind (NIB), USA products, it wouldn't matter to them. The School for the Blind was well known for quality.

    Our submitted bids weren't accepted apparently because we never heard back. I didn't know if I messed up on the submissions or they chose an alternative of which there were none on the menu. I heard nothing from FEMA but my consultants told me that was usual for them. They operated on their own agenda and obviously had need of our vests, probably our back braces. Let it lie for now and revisit it after the first of the year. No prospective GSA contact would do anything before then.

Chapter 54

Adjustments

Let's pause for some perspective. Things weren't going as planned and all my partners had other things to do. Don had a business to run: the others actual jobs. Dick had been the Dean of Big Ten football officials for years and now had retirement to enjoy among his multiple homes. Will had moved to suburban Detroit and became a mortgage broker and his wife headed up a national charity. Pat and his wife had health problems and Joe passed of dementia in a facility out west where one of his sons lived. Knight and Hornung had dementia and kept their wives busy providing care at home. Oscar had a menu of ailments and Van was in Phoenix. His brother Dick had had a stroke requiring care and attention. Dewey was as busy as ever as an unpaid public servant and was starting to slide. Sal was able so far as I knew but had long drifted from the loop. All remained supportive because of our long-term relationships and, I would like to think, their respect for me.

As for me, I had a degenerating neurological disease, progressive and debilitating, with no cure and was in constant pain. I am not complaining, just stating facts. My biggest bitch was the constraints it put on Becky. She deserved much better than she got and she did everything for us and by us I'm including Pure-Pro members. She set the tables for me to do my thing with skills that I had to acquire--they didn't come naturally-

-and hone to the fullest of my potential when I represented Pure-Pro, especially one: <u>patience</u>.

As I have said, the very first time I saw the Night Armor vests I thought of Trailorboards and its <u>promotional</u> <u>potential</u>. For Christ's sake, there was the <u>value</u> of the thing. Certain people saw it; others didn't. Without it, as successful as Pelotonia became, they wouldn't scratch the surface of their true potential.

Now it was off the table because I had plans of my own. Pelotonia had just come off a very successful year exceeding $10,000,000 for the first time. It was inspirational to me. I was a big fan to the point I was going to emulate them. What a concept. A bicycle tour of the state to raise attention and of course money for a cure for cancer. But wait, people who would sign up to ride that far probably rode close to everyday, usually in the early morning or in the evening for those who worked. Maybe they would be interested in a light weight LED lit protective vest when they rode in the dawn or dusk for safety purposes. One that flashes! Hey, maybe they could even wear it on the tour, let people know who they were. Put a logo on it with the lights flashing to kind of promote the event to every car they passed, every city, town or neighborhood they passed through. Maybe some sponsor logos around the event's. I've got it: have the promoters of the event sell the vests to prospective sponsors. Every rider to wear every day that they rode throughout the year. Get those going to or coming from work's attention. Reach millions promoting themselves and safety as well as the event's cause. Make sense? Thought so.

Only my concept featured other causes: neurological diseases, the fastest growing killer in the world with no known cures for any of them and no major events to fund finding cures. They were killing my friends and one would be killing me if I needed further incentive. I'm going to consolidate here so as not to lose my audience. What follows happened over the course of several years and I wouldn't get support until finally the NFL Hall of Fame judged my event to be just what they were looking for. Their consultant's exact words when I met with him in Canton were: "You don't have to sell me, I'm sold!" The saga part was in between and then beyond. Of course, time marched on in the interim. The China-USA situation only worsened.

Based on my own experience and advice from experienced consultants that I trusted, as well as other prime vendors attracted to our vests, I narrowed my GSA target base to the military, the airports and of course FEMA, then to the other disaster services. To get FEMA would open all the doors and the size of their order would establish Pure-Pro as a player. Of the services, the Coast Guard showed the most interest although all had some. I had sent them samples and they tested the vests under extreme circumstances and were amazed. From the air at night, our vests worn by Guards on a cruiser could be seen from ten miles away. Cruiser to cruiser from five miles. <u>They</u> wanted <u>me</u> to get the word out to the other services so <u>they</u> wouldn't be the first to order. That's what I was faced with. Dozens of times, servicemen I had developed relationships with serving as buyers/screeners had completed their service by my next call. Day after day after day in all the services. If I could do the Expos, by now we would have been established. I estimated selling 50,000 vests per year to start then hand it off to the Prime Vendors and the School for the Blind. I figured I had made over 5,000 contacts in the GSA market over the years to those I thought to be potential candidates for our products; and <u>at least</u> half enthusiastically recommended Expos. Early on, I had tried to get "Disabled Veterans" status for Pure-Pro but that required over half our principals to qualify. Only Kramer and I qualified. I tried using Hornung and Knight (Army basketball coach) and of course Rosser our Medal of Honor Winner, but they weren't principals, although Rosser's involvement did matter and helped our cause. As yet not enough for a breakthrough

A now-funny story comes to mind about our luck at the outset. Maybe it set the tone. When we got our very first vests from Dick's suppliers years before, we were blown away. They were great. It was just before Christmas and our Joe O'Donnell and Red Berenson, the Michigan Hockey Coach and NHL immortal that we'd gone to school with back in the day, were about to embark on a North Pole canoeing expedition over the course of a week in Alaska. It was an annual event for Red. Just when you think you have heard it all. I expressly <u>told</u> Joe to be sure to take a couple of our vests just in case. Of course he forgot and of course it was their worst winter in years. They got lost in the raging waters for days. They were off schedule and the COAST GUARD had supposedly been monitoring their progress nightly. The Coast Guard finally found them safe but barely, vest free. Maybe that was an omen. If only. It took them weeks to recover. I still haven't.

When I first came to Columbus to begin my political career I naively thought that the purpose would ultimately be to <u>solve</u> the world's problems piece by piece. It never was even then. Many politicians' objectives were to <u>take</u> <u>advantage</u> of the world's problems to <u>get</u> <u>theirs</u> and it has expanded exponentially throughout the years. Nowadays nothing gets through without a cut, especially among the party in control, most especially when it's the Democrats. I've learned over time that America's biggest threat is within its own government and <u>ours</u> is the one the rest of the world looks up to? And that's just the starting point. Throughout history all great powers dissolved from within <u>before</u> they were conquered for lack of leadership. We just threw our last great leader to the curb. We have a turd at the helm now. Our biggest threat is a horde of enslaved barbarians from the East dominated by the Communist Party. During our present regime they will take control of our economy unless there is a rebellion before we disintegrate internally. We are currently catering to them.

Chapter 55

Family Matters/Opportunity Anew

Logan and Laura Gall were married on Becky's 65th birthday September 18, 2015 at our parish St. Andrew's Catholic Church in Upper Arlington. Their reception was an elegant affair at a beautiful venue at The Boat House which is located at the confluence of the Scioto and Olentangy Rivers. Most of their friends from high school and college attended. Laura is from Westerville, another suburb where they lived until June 2021, when they moved to their dream home in Powell. We were and are so proud of them. They produced our two beautiful grandsons Pauly, three, and Tommy, one. They are smart and healthy boys and apparently polar opposites. Laura's parents, Ken and Ann, are great people and have a home in Marblehead, Ohio on Lake Erie. They still reside in Westerville pending upcoming retirements. Everybody is healthy; me too, just disabled. We see the boys every week. Other than what is facing the nation we have no complaints.

When they come over, Pauly takes control of the house and inquires, and inquires, and inquires and then inquires. T-Bone as I call Tommy sits and looks, grabs a toy and hits me with it between meals. I have an electric scooter for tours outside that Pauly takes control of for our ventures to the park and playground, where occasionally we will run across Shemy, Megan and the Bo clone they are raising. That's of course Glenn Edward the IV, now in

Hastings Middle School, where Logan attended. If I could contribute to it, it would be the life I dreamed of.

We lost our precious Beagle Dog Digger on September 28, 2020 at the age of fourteen and a half. She had months of discomfort with liver cancer and issues with her gall bladder. We would sneak all her meds in doggy pill pockets and that was pretty much all she would eat. Her poops were pretty much just blood. Logan called Becky at work that day and told her, "Mom, this is it. She's trying to tell us she has given it all she has." Within a couple hours of that call, Becky and I were at the vets on that dismal, rainy Monday afternoon, saying our last goodbyes. As we cradled and kissed her, her loving little heart beat its last beat at 5:02 PM. We are so very grateful for all those years of her pure, unconditional love and devotion. She was a great little friend and Becky often says that little dog got into her soul. It was months before she could even talk about Diggy without sobbing. I know many of you have experienced the same sad loss. If only she were still here. Log and Laura's dog Einie really misses her too. He just mopes around when he is at our house.

Other than family all I think about is our quest; that's all I have left. Pure-Pro Products, LLC is on cruise control as the Chinese problem festers. We will either get orders and be able to fill them or we won't. I keep my hands in and don't bug which now at this stage I always have to control. I am going to condense things dramatically now because what I'm setting you up for is my life's crown jewel and I couldn't stand to retrace my steps and I would lose you readers at the gate if I tried.

College athletes, specifically football, were approaching a crossroads back in 2017. So was the NFL. Left unattended, neurological diseases would wipe football off the map. None of the schools were going to do anything about it--believe me, I checked--until it hit, then they would panic and compound the problem. The schools are already infested with our enemies and sports isn't on their agenda, other than as a target. Over the years I had been focused on a remedy and I am a passionate man, incentified. It was simple but <u>couldn't</u> be credibly refuted and no alternative existed. We had to find a cure for neurological diseases, primarily but far from exclusively--head injuries. Neurological diseases were the fastest growing killers in the world and there were no cures for them. Very few effective remedies and nearly all the major collegiate research hospitals had either reduced or restricted their research budgets for doing so. Some major universities had completely stopped. I could cite them but I won't. Shaming them wouldn't help and they would be the prime beneficiaries of my plan.

It was Pelotonia on steroids juxtaposed. Instead of starting at the bottom at the neighborhood area, start at the top with the NCAA and the NFL. At just the right time, out of the blue and late of the Downtown Athletic Club, came Art Gase, my old Eastern Michigan recruit. He was living in Miami, Florida and was a successful businessman. He was visiting a niece in the Columbus area, got in touch with me and invited us to lunch to thank me for making his life possible. Becky and I would be delighted. His brother Bill, the Grape Ape, had played at Toledo as well but was severely disabled with a neurological disease, hospitalized. His son Adam was the Head Coach of the Miami

Dolphins, whose owner was Stephen Ross, Michigan's largest benefactor and namesake of the Ross School of Business at Michigan, the nation's number one business school. Hmmm, could there be a connection here? We were in school at Michigan at the same time.

    I laid out my plan which I am about to do here and Art was impressed. He told me to send it to him in Miami and he would have Adam get it directly to Ross. I heard from Jason Jenkins who was Ross's executive assistant the next week. Could the ball be in play? There was an interest.

    We would raise money for research to eradicate neurological disease. Just as in politics it would all depend on the ultimate messengers. The right people had to deliver it, fully convinced themselves, to the ultimate decision-makers. My plan had one big advantage, two really: since there weren't any others and our vests were perfect. It was a Disaster Plan for sure but ultimately that's what we faced. We offered a bicycle tour, featuring riders wearing our LED vests, with sponsor and cause logos above and between flashing LED lights made by the School for the Blind from Pure-Pro Products. They would ride from the NFL cities Pittsburgh, Buffalo, Cleveland, Cincinnati, Indianapolis and Detroit to Canton during the Hall of Fame week previous to the Enshrinement for the 100th Anniversary year 2020. Besides the Hall of Fame and the aforementioned NFL cities, the entire NFL itself, plus the NCAA and all Division One teams to start, and all their TV sponsors and the Networks themselves and all <u>their</u> sponsors would participate and be donors. <u>Initially</u>, vest purchase orders, once designed, would go out, logoed up, with season ticket applications with full opportunity for prospective sponsors to join in. Figuring season ticket applications for just the six inaugural teams riding, we would have 300,000 prospective riders. The teams could choose to sell the vest for $50.00 apiece to sponsors and/or riders, with the selected cause and team logo flashing, on the days of the Event as well as the other days of the year that they rode. The then six major NCAA Conferences could do the same in support and offer events of their own in the future, same modus operandi. The TV networks' own sponsors could be solicited immediately for the Inaugural Event on the NFL's Centennial Celebration year. Nike and the other sports equipment companies would be critical, since they had been focusing on head injury protection for years, having seen the handwriting on the wall. Properly done--which the Inaugural couldn't possibly be, too much communication and continuity would be required--estimated the potential to be $1,000,000,000. Fine tuning in successive years would get us there. My plan featured the cause and its sponsors with the NFL Hall of Fame being central to it all. I'd just been handed access to the one man who could make it all a reality: the owner of the Miami Dolphins, a classmate at Michigan.

To this day I have never heard from Stephen Ross. His Executive Assistant Jason Jenkins responded for a while, enthusiastically at first, then nothing. He had read my materials, saw the potential and passed it along. I tried the Lions; the Ford CEO was Jim Hackett, formerly the Michigan Athletic Director. Ford owned the Lions. His Executive Assistant seemed embarrassed when she informed me of his lack of interest.

Finally I got through to the Cleveland Browns' owners, the Haslems, Jimmy and Dee, who had recently purchased our Columbus Crew Soccer Club along with Dr. Pete Edwards an orthopedic surgeon and longtime team doctor. I am truly grateful to him because he, through the Haslems, opened the Hall of Fame door for me and introduced my materials to them. Upon their advice I gave the Hall a call.

I was told to call Ms. Pat Lindesmith, Chief Partnership Officer. The Browns had provided my information--absolutely no fat--which has always been my style. She had reviewed it and passed it along to their consultant Jeremy Hogue, President and CEO of Sovereign Healthcare Alliance in Mission Viejo, California, who was exploring such options as it had long been apparent to him and the League that head injuries needed to be dealt with. He was due in the next week, could I come up to meet? It was now June: just over a month until the Hall of Fame game. Of course I could. It would be the furthest I had driven alone in years, nearly 100 miles, but nothing was going to stop me.

They met me at the entrance of The Hall, valeted my car and had a wheelchair ready. If you have never been to The Hall it's not big city at all despite its elegance. Besides Timken Steel it's Canton's heart and soul, a must see. As they wheeled me in, Pat Lindesmith and Jeremy Hogue came to greet me with big smiles and outstretched hands. As I mentioned earlier, Jeremy's first words were "You don't have to sell me, I'm sold." We met, fine-tuned and planned for the League Meeting at the Hall of Fame Game two weeks away. I was invited but I wanted it to be

Jeremy's thing and he had it down. I knew from long experience that the one unknown or unnecessary person in the room could queer a deal. I would be a distraction, an outsider with my wheelchair to the same people that ignored me for years. I had made the right decision. After the game, at their business meeting, the NFL committee waved Jeremy off. They were so excited that they had secured Beyonce and Jay-Z and J.Lo for the next year's Centennial Super Bowl Game Halftime Show that they didn't have time to discuss their ultimate future, embarrassing their hired consultant in the process.

Jeremy never called me I and smelled the rats. I called him the next week and failed to connect. Later I called Pat and she confirmed it, somewhat embarrassed. Put yourselves in my place. I had to back off. Not stop, just back off. Jeremy later emailed and apologized.

The mamas of the world weren't backing off though; their sonnies had been getting their dicks knocked loose and their brains scrambled long enough and they had had it. All across the country there was an uprising gaining momentum. High school football was imperiled even here in Ohio, which is a hotbed. At Upper Arlington, potential stars were asking coaches if they could play just in games because mommy wanted them to play on the golf team instead during the week to stay safe. In the historically strong city league, traditional rivals had to join up to even field a team. This was streaming across the nation led by the Left and had to be given attention. I made a plan for that, too, when the time came. For now, we had been dismissed.

Let's step back. I didn't wish to attend the NFL meeting at The Hall of Fame for reasons beyond Jeremy being an advocate hired for that purpose and well informed. In my prime I was an intimidator. I ran meetings. I was never intimidated, as you have seen. Now I was a cripple, an invalid physically, but mentally close to my prime. I represented Pure-Pro Products, LLC and its Foundation, "The Hall of Fame Legacy Foundation for Neurological Research," which our event was going to fund with proceeds from "The Tour for the Cure." Our credentials were: Ron Rosser, Medal of Honor Winner, Paul Hornung, NFL, NCAA Hall of Fame, Ron Kramer, NCAA Football Hall of Fame, Bob Knight, NCAA Basketball Hall of Fame, Oscar Robertson, NCAA, NBA Hall of Fame, Tom Van Arsdale, NCAA Basketball Hall of Fame, Joe O'Donnell, Buffalo Bills Hall of Fame and Sal Bando, Oakland Athletics Hall of Fame. The meeting was held in the NFL Hall of Fame Office after the Hall of Fame Game with the owners on a Beyonce/Jay-Z/J.Lo high and for us to be dismissed out of hand for bringing them the only solution to the biggest problem they had ever faced and I should be there? Nah. Jeremy had been embarrassed for accomplishing the task they had assigned him.

 The Hall had other resources I coveted too. The world's richest man at the time, Jeff Bezos, had his brother Mark helping The Hall with its Village development intending to house members in need and down the road. This was a noble objective at Hall of Fame Village. I viewed him as a stalking horse for opportunities for his brother as well as one who could make our event happen in a heartbeat. The word was out that Jeff was out for a TV network to complement his Washington newspaper, hell maybe even the NFL itself. In my mind things didn't look good for the NFL, not with their arrogance. The second resource was John St. Pierre, CEO of Legacy Global, who from his credentials could stage our event. He too was currently working on the Village. Their creds are attached. See if you agree. But now our event wasn't on the table. The NFL was ignoring its biggest threat down the road, player well-being, then, players.

On Sunday, November 11 to celebrate our grandson Pauly's first birthday, we were set to attend his birthday party at a local pizza place with Laura's parents and relatives. Several days before Becky was noticing some erratic behavior on my part, mostly lack of coordination. That Sunday morning, realizing there was something critically wrong, and, as always, using her best judgment she summoned the Emergency Squad. They took me to the OSU Emergency Room and after a battery of tests admitted me for several days for observation due to an Ischemic stroke. This occurs when a vessel supplying blood to the brain is obstructed. It accounts for about 87 % of all strokes. Fortunately there was no damage but it was life changing, as I decided to quit drinking. Pauly's first birthday didn't go as planned but could have ended up much worse. I had been pounding for sixty years, but stopping turned out to be easy for me. My mind works that way. I still have never tasted coffee or cigarettes. I replaced the beer and wine with zero alcohol Budweiser and alcohol free Fre' Red and Merlot wine bottled by Sutter Wine. If only they could come up with an alcohol free Bourbon. Anything I do, I do to excess. Now, that would be Gatorade and fruit juice. Becky's motto for me is "Anything worth doing is worth over doing." I wished that history applied to successful ventures.

Chapter 56

Last Chance

Next on the Agenda for the NFL and NCAA, and therefore Pure-Pro, would be the inevitable "Pay to Play" Name, Image and Likeness (NIL) legislation. They were reluctant. It was inevitable in our minds. We never gave up on the Tour, just put it on hold. They had been dodging it for years. The mommies were a force and the sonnies were diversifying on their orders, so <u>no more football</u> unless sonny has some skin in the game. Better to face up to it now and give a little than wait it out and lose a lot. The high schools were already hemorrhaging. It had to be legislated federally or the inevitable state legislation, different in every state, would prevail. You could ultimately have fifty different standards blowing recruiting and competition to hell. The Federal legislation was our target.

July 17, 2020

The Honorable Mike Dewine
Governor, State of Ohio
77 South High Street, 30th Floor
Columbus, OH 43215

Dear Governor Dewine:

Wednesday's address to Ohioans regarding Coronavirus control was exemplary and effective in achieving its objective of alerting Ohioans that their fate is in their hands if they simply follow the guidelines you have put in place until that goal is achieved. The tenor was perfect, no scolding, not "BEGGING," as so reported in Thursday's *The Columbus Dispatch*, just a simply folksy "Fireside Chat" given in July. Best of all no threats. Very effective and I think it will get the job done. Congrats.

I'm a former political consultant/lobbyist (from the Rhodes Administration until about 2005) and we've crossed paths several times along the way. About 15 years ago I contracted a Neurological Disease (Inherent Neuropathy) that is both degenerative and incurable and was forced to change paths. Together with some old friends and former fellow athletes we formed the internet company Pure-Pro Products, LLC (www.pureproductsllc.com) which markets safety products to the GSA market. Turns out now most of us have neurological diseases and are incapacitated, as well (Bob Knight, Paul Hornung), but my mind is largely unaffected so I'm the Chairman (Dewey Stokes is also a member; we were together the last time we met). Together several years ago we designed a fundraising mechanism (based on Pelotonia) that fully deployed could raise billions of dollars for neurological research to find a cure for Dementia, Alzheimer's, ALS, Parkinson's, etc. by utilizing the NCAA, the NFL, the Veterans' Administration, the Networks and all the respective sponsors in an annual event that has already been vetted by the NFL Hall of Fame.

Critical to this and to where you could be of assistance should you so choose, a bill being sponsored by Congressmen Anthony Gonzalez and Steve Stivers (but written largely by us) is being introduced next week (07/21) in the House. A critical clause in the bill, which involves establishing guidelines for the national "Pay for Play" law to take effect next year, is that 3% of all monies paid to both players and schools by agents or companies be set aside to fund either research or an event to promote research for a cure of neurological diseases (of which there are currently none).

Now, as you know, Gonzalez is a freshman and Stivers a bit of a pariah (2018 election) and we are going to need a lot more legislative clout to get this approved and advanced, especially in an election year with so much at stake. Others in our company are pursuing stronger sponsorship but I'm concerned about holding up my end as chairman. Anything you could do or even suggest would be most appreciated. Neurological Diseases are the fastest growing killers in the world with no known cure and many of these colleges have research centers that could perform but for lack of funding. Many others have given up.

Based on your experience and access over a long and distinguished career in both Washington and Ohio and on the merits of our objective and its prospective impact, as well as being an Ohio company I would hope you'd see fit to provide the assistance and direction at your disposal to make our objective a reality. Please let me know at your earliest convenience.

Respectfully,

Dan Clevenger, Chairman
PURE-PRO PRODUCTS, LLC
614-459-8827
614-288-1062 (cell)
Email: dclev@columbus.rr.com
www.pureproductsllc.com

I didn't care what the final Federal bill mandated, so long as three percent of every dollar paid from the payors whoever they may be, to the players, prospective athletes or schools would be set aside to be placed in our foundation, "The Hall of Fame Legacy Foundation to Fund Neurological Research" to prevent and find cures for neurological diseases. The distribution of these funds, billions of dollars over the years, would be determined by a select board of NCAA University researchers. Pure-Pro

Products, LLC would get a share of five percent of the three. Since I had skin in the game and couldn't actively lobby, an associate of mine, unconnected to Pure-Pro, knew of two Ohio Republican Congressmen Alex Gonzales and our own Congressman Steve Stivers (whom I knew), who could sponsor the bill, which they did. I was told our three percent clause was included, by a trusted ally acting in our behalf.

Since ours would likely be the only research clause in any of the bills introduced and we already had our Foundation lined up, things looked good. Gonzales had played football at Ohio State and his father had played at Michigan. Alex then played for ten seasons with the Indianapolis Colts. He had been one of Peyton Manning's favorite targets. Since Peyton was up for induction into the Hall of Fame in their 2021 class we figured him for interest in promoting our bill when it came up. He had already shown those inclinations, having had Alex as a guest on his television show showing Peyton around the U.S. Capitol. It was well done and received.

Because of the 2020 "Election" and the resultant transition and, of course, the Pandemic primarily, there has thus far been no federal legislation activity on the 2021 bill. I can't be involved, since I am an interested party and my conduit and I have "parted company." Current status, uncertain. It should and could stand on its own, but this is politics and my conduit breached my trust. I have no idea of its status and Stivers just retired.

Even if our Hall of Fame proposal was accepted, the Inaugural Tour for the Cure would have fallen victim to the Pandemic, last year and this. It's too late now. The new regime, unless stopped, will ruin sports. It is one of their goals. Taxes will be so high as to render attendance unaffordable and the economy will founder. Television had done such a bang up job on its game presentations that the average fan won't miss what he can no longer afford and ticket prices, no longer affordable, are unlikely to be lowered, as the teams took a bath last year. They will want to make it up and won't be able to. The player pool will diminish throughout until "Pay for Play" passes federally, which now fewer of the "partners" can afford. The new administration couldn't care less. You will never hear anything about this in the media. Everything will be peaches and cream or Trump's fault as our country founders.

With the Pandemic and the Chinese embargo, the GSA market for our vests was put on pause, even though now access to a source had been resolved by the addition of two great guys interested in the GSA product market in America's private sector: Tim Cline and Mills Hawkins, both former collegiate athletes. But even they were back and forth on how secure those Chinese sources were and they had a man in China. I couldn't see a resolution in my lifetime, only further deterioration. We disbanded Pure-Pro Products, LLC as of 12/31/2020. A colossal failure.

The only thing we had left was the Foundation. If our Pay to Play legislation ever passed, 95% of the 3% would have gone to research. If we were recognized for our contribution, 5% of the 3% would have gone to us. It was no longer likely to happen. I need to point out that the situation we found ourselves in with Pure-Pro is all on me. Had I not developed neuropathy I could have pulled it off. You had to have <u>presence</u> and that used to be my strength. For over fifteen years I had been "out of sight, out of mind" professionally. Gradually accepting it, hurting us all along. In my defense, my original skill set was what was needed. Each of my partners had their own and those were needed too, to a lesser degree until our company was fully functional, a status we never attained. True, every evolving set of circumstances was against us from the start. These are what successful companies deal with and overcome and we didn't. I couldn't. The one thing I will take from the experience on a positive note is my "Tour for the Cure" strategy was perfect. Representing my partners was my highest honor.

Chapter 57

A Skunk in the Woodpile

Cullen and Marsalka had both died but their brethren still stalked the earth and one of them was a fellow Michigander. I won't say "Michigan Man" because that connotes "honorable" and I don't intend to expose him either. Enough of the brethren already have his number. He never conned me. I can't prove he cheated me. He just always lied to me; guaranteed our three percent clause was an NIL Bill feature among many others. I liked him but I had liked Cullen and Marsalka too. I feel sorry for him. He is an alcoholic and needs to quit and reform his ways. He is currently desperate and delusional. It appears he cheated me, my partners and our Foundation out of a large sum of money, millions of dollars, on the <u>distribution</u> of some then desperately needed Pandemic products. I had arranged a contact in his behalf and allegedly ours for a fifty-fifty percent split, our share to the Foundation with my distributor friend, by now a Fortune 100 company CEO in the healthcare field. Unbeknownst to me, my "ally" included his Hedge Fund Manager cohorts and excluded us. The Circle of Life huh? I just can't seem to come out ahead with Hedge Fund Managers involved. Or this guy.

There was absolutely no mention of our three percent clause in the Gonzalez NIL Bill summary. Even worse, since I had a vested interest in the NIL Pay to Play Bill sponsored by

Congressman Gonzalez, and was disabled besides, I couldn't legally lobby for its passage in Congress. I arranged through a formerly trusted intermediary for my to-be betrayer, who was an uninvolved third party, to represent our strategy to the congressman, which he said he did. He assured me that our three percent clause was a featured element. If it was, it would guarantee that the Gonzalez Bill would jump to the top of the options for passage. The NIL Bill summary showed there was no such clause mentioned. That clause was originally the only chance the Gonzales Bill had to be considered because Gonzales had heretofore been an underachieving freshman Republican legislator whose sponsor partner--was the more senior Republican Steve Stivers--had retired. Now his sponsoring partner is Democrat Emanual Cleaver, D-Mo. Then Gonzales voted to impeach Trump, gaining more Democrat support, but suspended his reelection campaign for 2022 after the backlash that caused. Our three percent clause, once a "guarantee," is nowhere to be found. Its inclusion would have assured the Bill's passage in the now Democratically controlled legislature. The Pandemic affect will blunt its impact anyway and sports as we have grown to know them will have a long time recovering. I challenge anyone to find a flaw in our three percent set-aside to fund neurological disease research element. It meant billions of dollars to the cause.

What I missed most because of my disability was going to the Michigan games on Saturday with my family and friends and seeing all the guys and their families. It never lost its charm. We would go from our lot on Main Street across to the old press box to see many friends, then over to the M Club lot to Brownie's, maybe George Pomey's. It was always great to see my longtime friend Tom Parkhill, who I have been close to for nearly sixty years, like the dozens of others. Not so much now, so I hear. I used to go to both the basketball and football reunions just to check in and connect. Some so successful; others so stricken, most in between. Good Ole Boys. Michigan Men.

My life now is my family and in that I was truly blessed. All healthy and fit and close. Logan and Laura were fifteen minutes away in their first home in Westerville and still are in Powell. Two wonderful boys. Becky has friends she can vacation with and I have in my house a Rogue Echo Bike and my scooter for nice days when I traverse the neighborhood greeting the dogs, kids and their parents. Some used to stay away because of my MAGA hat I always wear. Not now. I would like to get one of Starling's Tug Boat horns but it won't fit on my scooter. I tell the kids fishing in the pond at the park next door that there's an alligator in the pond—eats a kid a week.

Robin Perry just passed and I talked with his wife Linda. Called old friends John Walker, Skip Hildebrand and Gary Kane to be sure they knew. I will have to check in on Ted Forbes, it's been a long time. Petroff and Kroll died years ago. Kroll wanted his ashes scattered in Thunder Bay near his birthplace Alpena, with a farewell toast. Kane and Robin did the honors. They rented a boat and bought a twelve pack of Kroll's favorite Tecate. Half a mile out they realized they had Tecate Lite and had to return to get the high-test. Principles, man. I was supposed to be there but they held up my end.

I talk to Parky a lot and he catches me up daily on his email chain. More and more of the guys and their successors are stricken with the curse of neurological diseases. I was lucky to get the one I got because my mind still somewhat functions. I am still a burden and that's my shame. I wanted to finish this book and I just did. A lot of dear friends from my past haven't been attended to yet because they just didn't fit into the flow of the saga. I will pay them tribute in the Wrap-Up Section, as many as come to mind. I'll forget some, sorry, my bad. I am going for a scooter ride now, maybe run into Shemy. Go Blue! Later Logan is going to bring the boys over.

FOOD FOR THOUGHT: Several pages previously I referred to an email from Stephen Ross to me and other alumni seeking a contribution to help him achieve HIS goal for our Alma Mater. HE ended up raising $8 Billion for Michigan, $1.5 Billion of it HIS. Yet my request for his attention to a solution to saving HIS BUSINESS gets ignored. So we're even. Ha! Now the Michigan Business School, number one in the country, is called simply The Ross School. When in December 2019 he had a fundraiser in his house in New York for Donald Trump's reelection campaign, Michigan officials started a campaign to have the Ross name taken off the Business School. Uh huh. Hang on.

I have beaten my last dead horse.

(A) Pure-Pro Night Safety Illuminated Vest

(B) Pure-Pro Night Safety Illuminated Vest

(A) Pure Pro ProBack

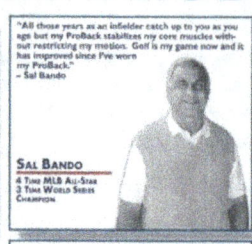

B) Pure-Pro ProBack

HALL OF FAME MARKETING	**PURE-PRO PRODUCTS, LLC** www.pureproductsllc.com	WORLDWIDE DISTRIBUTION

Dan Clevenger, Chairman
PURE-PRO PRODUCTS, LLC.
614-459-8827
614-288-1062 (cell)
Email: dclev@columbus.rr.com
www.pureproductsllc.com

Chairman and Co-Founder of Pure-Pro Products, LLC based in Columbus, OH and Ann Arbor, MI. Started in 2008 by a select group of longtime friends and former athletes, some of Hall of Fame status, after their retirements from their respective careers looking for an outlet to pursue a venture together to benefit the general public as well as themselves on a grand scale. Mr. Clevenger was an economics major and varsity basketball player at the University of Michigan and later an Amphibious Reconnaissance specialist in the Marines. Upon discharge he returned to Detroit where he got into sports broadcasting and marketing for Detroit's professional sports teams until 1978 when he was lured to Columbus to participate in a gubernatorial campaign, later aborted, and, having had a thirteen term congressman (Ohio's Cliff Clevenger) in the family, decided to stay and establish his own career as a political consultant/ lobbyist/ investment advisor until 2008 when after a wave of sports injuries began to take their toll and after repeated surgeries and an ultimate diagnosis of Inherent Neuropathy, a neurological progressive, debilitating disease, non-fatal but with no known cure forced him to the sidelines physically. Similar neurological disorders influencing former peers of more serious consequence (Dementia, Alzheimer's, ALS, etc.) appeared on a consistent basis, some affecting the LLC membership itself. He decided to do something about it.

Pure-Pro's featured product is an LED illuminated Night Safety™ vest, championed by our associate Bob Knight (www.pureproductsllc.com), which we market primarily in the GSA market. FEMA thinks it's the best nighttime safety product in the world and AAA feels it's the best outside promotional product available.

Dementia is the fastest growing killer in the world with no known cure, followed by Alzheimer's and ALS and many pharmaceutical companies have even suspended research. That's what they used to say about cancer until ten years ago when a group of cancer survivors in Columbus started Pelotonia, a bicycle tour of the state one weekend a year, which has raised nearly $200,000,000 with primarily grass roots efforts in ten years and cures are being found repeatedly.

614-459-8827 • FAX 614-459-8755 • 1490 Lafayette Dr., Ste. A • Columbus, OH 43220-6802

(A) Pure-Pro Clevenger Bio

Page Two

The Neurological diseases affect primarily athletes (football) and Veterans, that's the NFL, NCAA and the federal government (VA), and they have no such events and have put very little effort in place. They have billions set aside to do so if they had the vehicle and incentive. Well, Pure-Pro does and we are putting it in place. It would involve the NFL Hall of Fame, the Ohio Health Foundation and Pure-Pro doing a Pelotonia type "The Tour for the Cure" event only putting the Event's logo and its primary sponsors' logo on our vests above our LED lighting, not only on the days of the Event but on every other day of the year when the riders train, see this link https://www.youtube.com/watch?v=GQVHvDLg7MU. Progressively, Events would spread throughout the League.

Think of the sponsorship millions available—the NFL, NCAA, their sponsors, the Networks, their sponsors. Our goal is to raise $1,000,000,000 by year three. There is much more to say if you are interested. In place, I believe the President would love this. This can literally salvage the NFL's tarnished image. Hopefully you can share our vision and assist us.

(B) Pure-Pro Clevenger Bio

440

Dan Clevenger

From: Dan Clevenger [mailto:dclev@columbus.rr.com]
Sent: Saturday, August 18, 2018 3:38 PM
To: Jennifer Jehn (jjehn@dolphins.com) for Stephen Ross; Annette Howe for Ford CEO Jim Hackett (thowe14@FORD.com)
Cc: Sara Donlon (for Congressman Stivers) (Sara.Donlon@mail.house.gov); Bret Adams (badams@adamspartnersltd.com)
Subject: Event Blueprint

https://www.10tv.com/article/pelotonia-10-years-strong-and-gaining-momentum

http://www.cantonrep.com/special/20180702/whos-who-on-hall-of-fame-staff

http://www.dispatch.com/news/20180816/new-national-veterans-memorial-will-open-at-end-of-october

Mr. Ross, Mr. Hackett:

    Hopefully my summaries afforded you a grasp of my concept and the links above a grasp of our prospective partners, at least initially. This is it for me and I intend for it to be the biggest thing of its kind ever done so it had to be a Michigan thing with an Ohio support base, just like it's always been, admit it or not. You two are the most influential Michigan Alumni and our guys and our friends add to the venture's credibility. Ohio Congressmen General Steve Stivers and Jim Jordan are honorable public servants and swamp busters that fight for their causes, not just provide good intentions, and we hope will be our liaisons to the president, who is critical to our success. Additionally, the Pro Football Hall of Fame is in Canton, the National Veterans' Memorial and Museum will have its Grand Opening here in Columbus on October 27th and the Ohio Health Foundation is here in Columbus, as well. Incidentally, Ohio is the only state that does not have a State Plan to promote our cause—yet. Once ours is in place it will.

    Michigan also offers current Hall of Fame Dan Dierdorf (when he's able) and certain inductees Charles Woodson and Tom Brady as Honorary Chairmen of the Inaugural Event of the "The Tour for the Cure of Dementia, Alzheimer's and ALS," probably in the early summer of 2020. I would advocate a Pelotonia (see link above) type event with teams from Buffalo, Detroit, Cleveland, Pittsburgh, Cincinnati and Indianapolis starting off with an event launch at the team headquarters of each city, biking to Canton over two days with a huge event in Canton some weeks prior to the annual Hall of Fame game.

    Each team would hire a professional Event Planner to plan and promote collaboratively their respective event and each rider would purchase one of our LED vests https://www.youtube.com/watch?v=GQVHvDLg7MU with the Cause and Respective sponsors logos and sell others. Pelotonia itself has close to 10,000 riders each year and they have nowhere near the promotional tools of the NFL, the NCAA, the VA, the Networks, our sponsors, theirs, year around in all their venues. Ultimately it's all in three things: planning, promotion and WHO asks for the money. Nobody is going to give me a damn dime, no matter the cause. Every team should have an Honorary Event Chairman of considerable fame who coordinates the fundraising efforts in each city. Also, as I've said previously, if you superimpose the map of each NFL and NCAA power conference over the map of our prime Neurological Research Centers there's one in over half. Plus, every state has a Health Foundation. Pelotonia was founded ten years ago by cancer survivors and has raised nearly $200,000,000. We don't have survivors. But we will be starting out with mega-corporations, media giants and the most popular sport in America with desperate need for a solution to the problem we target.

1

Event Blue Print Email

Dan Clevenger

From: Stephen M. Ross and Richard Rogel [victorsformichigan@umich.edu]
Sent: Thursday, October 04, 2018 9:37 AM
To: Dan Clevenger
Subject: U-M breaks $5B fundraising record

We are thrilled to share terrific news with all who donated to the Victors for Michigan campaign.

President Mark Schlissel announced this morning that the University of Michigan has shattered records as the first public university to raise **$5 billion** in the most successful fundraising campaign of its history, including **$1.1 billion** for our students. Every single gift has made a collective impact toward this remarkable achievement.

While we still have three months left in the campaign, this is truly a moment to celebrate. Thank you again for your support of the university and its mission.

Stephen M. Ross
Chair, Victors for Michigan campaign

Richard Rogel
Co-Chair, Victors for Michigan campaign

Contact   Privacy   Unsubscribe
© 2018 The Regents of the University of Michigan

Ross--UM Breaks $5 B fundraising record email

Dan Clevenger

From: Lindesmith, Pat [Pat.Lindesmith@profootballhof.com]
Sent: Tuesday, June 18, 2019 1:45 PM
To: Dan Clevenger
Subject: Re: A Brief Summary of the Campaign Order

Dan,

I truly appreciate your detailed thoughts and information and passion to make a difference. As I've shared with you in our conversations, the Pro Football Hall of Fame is working in many areas to establish a HOF Health organization. I have forwarded all of your materials to a consultant that is helping us in this area. Once we have fully vetted the opportunity we will be back in touch with you to determine next steps.

Best Regards,

PAT LINDESMITH
CHIEF PARTNERSHIP OFFICER & SENIOR VICE PRESIDENT OF GOLD JACKET RELATIONS
D: 330-588-3632   C: 330-327-4892
Pat.Lindesmith@ProFootballHOF.com
Tickets | Shop | Facebook| Twitter | Instagram
Honor the Heroes of the Game, Preserve its History, Promote its Values & Celebrate Excellence EVERYWHERE

Lindesmith Hall of Fame Email

NFL, NCAA team up for safety improvements

The Associated Press

INDIANAPOLIS — The NFL's top medical experts are asking college football physicians and trainers to help make the game safer. They want the NCAA to pitch in, too.

Dr. Allen Sills and Jeff Miller, the NFL's executive vice president for health and safety initiatives, spent Monday and Tuesday in Indianapolis sharing data about their findings on the prevention and treatment of injuries. It's the most formal presentation league executives have had with college officials, and Sills and Miller hope this presentation leads to a broader conversation that includes discussions about lower-body injuries.

"We're able to show them what we're working on and what we're finding and how we're applying that knowledge into the day-to-day care of professional athletes," Sills told The Associated Press during a break. "I think we hope this is the start of even more regular interaction between the two organizations because we share the exact same goals, which is improving the health and safety of players."

The two-day meeting included participants from the NFL's health and safety team, the NCAA's Sport Science Institute and medical staffs from schools in each of the power five conferences. It comes amid a rapidly evolving landscape of injuries in football. Sills is the league's chief medical officer.

Over the past decade, Miller estimates the NFL made between 50 and 60 rules changes to enhance player safety. Members of the league's competition committee now routinely contact the medical team before considering making additional changes.

Plus, as Sills and Miller have collected more data they found NFL coaches and players increasingly receptive to their recommendations and conclusions.

Players, they say, are asking more questions about equipment, such as helmets. Coaches and assistant coaches, they add, have shown greater interest in how they can reduce the number of injuries at practices.

NFL, NCAA team up for safety improvement

Brand expert Bezos helps build media company

NFL aims for $25B in revenue by 2027

By Scott Soshnick and Eben Novy-Williams
Bloomberg News

NFL executive Brian Rolapp has an old photo on a wall of his office. It shows a group of prep-school football fans so captivated by a game that they ignore a building engulfed in flames behind them.

"Without exaggeration, it sits in a place where I look at it every day," said Rolapp, the chief media and business officer for the National Football League.

For years, pro football has inspired that kind of passion in millions of fans. The NFL generated about $15 billion this past season, making it the king of U.S. sports. And the league is about to lean even harder on its fans, aiming to boost its annual revenue to $25 billion by 2027. That might test the limits of a sport grappling with shifting TV habits and controversies surrounding brain injuries and the national anthem.

But tailwinds could help the NFL and commissioner Roger Goodell achieve their growth targets. The spread of legalized sports betting across the U.S. promises to lock in fans and keep them riveted to games. Tech companies such as Amazon and Facebook, meanwhile, have emerged as bidders for big-dollar broadcast packages.

"Roger's aspirational target of $25 billion is starting to look pretty good," said Marc Ganis, a sports consultant who advises the NFL and a number of its owners on business strategies.

According to the league, NFL regular-season games, excluding those played in London, averaged 15.8 million viewers. Moreover, 45 of the top 50 telecasts this season were NFL games. The AFC championship game, in which the New England Patriots defeated the Kansas City Chiefs to advance to the Super Bowl, drew almost 54 million viewers.

That's more than double the number of people who watched the Macy's Thanksgiving Parade or the 2018 Oscars.

"There's nothing left in media that will aggregate that many people," Rolapp said.

Just how valuable NFL games are to the broadcast networks and digital newcomers such as Amazon and Facebook will determine whether the commissioner hits his revenue target.

The NFL reaps about $5 billion a year from its TV contracts with CBS, NBC, Fox and ESPN. All indications are that the league will get a lot more when the contracts expire after the 2021-22 season.

Ganis, the consultant, expects the league's next TV deals to yield increases in excess of 50 percent. On top of that, he expects that a new billion-dollar package of games will go to a digital distributor such as Amazon, which now pays $50 million a year to show "Thursday Night Football," which helped the league boost online viewing by 86 percent.

Online executives aren't the only ones clamoring for a tie-up with the most visible and valuable U.S. sports league.

When Papa John's and the league ended their relationship after the company's former CEO blamed player protests for sliding sales, it took the NFL just 24 hours to announce a new, bigger deal with Yum Brands' Pizza Hut.

More widely, the NFL has added seven leaguewide partners since January, including its first casino partner, Caesars Entertainment, and its first presenting sponsor for the conference title games, Intuit. The NFL and its clubs brought in a record $1.32 billion in sponsorships in 2017-18, according to consulting firm IEG, significantly more than the National Basketball Association or Major League Baseball.

That doesn't count the league's newest partners, including home-improvement giant Lowe's, which chose the NFL after exiting a 17-year relationship with NASCAR.

"Let's face it: The NFL is dominant," Lowe's Chief Marketing Officer Jocelyn Wong said. "It's the largest, most avid fan base. That was very important to us."

NFL commissioner Roger Goodell has said his goal is to increase the NFL's revenue from $15 billion to $25 billion by 2027, an aspiration that seems more attainable when considering broadcasting deals, sponsorships and still-strong viewership.
(DAVID J. PHILLIP/THE ASSOCIATED PRESS)

NFL aims for $25 B in revenue by 2027

MEET THE PEOPLE BUILDING JOHNSON CONTROLS HALL OF FAME VILLAGE

St. Pierre ties LEGACY Global to Hall of Fame

By Tim Botos
The Canton Repository
GateHouse Media Ohio

LEGACY Global Sports was less than an enigma when Pro Football Hall of Fame President David Baker was introduced to them.

It was during the Super Bowl XLVII festivities in 2014. The game itself wasn't much of an event; the Seahawks pounded the Broncos 43-8 at MetLife Stadium in New Jersey.

"He'd never heard of us," recalled LEGACY Global Chief Executive John St. Pierre.

Not surprising.

The company is involved in everything from running lacrosse and hockey tournaments to creating films to spotlight young athletes for college coaches and recruiters.

"We're probably one of the largest, fastest-growing companies no one has ever heard of," St. Pierre said.

The company employs 450 people worldwide and boasts of being involved in events that featured a combined one million young athletes.

They also became the first outside business to partner with the Pro Football Hall of Fame on Johnson Controls Hall of Fame Village project, following discussions after that first encounter. The idea was to bring athletes from across the world to Canton.

The sports complex, which currently features five multipurpose turf fields south of Tom Benson Hall of Fame Stadium, has served as a worthy site for soccer, lacrosse, rugby and football events.

More than 130,000 athletes, family members and fans visited last year, with 80 percent of them from outside Ohio, according to information provided by officials at the Hall of Fame. This year, the Hall expects as many as 170,000 people through 40 events, camps and leagues.

Among the large draws are the Pro Football Hall of Fame Academy, where attendees can receive coaching, skills training and character development from some of the top names in football, and a World Youth Football Championship in December.

"That's 26,000 hotel room nights this year," said Pete Fierle, chief of staff and vice president of communications at the Hall of Fame. "LEGACY Global Sports is a worldwide leader."

St. Pierre played college hockey at the University of Southern Maine. After college, he moved to Chicago to work as a general manager at FirstService Franchise Corp. In the late 1990s, he was an executive for the internet company handymanonline.com, then at worldatmydoor.com before co-founding LEGACY Global Sports.

"The national youth sports market is worth $15 billion a year now," he said. "For a long period of time, the industry was very fragmented ... what has changed over the year is the expectations of parents. They want to get top quality at top value."

LEGACY Global was founded almost by accident. It began 15 years ago, when St. Pierre and two others helped a youth hockey team organize and create an itinerary for a trip to Sweden.

From there, the company expanded into other sports, including basketball. Along the way, it has purchased existing organizations, leaving the names intact, but taking over the operations.

St. Pierre ties LEGACY Global to Hall of Fame

The Columbus Dispatch 11/19/2021

Pelotonia cyclists raise $20 million

Pelotonia participants ride past the Ohio Statehouse on Aug. 7. The race returned to its in-person format this year after being held virtually in 2020 because of the pandemic. NICOLAS GALINDO/COLUMBUS DISPATCH

Monroe Trombly Columbus Dispatch | USA TODAY NETWORK

Pelotonia announced Friday that it raised nearly $20 million this year for cancer research.

That's almost double as much as the previous year, when COVID-19 forced the nonprofit to cancel its annual bike ride and introduce a virtual platform.

The haul represents a return to normal for Pelotonia. The bike ride fundraiser, which started in 2008 and resumed an in-person event this year, generated more than $23 million in 2019 but dipped to $10.5 million in 2020.

In August, more than 6,000 people signed up to participate in rides of varying lengths, while nearly 4,000 more participated virtually, according to Doug Ulman, the chief executive officer of Pelotonia and three-time cancer survivor.

"Frankly, this community over the last 13 years

"One of the biggest things we learned from last year was that even if you take the pandemic out of the equation, people want to be able to participate in a way that's meaningful to them."

Doug Ulman Chief executive officer of Pelotonia

has been so generous, and when you go through a situation like the pandemic, you're really not in

See CYCLISTS, Page 12A

Pelotonia cyclists raise $20 M

Why Householder kept job amid bribery charges

Jessie Balmert
Cincinnati Enquirer
USA TODAY NETWORK

Rep. Larry Householder, R-Glenford, was arrested in a $61 million bribery scheme. Other city council members accused of bribery have been suspended while Householder remains in place. FRED SQUILLANTE/COLUMBUS DISPATCH

COLUMBUS – Former Ohio House Speaker Larry Householder, three city council members from Cincinnati, four from Toledo and one from Cleveland all face criminal charges in connection with allegations of bribery and corruption on the job.

All are innocent unless proven guilty but only one, Householder, can't be suspended from his job under Ohio law.

State law allows Ohio Attorney General Dave Yost to file a request with the Ohio Supreme Court to suspend local officials accused of felonies related to their official duties. But that law doesn't apply to state lawmakers and other statewide elected officials.

Householder is accused of participating in a $61 million bribery scheme that helped elect him to lead the Ohio House of Representatives, pass a $1 billion bailout for nuclear plants and defend that law against a ballot initiative to block it.

"If the Legislature would like to give me the authority to go to the Supreme Court and suspend him (Householder), I'll do it the same day but I don't have that power," Yost said in a Tuesday interview.

How to remove an elected official

Yost has initiated or threatened to initiate suspensions against Cincinnati's P.G. Sittenfeld, Jeff Pastor and Tamaya Dennard, Cleveland's Ken Johnson and four Toledo councilmembers accused of trading their votes for bribes. In most cases, the officials resigned or agreed to the suspension.

If the process proceeds, a trio of judges reviews the circumstances and can suspend officials, even if they haven't been convicted of the offense. While suspended, officials can collect taxpayer-funded salaries.

The process doesn't apply to Householder as a state lawmaker. If Householder is found guilty, he would be forbidden from serving as a legislator because of the felony conviction. Absent a conviction, the Ohio Constitution allows House lawmakers to expel Householder with a vote of two-thirds of members for "disorderly conduct," a broad term that could cover Householder's alleged actions.

Speaker Bob Cupp, R-Lima, has asked Householder to resign, saying that would be "the honorable thing to do." But Cupp hasn't called for a vote to remove Householder, which would require 31 GOP "yes" votes in addition to 35 Democratic ones.

Householder doesn't have the same power in the 99-member Ohio House as a council member might on a nine-person panel, Yost said, but his vote can swing whether a bill passes or doesn't.

Would a change help?

Rep. Jeff Crossman, D-Parma, said he has considered a bill to expand Yost's authority to suspend state lawmakers as well, but that could raise concerns about the separation of powers.

Yost said that's a concern he shares, but one could argue that the Ohio Supreme Court's panel provides enough protection for state lawmakers against overreach from the executive branch: Yost's office.

"As a practical matter, the General Assembly is going to guard the right to decide whether to expel a member or not," Yost said. "They clearly have the ability to address the situation if they want."

Crossman said he wasn't sure if a suspension would adequately protect Householder's constituents anyway. "It's denying these folks representation."

"It's just a sad situation," Crossman said. "I wish the Republicans would step up and clean up this mess. They just haven't shown the willingness to do so."

Crossman plans to reintroduce a bill that prevents lawmakers charged with a public corruption offense from taking office. His prior proposal received no hearings last year.

Meanwhile, Householder is receiving an annual salary of $67,493 and introducing legislation to bring "checks and balances" to health orders.

No House Republican vote on expelling Householder yet

Jessie Balmert and Anna Staver
Cincinnati Enquirer
USA TODAY NETWORK

COLUMBUS – After a three-hour meeting Tuesday, House Republicans decided not to immediately remove former leader Rep. Larry Householder, but deliberations continue.

Householder, of Glenford, is accused of racketeering in connection with a nearly $61 million bribery scheme to elect him to lead the Ohio House, pass a $1 billion nuclear ballot and defend that law against a ballot initiative to block it. He has pleaded not guilty.

House Republicans met for the first time as a group Tuesday to discuss whether Householder should be removed. The expulsion process, spelled out in the Ohio Constitution, requires 66 lawmakers to "punish its members for disorderly conduct."

The Ohio House comprises 35 Democrats and 64 Republicans, though it's unlikely Householder would vote to remove himself. That means Republicans need at least three Democrats to support expelling Householder but can likely count on many more.

House Republicans hold a variety of views on removing Householder, ranging from vehemently supporting expulsion to wanting to keep him in the chamber. Householder himself has said removing him would be "unprecedented" and "subvert the will of 31,000 local citizens" who elected him in November.

Rep. Larry Householder, R-Glenford, won't be removed by House Republicans yet. FRED SQUILLANTE/COLUMBUS DISPATCH

Those disparate views played out in Tuesday's meeting, which Green Township Rep. Bill Seitz called a "very civil and spirited discussion." Householder attended. House Republicans didn't plan to vote to remove Householder Wednesday, but the option is still on the table, said GOP lawmakers involved in the discussions.

Democrats could try to force a vote on the House floor once again, but it will not pass without Republican support. On Monday, Reps. Jeff Crossman, D-Parma, and Michele Lepore-Hagan, D-Youngstown, introduced a bill that would require lawmakers to reimburse the state for money they received in between an indictment and felony conviction for public corruption.

A spokeswoman for Speaker Bob Cupp did not respond to questions Wednesday morning about next steps.

THE COLUMBUS DISPATCH MARCH 19, 2021

No House Repub vote on expelling Householder yet

THE COLUMBUS DISPATCH MARCH 21, 2021

Journalists, family member differ over Neil Clark's lobbyist legacy

Capitol Insider
Darrel Rowland
Columbus Dispatch
USA TODAY NETWORK

It's hard for many state government veterans to believe that Neil Clark, the man who personified the term "super-lobbyist," is gone, due to an apparent suicide.

He will be remembered for both his effectiveness and ruthlessness in Ohio politics – especially when the Republican joined former Ohio Democratic Chairman Paul Tipps in forming the independent lobbying firm State Street Consultants. The powerhouse duo's association eventually dissolved in a nasty legal battle.

Clark

Clark's place in state history is assured by two things: His involvement in the 1990s "pancaking" scandal when illegal multiple honorariums were paid to legislators, and his federal indictment last year in connection with a $60 million effort to boost the political resurrection of former House Speaker Larry Householder and subsidize Ohio's two nuclear power plants. Both Clark and Householder pleaded not guilty.

But Jeff Mullen, whose wife Diane is a sister of Clark's widow Colleen, said Clark's obituary accurately cites his "unexpected acts of kindness and generosity to strangers. He paid medical bills, bought groceries, gave money, clothing and goods to people who needed help."

Mullen, who lives in Holmes County, recalled the effort Clark would put into making intricate mosaics.

"He would really look into the soul of someone or something and try to portray it. He gave me and Diane a present of a mosaic of our choosing two Christmases ago, but he had to abandon all that when he was indicted. His art was really good, and from his heart."

"In the end, he had none of the riches that would accompany a crook. Now look around."

'He had power'

Mary Anne Sharkey, who headed the Cleveland Plain Dealer's Columbus bureau during Clark's rise to power in the 1980s, recalled that he "did not mind being called a rogue or an influence peddler or a backroom operator, all apt descriptions, as long as the story or headline included the word 'powerful.'

"He reveled in his bad boy image and bragged his Sicilian father was in the Cleveland mob as a way of asserting street cred. ... Whether people praise him or not, Neil was powerful through prolific campaign contributions, browbeating of legislators and bureaucrats, and command of the legislative and budget process.

"And he had power – more than the House speaker, more than the Senate president, and more than any other lobbyist on Capitol Square."

Cutting deal with Householder

Clark was a kingmaker as well as a lobbyist, says Lee Leonard, who covered the legislature for more than three decades with The Dispatch and UPI.

"He helped negotiate a deal that prevented a terrific battle for House speaker (in the early 2000s) between Larry Householder and Bill Harris when a vacancy opened. Sen. Dick Schafrath (former Ohio State and Cleveland Browns lineman) was persuaded to resign so Harris, a representative from Ashland, could move to the Senate and Householder could be speaker. Harris became Senate president and we all know what happened to Householder."

Leonard also noted that "Schafrath originally got to the Senate because the Senate Republicans, with Neil involved, wanted to keep state Rep. Tom Van Meter (also from Ashland) from returning to the Senate, where he brought a fighting conservative view and sometimes disrupted things.

"The Senate GOP leaders wanted to work with Democrats to get things done at that time. 'Nothing in the legislative process goes through if you stomp your feet,' Clark said at the time. So they backed Schafrath in the primary and he won."

Willing to enrich lawmakers

Mike Curtin, who covered the Statehouse as Dispatch public affairs editor before become Dispatch editor, associate publisher and a two-term state representative, said the rise of Tipps and Clark as independent lobbyists coincided with the explosion of money in legislative politics.

"Tipps and Clark recognized the value of being rainmakers. Not only representing high-end clients in search of inside track access at the Ohio General Assembly, but making sure these high-end clients understood the importance of being leading contributors to assure (Democratic Speaker Vernal G. Riffe Jr.'s) and (GOP Senate President Stanley J. Aronoff's) continued leadership.

"Unfortunately, Vern and Stan grew to enjoy too much the good life. Tipps and Clark understood these vulnerabilities and took advantage of them. They not only helped raise big bucks for the (legislative) caucus funds, but they helped enrich Vern and Stan personally. The pancaking scandal is the example that got the most attention from the press, and helped lead to the downfall of both leaders"

"Neil and Paul were the foremost examples of independent lobbyists willing not only to push the ethical boundaries of lobbying, but to bust right through those boundaries," Curtin said.

"The need for ever-larger amounts of money in the system, combined with the willingness of lobbyists like Tipps and Clark to use their old friendships with legislative leaders to enrich their political funds and to enrich them personally, is what led to the current state of affairs, and to Neil's tragic end."

Journalist, family member differ over Neil Clark's lobbyist legacy

HOUSE OF REPRESENTATIVES

UNDER THE SPONSORSHIP OF

REPRESENTATIVE C. ALLISON RUSSO
HOUSE DISTRICT 24

On behalf of the members of the House of Representatives of the 134th General Assembly of Ohio, we are pleased to extend special recognition to

DAN CLEVENGER

on the occasion of your Eightieth Birthday, August 6, 2021.

Your birthday is a time to reflect on the many and varied events of your life and to take pride in your numerous achievements and your contributions to the world around you. Indeed, you can look upon your life with great satisfaction, for you have readily shared your energy and enthusiasm with your family, friends, and community and have enriched the lives of all who know you.

The hopes and dreams, joys and challenges contained in your life experiences have continually enhanced your personal growth, and you are truly deserving of high praise for giving of your time and abilities far beyond what was required or expected. Diligent and painstaking in all of your endeavors, you can be proud of your tremendous record of accomplishment and of your tireless efforts in behalf of others.

Thus, with sincere pleasure, we wish you a very happy birthday and salute you as an outstanding Ohioan.

C. ALLISON RUSSO
REPRESENTATIVE
HOUSE DISTRICT 24

ROBERT R. CUPP
SPEAKER
OHIO HOUSE OF REPRESENTATIVES

State of Ohio Award (80th Birthday)

FINAL SUMMARY

Chapter 58

The Final Fate

The following documents confirm our quest, a noble endeavor come up short. I hope all my predictions don't come true for our future generations. A helluva thing to come up short on your last professional effort, especially one so critical. The timing initially perfect, rendered it unachievable at the end which is why I fear for our future. Our own country harvested the obstacles and our enemies will pounce.

I will stick to the one thing I excel at, being a good Grandpa. Bring 'em on! Does surviving a saga make me a sage? May God watch over us.

The Final Irony—From the beginning if I had gotten everything I wanted from everyone I asked along the way at precisely the time I asked regarding the "Tour for the Cure" our Inaugural Event would have fallen on the NFL's Centennial Celebration. And of course that was just as the Pandemic Lockdown began. I still had the touch. Fate had stacked the deck.

REGRETS

Throughout this account of my life experiences I have accentuated that I have always spoken for myself when representing opportunities that would benefit those targeted by what I offered. That was simply because they and I had the most at stake. I didn't want anyone else representing me making the presentation, nor did I wish to speak with anyone not making the decisions. I had a reputation to live up to, as you have read.

If you have read closely it becomes apparent that in the two biggest opportunities of my life and in the lives of millions of others, the presentations of what I proposed were made by others. I rationalized that my disability and my unfamiliarity with my targets put those others that I trusted in a better position to achieve my objectives. Please follow along closely now, learn from what I already knew. Attend to the most important things in your life your damn self and live with it. It is much easier than what I am faced with now. Never let others deliver your messages. And do it in person!

The first major mistake was me not personally making the "Tour for the Cure" presentation at the NFL Hall of Fame. I rationalized that Jeremy Hogue was a Healthcare Professional hired by the NFL to find a solution to the Neurological Disease rampage (primarily then, head injuries) threatening their sport's future. Maybe I was swayed by his very first words to me, "You don't have to sell me, I'm sold." Maybe I rationalized that on Hall of Fame Game weekend their agenda would be full and my attendance would undermine Jeremy's presentation, or maybe I was afraid I just didn't have it anymore. But he worked for them and they blew him off and his was a plumb job. I was an old cripple. For the foreseeable future there would always be players. Beyonce and J.Lo were on tap.

The second mistake was far worse and involved the NIL Legislation. Our 3% clause had no credible opposition, once explained, and would have raised billions for Neurological Disease research over time. And it would be a Federal Bill, rendering all those state bills null and void and positioning football as a healthcare savior. The media would lionize both Congress and the NFL.

Our landmark NIL Legislation was ostensibly presented to Ohio Congressman Anthony Gonzalez by a "trusted" ally who "loved its potential" and was actually enshrined in the same Ohio High School Sports Hall of Fame as Congressman Gonzalez (different eras). He assured me Gonzalez was "all in" and saw its potential. Since our Bill did more for Gonzalez than he, without it, could do for us, and since I couldn't lobby my own Bill to Congress, I trusted we were in good hands. Gonzalez would vote to impeach Trump after the Democrat led January 6th debacle and will not seek reelection in 2022.

I see no evidence to this day that Congressman Gonzalez ever even saw the Bill. It would've been his savior. Ours too.

Fool me once, fool me twice.

THE MISSING CHAPTER

I considered including this chapter much earlier in the Second Half section but didn't because it's a "shoulda, coulda, woulda" set of circumstances that ultimately didn't materialize. But it fits with the rest that did and is both funny and frightening. Maybe you had to be there and know the people but you have already run across a couple so here goes.

About five years after the Trailerboards experience and I was well established in Columbus, Russ Mook and I went to a preconference football game in Ann Arbor, alone, no entourage, just to get away, to see some ball and drink some beer. Russ and I had a connection that tended to bring out the worst in both of us. Why not tempt fate?

At halftime we ran into Tureaud who now had a "farm" between Ann Arbor and Saline for game day business purposes and had "branched out" his portfolio to include endeavors with Detroit based Motown. I knew all about Motown's "portfolio" from my days in Detroit--also Ken's hometown--and a caution button went off. Ken seemed already too "connected" to their products. He was having an Open House at the farm after the game and we were invited.

The game was a blowout and Russ and I arrived about 5:00 PM to a packed house. A huge pond with a lighthouse was central and a barbecue pit was turning out ribs and corn. I knew next to nobody but recognized many from the

Detroit streets and newscasts. I briefed Russ. I also hoped Ken had this under control, not vice versa as I feared.

Russ thought the whole thing needed some perspective and suggested some from the Lighthouse, about four stories high and currently vacant so I grabbed a six-pack and we ascended. About five minutes later, up came the Motown power base, all familiar to me but seemingly surprised by our presence. They had been chatting on the climb but went silent upon arrival. Five in all.

As usual, I interjected myself with a greeting that fell flat and changed my mood but did get a smile from Russ. That one. There was danger afoot. Russ slowly walked over to the edge and looked down, then over at them, still featuring his maniacal smile. I swear, the Lighthouse started ticking. Who were we? The main Motown honcho saw somebody down below he had to talk to. Down the ladder he went with two of them. The other two stayed, glaring at us. Russ looked over at me. I waited for him to laugh first. Then we both did. Ole Roosky. We pitched 'em. Splash!

That spring Bill Laskey told me he had run across Ken in the Lansing Airport seemingly hiding from someone, too busy even to speak. Later that summer, if memory serves me, Ken was killed in a mysterious car "accident" on his way home to the farm. That mystery remains unresolved.

There were a lot of these.

EPILOGUE

I don't lay claim that the way I chose to lead my life is a recipe. Retrospectively it was the right way for me because now given my set of circumstances I am a happy man. There must be a lot of people out there living in shame if they have a conscience. Think about the horror they have wreaked on their fellow men in the name of greed under the guise of the "greater good." I came as close to doing *my* best as *I* could have is how *I* rationalize it.

Here are several examples. When I first joined the Brown Campaign, on my downtime I became interested in the Ohio State University's Endowment Fund, if only to compare it to Michigan's. I was astounded at the disparity with the larger OSU's Fund *far* behind our own. I expected a disparity in UM's favor because of our Alumni Base relative to OSU but nowhere near the actual margin of ten to one. It didn't take much research to find out why—patronage. Political appointees (whom I knew) were running it and openly spending the principal which is statutorily illegal. When I made my findings known in the office, nobody said much, but the managers were quietly replaced months later. At that point I realized it was because of me.

Fast forward fifty years and now OSU has already allocated over a hundred million dollars to former athletes that claim they were abused by a former team doctor long dead over a generation ago as previously detailed. OSU is actually advertising for more claimants and the total will grow. The only sources of revenue I am aware of for a public institution are taxes and/or endowment fund donations If I am a resident or a prospective donor, I'm pissed. Because of me, through a conduit, I was a relevant factor in Michigan's limiting claims and payouts, then closing the door when responding to similar additional claims years after my time as a student athlete, settled last year. What taxpayers authorized this? Which donors? To freeloaders. What's that old word? Ah yes, dignity. Remember? Where is it? Taxes and donations aren't paying these freeloaders, the Deep State is. They're running our colleges.

Then revisit Pelotonia, $250,000,000 raised by cancer victims via grass roots methodology over thirteen years and through the Pandemic. What if OSU had joined in at the outset, or even now? Oh, they'll accept the money, after all, it sustains them. They have even approved the Event, praised it on occasion and have put the proceeds to good use. Many cures for cancer have resulted.

Yet the OSU Neurological Disease Hospital is next to discredited. I know because they have all but abandoned its salvation. The remaining doctors are my source of information. The ones they have hired from Michigan to revive it have left. Several years ago I tried to generate interest in the "Tour for the Cure" at the top and they (OSU) inquired of what my financial contribution would be. No need to elaborate further. I wasn't of a mood to pay to raise money to salvage their Hospital with my strategy. How was that rational?

These abuses of power are relevant here only because they involve me in a small way. Most of you readers could match or exceed them with experiences of your own. Think for a minute what our leaders have access to and of the schemes of empowerment at their disposal involving our deadliest enemies. Reflect on who constituted our leadership. What horrors await?

Finally, I spent three years trying to get a credible introduction and recommendation from the NFL to the Hall of Fame to introduce personally my "Tour for the Cure" solution to their acknowledged biggest problem, the prevention and cure of Neurological Diseases. They even sought out a leading medical expert to find the answer nationally, Jeremy Hogue, whom you have met. With all my connections to the NFL hierarchy, how would I finally connect to be able to present my strategy to the Hall of Fame, charged with the screening of options by the NFL?

The Columbus Crew is our professional Soccer Team with a considerable fan base and always looking for growth and expansion, especially since they have solidified ownership which was a problem in the past. The catalyst has been Dr. Pete Edwards, formerly the Team Doctor and now an owner, along with Jimmy and Dee Haslem who are also the principal owners of the NFL Cleveland Browns. Their goal is to maximize the Crew's potential in the Soccer World like the Haslems are doing with the Browns.

Dr. Edwards heads up an Orthopedic Medical Group less than two miles from where we live. Becky and I have frequently advantaged their services. Neither of us have utilized Dr. Edwards personally but many of his doctors have served us well. As a last resort I called Dr. Edwards and spoke with his receptionist. She asked me to drop off a summary of what I proposed and she would make sure he got it. I dropped one off making sure she would see I was disabled (hey, if you've got it flaunt it). A week went by and I hadn't heard so I called and she said he had forwarded it. Another week passed and I got a call from Pat Lindesmith of the Hall of Fame inviting me up to meet with Jeremy Hogue the next week. I wouldn't have to sell him he was sold.

Upon completion of this book I called Dr. Edwards to thank him. He couldn't recall his intervention. Busy man. I was forgotten about in three years. So much for immortality.

IN GRATITUDE

To Tom Van Arsdale for his Forward, lifelong friendship and introduction to Michael Daswick, who put this book in order, tolerating me all the way. He'll need some time off. And of course to Becky, enough said. Das's son Tyler provided the same for Tom's *Journey Man,* a journal of his illustrious career, a great read. I've got a barrel of commas to get rid of if anybody needs some. Both Tom and Das live in Phoenix and have the requisite mountain retreats for when it gets ungodly. Tom and his brother Dick are painters and their Van Arsdale's Arts Studio and Showroom is located in Scottsdale. Tom's done some work for us, a fine portrait of our last dog Digger. More to come. I have listened to Das as we have prepared *Fate Stacked the Deck* for distribution. I got to say what I wanted said because of the value my experiences with those included had on me. I tried to make it all fit. It was my journey.

To Michael Daswick, who should thank me for providing the challenge of his life.

To Catherine Adams, who cleaned up my manuscript and provided her experienced insight.

To new friends.

May God Bless you all.

Clev

A TRIBUTE TO PELOTONIA

My story was finished after the Final Summary and I segregate this because everything in my book, to the best of my recollection, actually occurred. The "Tour for the Cure" never did. Now never will. I have to at least set the stage.

Pelotonia not only occurred, it endured, overcame and matured (see attached articles) to established standard, by any status a monumental success. The Hall of Fame game is this week and nobody notices but Pelotonia's annual event is on the horizon and here in Columbus everybody is pumped.

From the start, Pelotonia originated in Columbus with the requisite launch events and teams of riders that paid dearly for the privilege to ride bicycles over routes spanning the state. They were greeted by crowds of supporters with complementary events of their own at various towns and cities along the way, Friday to Sunday. Originally each rider, largely cancer survivors, had a considerable quota to raise to qualify for the privilege to ride hundreds of miles to raise money to find cancer cures <u>if</u> they made their quotas. They formed teams to enhance their fundraising potential and had shirts made to identify their teams, all on their own advised by their founder. He was a fellow survivor whom I am now officially upgrading to GAH because what he organized and inspired was incredible. The money was there and they dug it out, year after year. Over $250,000,000 to date. He is long gone now but his successor is a visionary and an even better leader.

I tried to get in early on with our vests as you have read, but was rebuffed. Try as I might I couldn't let it go. As my disease progressed "The Tour for the Cure" became an obsession and I thought I had the connections at the top to make it happen. I juxtaposed the Pelotonia grass roots strategy to those at the top I thought I would have ready access to. Turns out I had the access but was rebuffed at every turn until I ran across Dr. Pete Edwards, whom I still haven't met. Go figure. Maybe soccer's not so bad.

I have attached a chart to make the distinctions between Pelotonia and the Tour obvious so I don't have to rebeat a dead horse. Both fully implemented there's no comparison. One was and is hugely successful and shortly will be again, with a bright future. The other never will be. One not only succeeded, it inspired a colossal failure that should have. Cancer will continue to find cures. Neurological diseases, the world's greatest killer, will continue their scourge uninterrupted with no cures in sight. Football, America's favorite sport, will suffer accordingly, along with the other problems they have got to face up to shortly, all self-inflicted.

So you go Pelotonia! Along with my family and friends you have inspired the Overtime section of my life and this book. Bottom line you did it. We couldn't.

	COMPARE	
Pelotonia (Bottom to Top)		**The Tour for the Cure** (Top to Bottom)
Started by 100 nameless cancer survivors from OSU Hospital		Started by the NFL Hall of Fame
		NFL Itself
		NCAA Colleges & Universities
Targets: Grass roots beginning door-to-door, small businesses, metropolitan area, city, state		Targets: Existing sponsors, Networks, their sponsors, governments, interested parties, affected parties, cities, states, fan base
After 13 years: $250,000,000 raised		Launch target: $1,000,000,000 raised

Doubling down: Pelotonia plans to increase fundraising to $50 million annually by 2026

Allison Ward
The Columbus Dispatch

Pelotonia plans to double its fundraising efforts over the next five years to $50 million annually for cancer research by the year 2026, the nonprofit group announced Wednesday.

The popular cycling event held every summer since 2009 raised $23 million in 2019. A virtual-only event brought in $10.5 million in 2020.

Without an in-person event to put on during the pandemic, Doug Ulman, Pelotonia's chief executive officer, said the organization was afforded the opportunity to really analyze where the nonprofit should be headed in the future.

A look back: Pelotonia tally drops in 2020, but CEO is 'ectastic' given the circumstances

"We took much of 2020 to do a strategic plan, which was an intense, deliberate process with our whole team," Ulman said. "We had the time and space to do a plan of where we wanted to be in five years."

That's at $50 million with hopes of being miles closer to Pelotonia's main mission of ending cancer.

Pelotonia leaders acknowledged that the high-dollar goal might be a stretch, but Ulman said they've already shaken up the leadership team, begun to identify new partners while strengthening relationships with existing ones, and considered adding other activities to Pelotonia's calendar besides August's cycling event in central Ohio.

Ulman will step down from his role as president of the organization to focus his efforts as CEO on cultivating those strategic relationships and partnerships locally and globally.

Joe Apgar, the current chief operating officer, has been promoted to president.

Pelotonia is in the process of adding four new positions, including a chief marketing officer, to grow its team from 14 to 18, which Ulman said is no small feat since the money for those positions does not come from the ride. One hundred percent of fundraising dollars go to Ohio State University's Comprehensive Cancer Center.

THE PERILS OF POLITICS

I had a life in politics but it never was my life, as you have read. For some it was. Neil Clark was the prototype lifer. His career was his life and it consumed him. Retrospectively, when we first met I think I could sense it. His era was beginning as my career was waning due to my illness and when Vern retired Neil took command and everything changed. No holds barred. But Neil wasn't the leader Vern was and his tactics emboldened the connivers and those consumed with ambition and greed. I am not going to go beyond that but Neil does in his autobiography *What Do I Know, I'm Just a Lobbyist*.

It's a tell all and a good read that will blow the lid off Ohio politics as soon as the proper protections are put in place. Don't mess with Neil. He knew when he wrote the book that is would set him free, that he was ready. He took his own life in an isolated area of Collier County, Florida as his book hit the market.

ADDITIONAL CAST OF CHARACTERS

Anne Chanay
My special Full Circle Girl, no better friend. Jesus awaits.

Bob (Pee Wee) and Karen Quarnstrom
Always special.

Don Corriere
"Putty" All American Wrestler, long time roomie, Mr. Discipline.

Paul Schmidt
Bohemo. Big old tackle would head up any cast of characters.

Mike Ehrenfried
A good friend and helluva hooper taken too soon.

Dick Schram
Scrotum, was far too big to Totem; a real sophisticate.

Buddah Birnbaum
The prototypical Jew and a helluva racquetballer.

Jim Zubkus
   A fleet end and a born Master of Ceremonies.

Pete and Mary Passink
   Two great friends; a super golfer and Mary, Bo's longtime Segundo.

Mike O'Neil
   Never studied for finals, never missed a class, the Uber student. Bryan, Ohio Man.

Dave Roeback
   Also from Bryan. He plus Fritz Fisher and Mike Joyce = NCAA Champs.

Greg Spangler
   The Candy Man from Bryan, my uncles seat. Frat brother friend.

John and Fran Atchison
   The perfect match.

Dave Tingley
   Had to get a Buckeye in there, a Zubkus friend and my associate.

Barry and Roy from Fritz's
   The original Odd Couple.

Ron Kocan
   Just to look at him you had to want to tickle him, then run like hell.

Bob Gray
   "The King of Goalies" brought us a championship.

All my Phi Delt brothers:
   Especially the ones that stay in touch. Means a lot.

Tom Bobb:
   An original. Andy Russell's friend, would fit right in.

All my high school classmates:
   More reunions to come.

Bruce and Sue Lund Allison:
   A high quality coupling out of the past.

Ron Pullian:
   Our longtime equipment manager; gave me my "M" gear. Good friend.

Ed Warnament:
   The Man of Rough Edges and Sweet Women. (Deceased)

Dan Glennie:
Kroll's "publicist" from Alpena and UM, a born MC.

Tony Badalament:
"Tony Bad." Kane's and my Muse.

John Mahaney:
"The Chief," Columbus Lobbyist Extraordinaire.

Judge Vince Brennan:
Detroit's finest, took care of his friends.

Lamar Hunt:
I could have worked for him.

Don Simmonds:
At least he doesn't have to account for Kerry.

Andy Novak:
A former pro boxer and womanizer. Idolizes Pepe LePew.

Adam Polen:
A young good old boy.

My buddies from the club,
Those that had my back.

Dick Miller:
Our longtime friend and dentist for both generations. So good to us.

Jayne Frilling
A fine lady and phenomenal singer.

Bill Rohrbach:
Tiffin's best ever, preceded me at Michigan.

Mel Hoerig:
Great referee. Got me my shot.

Jerry Maxwell:
A flawless man.

Dick Allen:
The upfront man. You always knew where you stood.

Quinn Allen:
My son's great friend, as his father was mine.

Danny and Chris Tarpy:
Always kind and caring, the model distributor.

Kwamme Christian:
Another Calvert Alumni three generations removed. Your turn.

Larry Barrick:
　　My first altar server partner and favorite Lake Erie Fishing Captain.

Grover Rohe:
　　My biggest high school fan—Grove could pick 'em.

Jake Sauber:
　　Our high school big man both football and basketball.

Dan Moran and Gil Farley:
　　Even bigger and crazier.

Jocko Hoffmann:
　　Our protégé, made me proud. A good friend.

Bill Neckrock:
　　A Saddam Hussein clone, naturally a Phi Delt and a Nemo's man.
　　Quoting Bill: "After five martinis I become invisible."

Frank Clappison:
　　My favorite hunter and soft hearted tough guy.

Bob and Ann Cronenweth Chandler:
　　Two class acts meant to be.

Jim Gallagher:
　　Old Michigan footballer lost over Lake Erie flying his own plane.

Charley Collins:
Another UM gridder lost tragically far too soon, and his wife Nancy.

John Yanz:
Big tough Chicago lineman.

Bill Keating:
Added to the Keating NFL legacy.

Jim Conley:
The classic captain of a Rose Bowl Winner.

Rich Volk:
All-American, All-Pro and All-class.

Frank Nunley:
Ole Fudge Hammer and '49er blaster.

Mike Maiberger:
Now there's someone who should write a book.

Jim Waterston:
If I ever need a bank president.

Jim Hayes:
Our original sheik.

Robin Gordon:
> An actress friend and my co-star in my own debut (I married her; I was a priest), unworthy of further detail here. My claim to fame was being rejected for a Pacino movie because I was too tall. (Who wasn't?) she had it all but we've lost track. That's show biz.

Guy Curtis:
> Football, Wrestling, Cardiology, Friendship always got his best effort and paid off in his legacy. Still going strong, the consummate Michigan man.

Bob Ufer:
> A Phi Delt Brother---and Michigan Legend. I can still hear his presentation of
> "The Victors." I could go out on that.

Dan Dierdorf:
> Could have been one of the originals in Pure-Pro. An all-time great.

Jim Brandstater:
> Helped along the way.

Dave Fisher:
> Prototypical fullback/character.

Jim Mermis:
My polar opposite style-wise but a good lobbyist and friend.

Jim Speaker:
A good friend and Veteran. A Master of Event Planning, perfect to pay tribute to all included.

Caring Wives: Husbands Victims of Neurological Diseases
Marsha Volk Kemp (Stan)
Ann Moeller (Gary)
Lynn Nunley (Frank)
Anne Marie Conley (Jim)
Karen Knight (Bob)
Angela Hornung (Paul)
Patti Freehan (Bill)
Dona Laskey (Bill)

So Many More.

FINAL THOUGHT

Something to Dwell On: Do you really think all these disasters are "natural?"

BIG FELLA!

FOR THE ROAD

Many of those who hopefully will read my autobiography are far more qualified to write their own. I did mine because everyone named within either had an impact on me or me on them and that constitutes life, gives a person value. I would like to say I did my best but didn't always. Who did? I listened and didn't always hear, or heed. Consequently I paid the price at the cost of others. Sound familiar? What comes around goes around. But I never intentionally hurt a soul.

CAREER QUOTE

"I might not have done everything right but I never did anything wrong."

Dan Clevenger
Columbus, Ohio
December, 2021